"*The Hero Within* is a gripping and well-written testimonial to how troubled youth can transform their lives positively through hard work, the right environment, and the support of caring teachers, parents, and volunteers. This book will also make all Coloradans proud."

—U.S. Senator Ken Salazar

"It's an inspiration to those of us who sometimes get discouraged by the enormity of the social problems we confront."

—John Suthers,
Colorado attorney general

"This is clear, evocative writing about critical matters—the care of boys in trouble."

—Kent Haruf,
author of *Plainsong* and *Eventide*

"*The Hero Within* is special reinforcement for putting the time, energy, money, and people resources into all children and how it yields great dividends for the future. I believe this book should be required reading for all taxpayers, policymakers, and practitioners."

—F. Jerald Adamek, director,
Colorado Division of Youth Corrections

"A wonderfully inspiring and heartwarming collection of personal stories of young boys and dedicated adults at the Colorado Boys Ranch where, for half a century, fragile, troubled lives have been heroically redeemed."

—Mike Rosen,
KOA–850AM news-radio personality

"We too often overlook the fact that these young people hold tremendous potential to be productive human beings and, if given the chance to find their niche in life, the ability to contribute in meaningful ways to our society."

—Chris Melonakis,
district court judge, Colorado

"The stories in this book are heartwarming and encouraging to those serving this way ... and to families burdened by what to do. The commitment to love, train, and grow these boys for the long haul, rather than seeking the 'quick fix,' is demonstrated beautifully in these stories. The heroes are both the boys and those who serve them!"

—Catherine Evans,
former juvenile court judge,
Dallas, Texas

"This remarkable collection of interviews and oral histories is a tribute to the vision of the Colorado Boys Ranch. Each story is unique and offers an important lens on the difficult passage to adulthood—and each gives great hope."

—Bernard E. Harcourt,
professor of law and criminology,
University of Chicago

"Everybody who cares about troubled youth has something to learn from this book. It gives valuable insight into an amazing history: building a facility for troubled boys far out on the prairie where they are helped and, thereby, given the possibility of a normal life as adults."

—Torill Tjelflaat, executive director,
The Regional Child Research Protection Unit,
Norwegian University of Science and Technology,
Trondheim, Norway

Thank you
for visiting
CBR!          Chuck

# The
# HERO Within

## Healing Troubled Boys
## at Colorado Boys Ranch

by
Cynthia Quicksall Landsberg
and
Judith Pettibone

Fulcrum Publishing
Golden, Colorado

Library of Congress Cataloging-in-Publication Data
Landsberg, Cynthia Quicksall.
The hero within : healing troubled boys at Colorado Boys Ranch / by
Cynthia Quicksall Landsberg and Judith Pettibone.
  p. cm.
Includes bibliographical references and index.
 ISBN 978-1-55591-611-4 (pbk. : alk. paper) 1. Colorado Boys Ranch.
2. Problem youth--Institutional care--Colorado--History. I. Pettibone,
Judith. II. Title.
 HV883.C6L36 2007
 362.73--dc22
 2007007513

Printed in the United States of America by Color House Graphics, Inc.
0 9 8 7 6 5 4 3 2 1

Editorial: Faith Marcovecchio, Katie Raymond
Design: Patty Maher
Cover image: Eldon Warren, former Colorado Boys Rancher

Fulcrum Publishing
4690 Table Mountain Drive, Suite 100
800-992-2908 • 303-277-1623
www.fulcrumbooks.com

*In memory of David Lawrence Quicksall, 1950–1991*

*Colorado Boys Rancher, 1964–1968*

One hundred percent of the authors' royalties from
*The Hero Within: Healing Troubled Boys at Colorado Boys Ranch*
will be donated to Colorado Boys Ranch Foundation/CBR
YouthConnect.

CBR YouthConnect
28071 Highway 109
P.O. Box 681
La Junta, Colorado 81050
719-384-8110 Toll Free 800-790-4993

To learn more about Colorado Boys Ranch, visit
www.coloradoboysranch.org or www.cbryouthconnect.org

# Contents

# Foreword

# Caring Brings Results

In 1959, the Colorado County Judges Association saw a need for a rural home where troubled boys could be given a second chance in life. The community of La Junta, Colorado, embraced that vision with open arms and welcomed the first boys to Colorado Boys Ranch in 1961. CBR, an orphanage for troubled boys, has evolved over the past forty-eight years into CBR YouthConnect, a nationally acclaimed psychiatric residential treatment facility.

Every boy who comes to CBR YouthConnect is hurting inside. He feels pain and uncertainty. He comes to us with problems that may be biological or environmental in origin, but he is most likely struggling with emotions such as anxiety and deep depression. He may act out impulsively with defiance and aggression or try to hurt himself. Imagine being trapped in that world without knowing how to get out.

The CBR motto has always been "It is easier to build a boy than to mend a man." We believe troubled youth have tremendous talents and abilities. It is our experience that these youth can make meaningful and sustained changes in their behavior and attitude. These changes offer profound human and economic benefits to society.

CBR YouthConnect is the name we have chosen in recent years to more clearly reflect what we do. *CBR* refers to our heritage as Colorado Boys Ranch. *Youth* are our focus. *Connecting* is our job. We help youth who are severely mentally ill, socially dysfunctional, and lagging educationally to reconnect with their families and home communities. We help them understand their feelings and connect them to what caused those feelings. We help them verbalize emotions instead of harming themselves or others. Youth develop emotional control, insight, and skills to build healthy relationships and achieve in their schools and communities.

The values of CBR YouthConnect include preserving the individuality and dignity of each boy. Trusting relationships forged between a boy and an animal at CBR in our animal-assisted programming allow great strides to be made in human relationships. Using neuroscience, psychotherapy, and an enriched learning environment, CBR YouthConnect is known for "the integration of treatments that work," but, most importantly, it is known for people who care.

There is an old saying: "Bloom where you are planted." It reminds each of us that life can take root and spring forth from many and varied places and circumstances. *The Hero Within* is about the troubled boys and their mentors whose lives were planted in the southeastern Colorado plains, at a place called Colorado Boys Ranch. These lives took root there and bloomed. Each life, each story, is a wonderful testimony to the belief that "Caring Brings Results."

—Chuck Thompson, president,
Colorado Boys Ranch/CBR YouthConnect

# Preface

# The Rescue and Rehabilitation
# of Troubled Youth

Widely misunderstood by Americans, the juvenile justice system has as its ultimate goal rehabilitation of young offenders, while the primary goal of the adult system rests in meting out fair and just punishment for offenders.

Prior to 1900, juvenile and adult offenders were frequently incarcerated together and given similar treatment. After a long litany of sexual and other abuses of imprisoned youth, America finally woke up to the need for treating the two populations differently. Despite the establishment of the first juvenile court in the Chicago area in 1899, it was not until 1974 that Congress finally acted to pass the Juvenile Justice and Delinquency Prevention Act (JJDPA). This law not only spoke strongly to the need for separating juveniles from adults for personal and public safety reasons, but it also went on to limit federal funding to those states that refused to comply with what were described as the "core requirements" of the act. Equally important, the JJDPA codified the overarching importance of prevention in heading off delinquent behavior before youth ever become ensnared in the juvenile justice system with its uncertain effects and results.

Prevention can take many forms. Of the many types of prevention programs, some are effective and others clearly are not. For example, studies have shown that programs that expose youth to incarcerated, hardened adult criminals in order to "scare

---

**Sixty-six percent of boys
and almost 75 percent of
girls in juvenile detention
have at least one
mental disorder.**

(The President's New Freedom
Commission on Mental Health, 2003)

---

them straight" are largely ineffective, while well-crafted and monitored mentoring programs frequently succeed in salvaging the lives of troubled youth. Unfortunately, the effectiveness of prevention is very difficult to measure and doesn't often generate compelling statistics that can sustain program funding when budgets grow tight. As a result, dollars for prevention are the first to disappear in tough economic times, with the undesirable yet undeniable long-term result that even more dollars will be required later to build more prisons and correctional facilities to incarcerate juvenile offenders.

Virtually unknown to the average American but of paramount concern to juvenile justice and mental health practitioners is the fact that more than half of all juveniles committed to juvenile facilities have diagnosable mental disorders. Of these youth, up to 70 percent also suffer from some form of substance abuse, often from attempting to self-medicate to alleviate the effects of the mental illness.

---

**Untreated youth with
co-occurring disorders have
high rates of suicide,
medical problems,
homelessness,
unemployment, and
incarceration.**

(The President's New Freedom
Commission on Mental Health, 2003)

---

In many cases, parents of these troubled juveniles felt they had no choice but to surrender their children to the juvenile justice system and court jurisdiction because they couldn't afford to secure the needed mental health treatment.

In the extremely complex arena of juvenile justice, ongoing research must be a work in progress. In recent years, significant and widely authenticated scientific studies have demonstrated that brain development in adolescents is incomplete and slower than previously believed. In essence, adolescents lack the maturity to make certain decisions normally expected of adults. These findings support the conclusions of juvenile justice experts, who have long contended that youth think and act differently than adults and therefore need to be treated differently. For juvenile justice generally, such findings could explain why youth commit some of their crimes. They could also eventually have an impact on how juveniles accused of murder and other felonies are handled by the courts. Currently, juveniles accused of serious crimes are frequently prosecuted as adults and sometimes receive sentences of life in prison without the possibility of parole.

Perhaps the single greatest quandary faced by juvenile justice experts today revolves around the disproportionate number of minority children being swept into the juvenile justice system. At virtually every step in the process, from law enforcement contacts to arrests and confinement, minorities enter the system in numbers much greater than their percentage of the general youth population. Throughout the United States, literally hundreds of thousands of dollars are being spent to study why this situation exists and what steps can be implemented in our society and culture to correct it. Fortunately, some model programs have been developed that show real promise in lessening the disparity, but much additional work and effort is necessary. As poverty, dysfunctional families, domestic abuse, and many other factors have deepened the crises for our youth, easy solutions for their rescue and rehabilitation have remained elusive. The best hope remains the evidence-based programs that have been proven to work and can be replicated in different environments. This, in combination with committed professionals and volunteers working daily and

> **African American youths are more likely to be sent to the juvenile justice system for behavioral problems than placed in psychiatric care.**
>
> (U.S. Public Health Service Report of the Surgeon General's Conference on Children's Mental Health, 2000)

tirelessly, will give many of our young people a second chance.

We cannot escape the fact that, for better or worse, like it or not, the kids of today will first weave and then become the fabric of tomorrow's society. These youth include uncounted numbers of economically, mentally, and morally challenged juveniles who desperately need a second chance, right now. Families and communities offer the best venue for hope; love, care, and respect remain the best medicine, rather than confinement. Where there is no other real family, or when the family can no longer cope, sometimes the right medicine can best be found in a caring group home, youth village—or a youth ranch.

—Bob Pence, member,
Colorado Juvenile Justice and
Delinquency Prevention Council,
past national chairman,
Coalition for Juvenile Justice,
Washington, D.C.

# Introduction

Can the pain within troubled boys be healed? We all have a stake in the answer. If we believe the answer is no, or if nobody cares, then young lives are wasted and prison populations explode. But I believe the answer is yes. Troubled boys do have the potential to become hopeful and productive citizens.

Who better to explain that transformation than the former troubled youths themselves and the caring adults who helped them succeed? They are the voices of *The Hero Within: Healing Troubled Boys at Colorado Boys Ranch*. Although some names have been changed to protect the privacy of individuals, these are stories of real boys and real results.

Each chapter describes the insights of an individual boy, a dedicated staff person, volunteer, or parent, or one of the variety of therapeutic programs at Colorado Boys Ranch, including animal-assisted programming, that help these boys overcome abuse, neglect, and mental illness or anguish. Helping professionals might call these chapters case studies. The rest of us would call them true tales. For either audience, *The Hero Within* is testimony to the resilience and perseverance of troubled boys and their mentors who have each found their own hero within.

Thousands of troubled boys from across the nation come to Colorado Ranch, transforming their lives. With these stories, my coauthor, Judith Pettibone, and I bear witness to the positive outcome that can be achieved when professional care and treatment is given and love and hope are bestowed. When boys achieve lives filled with peace and hope, society benefits enormously. *The*

*Hero Within* contains good news. Prisons need not boom. Lives need not be wasted. Troubled boys can be healed.

—Cynthia Quicksall Landsberg

# Rooftops

# Richard

*In jeans and a T-shirt, his light-brown hair slicked back into a ducktail, the thirteen-year-old boy waited for the station wagon that would take him to Colorado Boys Ranch. It was 1961, the same year that* West Side Story *first appeared in movie theaters, and a ducktail hairstyle could make even a small boy look tough. But at that moment, Richard, the very first boy to be sent to Colorado Boys Ranch, wasn't concerned about his looks. It was his pigeons he was worried about. "I had to make sure that my pigeons got taken along," he says. "They're called commies. I used to catch them up on the roof."*

It is now more than four decades later, and Richard hasn't climbed any rooftops recently. Nevertheless, working as a computer consultant on the forty-sixth floor of a downtown Denver skyscraper, Richard is literally, and figuratively, at the top of his profession. From his lofty perch, Richard can look down through the window and see the Five Points neighborhood, where he once lived a marginal life in the projects with his mother, stepfather, and half brother before he was sent to live at Colorado Boys Ranch.

After a long day working with statistical analysis systems, Richard often skips dinner but saves his appetite for dessert. He likes to go to a fashionable diner a block away from his office tower. Sitting in a booth at the restaurant, Richard recalls what was foremost in his mind on that day when his mother relinquished him. It was the pigeons.

"I started collecting pigeons when I was really small. I was living in the projects near Larimer Street," Richard says, waving his hand toward the neighborhood that surrounds the bustling eatery where he now sits. "Larimer used to be Denver's 'wino' district. At that point in time, it was a bunch of old broken-down hotels," he says.

Richard pauses to greet a waiter who knows him by name and then returns to his subject. "We used to collect pigeons under the viaducts," Richard continues. "I was small at the time. We would get inside those steel girders, which took us underneath the bridge. We were about forty feet above the ground. That's where the pigeons build their nests. You wait until they're almost ready to leave the nest, almost ready to fly. We'd get our bags and cart them home. We'd find corn to feed them where they were unloading train cars. You'd just pick it up. You didn't have to pay for it. The pigeons were something in terms of a pet," he explains. "I couldn't have dogs or cats in the projects."

There were a lot of things Richard didn't have in his early years. A father was just one of the things he lacked. "My mother had five children, each one with a different father. I was number four," Richard says matter-of-factly, "fourth on the list." Richard remembers being told his mother may have been in a mental hospital when her two oldest children were put up for adoption. An aunt raised the third. Relatives and foster parents raised Richard until he turned four and a half. "That's when my mom met my younger brother's dad. They got me out," he says. "After that, it was kind of marginal."

Richard's marginal life included a stepfather who "was drunk all the time" and a mother who worked nights and slept during the day. With no supervision, Richard roamed the streets and viaducts of downtown Denver at a tender age. He was often gone for the entire day and into the night.

"We used to scavenge a lot of things in that area," Richard recalls. "The railroad tracks are right there. We used to go down to Denargo Market. You could get produce. If you go around, you can catch stuff that's been discarded: a tomato here, a cucumber there, a watermelon. You can bring a wagon and pull back a wagon full of vegetables."

When asked if the vegetables were for himself or his birds, Richard replies, "For myself and for the family. We didn't eat a whole lot," he says, and glances down at the menu.

Already sure of what he wants to order, Richard sets the menu aside and describes his early life. He paints a verbal picture of his mother, who, like a harried mother bird bringing back scraps to her chicks, brought home pieces of toast from the hospital where she worked the night shift as a nurses' aide. "Those pieces of toast, when she brought them, were my breakfast for a year, maybe two, because there really wasn't any food," Richard says. "The real treat was an occasional strip of bacon. There were times when I wanted to eat. I'd go home, but I'd have to make my own mashed potatoes, because my mom didn't do a lot."

Richard confesses to having a lifelong craving for real milk, since the only milk at home was occasional government-issued powdered milk. "Meadow Gold, the dairy, was in the neighborhood," he smiles. "We used to get in their back cages and get ice cream." As Richard tells the story of his childhood hunger, the waiter reappears and Richard declines dinner but politely orders dessert, with ice cream.

Richard's childhood life on the margins included scavenging not only for vegetables and ice cream, but for toys as well. "Cereal companies used to have prizes in boxes," he says. "If they had too many toys, they'd put them off to the side. We'd get in there and cart them off."

To supplement the meager family income, Richard panhandled in downtown bars, sold newspapers on the streets, and collected bottles and cans. "Half the time we were on welfare," Richard says as he toys with the dessert the waiter has set in front of him. "We had to hide when we heard a knock at the door, because creditors were there."

Scavenging for food and playthings turned to stealing. "I used to steal a lot, okay?" he says, his light-blue eyes narrowing as he peers across the table and nods his head, searching for understanding. "I was good at it," Richard makes clear. "Those pants I had had an inner flannel lining," he explains. "You cut the pockets. You can put something in between your pant and the lining. You could stick a lot of stuff down there, even arrows for my bow. No one would ever see it."

Richard's mother never seemed to notice or care where the loot came from. Richard's stepfather was often incapacitated by alcohol. "My stepfather drank away most of the little money we had. He was getting to the point where he couldn't keep a job because he was drunk so much," Richard recalls. "I remember Mom calling in sick for him many Mondays. Too much weekend."

When Richard's mother did take notice of him, it wasn't always good. Sometimes she beat Richard with a belt. When that didn't achieve the desired effect, she whipped him with an extension cord. "That hurt," Richard says.

Richard recalls that during those difficult years in the projects, there was one person who made a positive impact on his life.

"Isidore Ortiz. He ran the summer recreational activities at Crofton Elementary School, across from the shelter. It's about six blocks from here," Richard says, pointing north. "He was into entomology. Insects. He had butterfly nets, and he used to give them out to us. We would go around the neighborhood and catch butterflies."

Within the confines of the inner city, butterflies and pigeons gave Richard a glimpse into the world of nature. And the concern that Mr. Ortiz showed for his summer students gave Richard a view of his own rightful place in the world. "He took me under his wing," Richard says.

Mr. Ortiz nurtured Richard's intellectual abilities in other ways as well. He helped Richard grow from a fledgling chess player into a champion. "I used to watch these guys play chess, and I thought, 'I can do that.'" Richard says. "Mr. Ortiz took me to a city tournament. The first year, I don't think I lasted past the first round. After the second year, Mr. Ortiz gave me a plastic chess set and said, 'Take this home and play by yourself. You know all the moves you're going to make.' By the third year, I was beating these big guys. I was smearing them," Richard laughs. "I went clear up to the top and won the first prize in my age division. I forgot what they gave me, but it was just the fact that I had the certificate."

The bond with Mr. Ortiz was broken when Richard was eleven years old. His mother moved him and his younger brother to Denver's west side. Two more years of financial struggle and neglect ensued. Richard was often left in charge of his younger brother. "I was the babysitter while my mother went and played around," he says. During those years, Richard's mother began looking for somewhere to place her two sons.

Richard was to become a second-generation orphan. His mother had been put in a Denver orphanage by her parents when she was a young girl. "It was during the Depression years," Richard says. "My grandparents put seven or eight of their sixteen children into an orphanage, all at the same time. The orphanage taught my mom some skills in terms of changing sheets and ironing, but she left the orphanage early.

"My mom was real strange in terms of emotional stuff," Richard says. "Anything emotional, she didn't come across. It was like I was in a different world from her."

Richard was thirteen, his brother seven when his mother succeeded in pushing them both out of the nest. At the time, Richard wondered why he was being sent away, but he acknowledges that if things had stayed the way they were, he would have eventually gotten into big trouble. "I ran around with a lot of fast friends," he says.

When asked whether he remembers saying good-bye to his mother that day when he left for Colorado Boys Ranch, Richard replies, "Kind of. Halfway."

The first cottage-parents at Colorado Boys Ranch were Mr. and Mrs. Estelle Robinson. Mr. Robinson recalled going to Denver to pick up Richard and his brother in April of 1961. "These first two boys," Mr. Robinson said, "one of 'em hesitated. He didn't seem to want to go, and yet, he wouldn't talk about it. Finally I asked, 'Why are you hesitating?' The boy said, 'I've got some pigeons on the back porch.' So I said, 'Well, let's just take those pigeons with us.'"

Richard, his younger brother, and the pigeons all got into the station wagon with Mr. Robinson and set forth for La Junta and a new home. They drove south along the Front Range through Colorado Springs to Pueblo. From there, they turned east and followed the Arkansas River and the tracks of the Santa Fe Railroad. They passed through a string of small farming communities until they reached La Junta. After crossing the river and a canal, they headed north for a few miles and arrived at the Boys Ranch, an abandoned military housing area.

Richard acknowledges that it was difficult at the Boys Ranch at first, but as the weeks went by and other boys began to arrive, things got easier. More cottage-parents came along, and Richard quickly felt he was part of a large extended family. "It was like having your grandparents there. You could go to almost any cottage-parent: Mrs. Gantt, the Robinsons, the Crows, or the Branfas. You had cooks and workers, like Schultz, the maintenance man. We used to follow along behind him and help with remodeling." When asked who was important to him at the Ranch, Richard replies, "Almost everybody."

However, there were hurdles to overcome, some of them self-imposed. Richard recalls his first day at La Junta Junior High, in 1961. Still wearing his light-brown hair combed back into a ducktail, Richard was introduced to all his seventh-grade classes by the principal. The ducktail was a labor-intensive hairstyle rarely seen in that small rural town. "It was long and combed back on the sides, but it came down in front and curled over," Richard recalls. "I had to get in the shower and comb it and let the water dry in my hair to the point where it set. A lot of people at school really didn't want to mess with me," Richard says. "I was the Denver boy."

But Richard found his niche in athletics. "Even though I was kind of small, I was very physical and athletic. Get me into a uniform. Football. That was usually how I could get back at all the big people," he says.

John May, an executive secretary of the Colorado Boys Ranch board and CBR's first administrator, sized up Richard's mental attitude and athletic ability and redirected that energy into boxing. John May had been a Golden Gloves boxer in his youth, despite a childhood bout with polio. "He knew the streets that I ran out on, and he knew that I didn't have any technical way to defend myself," Richard says. "He knew I could thrash, but it's not the same. When you box, when you fight, you have to do it with a cool head. You can't be emotional. You can't be uptight.

You've got to be in control of your wits," Richard explains. Richard carried John May's lessons through life.

"John taught me how to box," Richard says, "how to weave, how to miss things, how to use your hands and to catch stuff, to direct it one way or the other to the point where it's not going to do any kind of damage."

Learning to redirect aggression was a skill that Richard needed, not just to protect himself in a scuffle, but also to fend off the peckish gibes that his mother hurled at him. Both before and after his years at the Boys Ranch, she often told Richard she wanted him out of her life. Separations between mother and son lasted for years at a time. He remembers one caustic remark that stung. "It was really acid," Richard states. But he tried to be philosophical. "Well," he told himself, "sometimes I have a mother and sometimes I don't."

Essentially fatherless as well, Richard found parental figures in abundance at Colorado Boys Ranch. "When I think in terms of father figures at the Ranch, John May is first and foremost," Richard says. "It was the way he treated me. From day one. He nurtured me. I could tell, in terms of the exchange, 'This is real. It's coming across. I don't have to worry about it. John will take care of me if something happens to me.'"

There were other men at Colorado Boys Ranch who helped to fill that fatherly niche. Seldon Jeffers, a pharmacist who owned a drugstore in La Junta, was another of the original CBR board members. Jeffers, a wise and discerning man, could demonstrate his concern for the boys at the Ranch without saying a word. "It was summertime," Richard recalls. "I was doing errands for the Ranch. I went into his drugstore. I was just barely starting to get some peach fuzz, a little, here," Richard says, and rubs his chin. "Mr. Jeffers took one look at me. He took me down the aisle. He picked up a razor and some shaving cream. He went and got some cologne. He put it all in a bag and gave it to me."

The local physician, Dr. Richard Davis, was another original CBR board member who cared for Richard in a tangible way. Dr. Davis, the original chairman of the board for CBR, screened all the boys' applications and took care of their medical needs. He did all of this voluntarily while running a busy medical practice in La Junta. Richard got to know Dr. Davis well after an encounter with a rattlesnake.

It was the third summer that Richard had been at the Ranch. After having recently put on about thirty-five pounds, Richard says he was "as strong as a bull" and looking forward to the football season. In late summer, Richard's brother woke him early one morning, urging him to come outside and see a snake. Still groggy with sleep, he followed his brother outside. Richard gingerly picked up the somnolent snake and held it carefully, as he knew to do. But the heat from Richard's hand transferred to the snake, waking the rattler up before Richard himself was fully alert. As Richard transferred the snake from one hand to the other, the snake bit him on the thumb.

Richard was taken to the hospital, where he stayed for ten days. A skin graft from his thigh failed to seal off the open wound, and Richard lost his thumb about two months later. Dr. Davis tended Richard throughout this ordeal and then helped Richard try to regain the weight he had lost during his hospital-ization. Richard did gain the weight back, but despite Dr. Davis's attentive care, Richard never grew another inch after that injury—at least in physical stature.

Richard did grow in other significant ways, thanks to all the father figures at Colorado Boys Ranch. "When I went to the Ranch, a lot of people opened up to me," Richard remembers.

One of the most memorable of these people was Everett Marshall, the former world heavyweight wrestling champion and a local farmer and rancher. Richard recalls visiting Marshall's property with the other boys. "Marshall had ponds with channel cat and perch," Richard recalls with a smile. "We used to go fishing almost every weekend of the summer at his place."

Marshall's property held an even bigger attraction for Richard. "He had a feedlot with grain bins," Richard says with a cunning smile. "They attracted a lot of pigeons."

Richard's pigeon collection had thrived since his arrival at the Ranch. "I had moved to the other side of the corrals and made a pigeon room. A guy from Eads who had fancy pigeons came through. He saw what we had, just basically common pigeons, really not worth a whole lot. But he traded us!" Richard says, still amazed, four decades later. "Homers! Kings! Fantails! Trumpeters! He traded us, one for one, and probably threw in some more too. That's where I got my initial stock, in terms of some upscale pigeons."

Although he enjoyed the horses and other animals that he tended during his daily chores on the Ranch, the pigeon room was where Richard went to find solitude. "I guess this ties in with my meditation, in terms of sitting still," Richard says. "I would just go up and sit in their cage and kick back. After a while, you get to the point where you are just part of the population. You can get them to feed out of your hand. There are times when you want to get closer and have more interaction. I could see who is messing with who, how they build their nests, how they feed, how they raise their young."

On days when the dirt roads on the Ranch were thick with mud due to melted snow, Richard remembers "picking up that extra clay on my shoes with each step" as he walked past the corrals to work on his 4-H project with his birds. Pheasants became important to Richard as well. "We built some pens, got some lamps, and had a lot of chicks. But the dogs got in and scarfed about two-thirds. I probably had fifty pheasants left. After that, I made sure the pens stayed locked. When the pheasant chicks were full grown, we took them out to Holbrook Lake and released them, with the help of the wildlife officer."

Richard's love of birds was not indiscriminate. His girl-friend's father had a turkey farm in Cheraw, not far from the Boys Ranch. "I wasn't really impressed with turkeys," Richard says. "A jet goes over and they all crowd in the corner and the ones under-neath smother to death. You have to be really careful of big noises with turkeys."

Along with his increasing knowledge about birds and their relationships, Richard began to pick up a lot about human inter-actions at the Ranch. Things like stealing, which had seemed commendable in his former world, no longer seemed right. "Once you get to the Boys Ranch, you realize, 'Oh, this is not a virtue,'" he says, shaking his head from side to side and smiling at his former idea of ethics and morality. "It is (a virtue) out of the world that you came from, because a lot of people admired you for it. It's a skill, so to speak. But once I got to the Ranch, I real-ized, 'No, I don't think this really holds.'"

"They were taking care of us," Richard explains. "We got three squares a day. We're going to school. We have all these activities. They're coming across for you in ways that nobody else really ever did. Why should you return the favor with some-thing ugly? It just does not fit in the scenario anymore. It's something that you've got to get up and over. I had to hold myself to a higher standard, regardless of peer pressure. You rec-ognize that the environment has changed and it's time for me to change too."

From these insights, Richard developed a personal motto: "At each stage of learning, we must give up something, even if it is a way of life that we have always known. That is a constant theme in my life's journey."

Interacting with adults, both on and off the Ranch, gave Richard a new sense of self. "They treated us almost like a normal family," Richard says. "We went to shows, football games, anything and everything. You're with people in public to the point where you know how to act. You're not your old ugly self. You learn to develop some social skills and self-esteem. You didn't have to come across really bad or macho."

Interaction with the other boys on the Ranch was just as important as interaction with adults, in Richard's estimation. "If you had a bad, ugly attitude while you were there, you probably got that attitude changed, because the other boys forced the issue," Richard explains. "You get to the point where you're clicking around with other kids. You still bump up against adults, but your peer, your peer is the thing. We had a bunch of different kids with different problems, but at the same time, once they get entwined within the group, they don't have to worry about that stuff anymore."

Not only did Richard watch over his younger brother at the Ranch, but he also became a big brother to many other boys. The Ranch director, when frustrated with a particularly headstrong youth, would often come to him and say, "Richard, why don't you go up and talk some sense into that boy?" Richard was happy to oblige.

But Richard wasn't always an angel himself. He describes one time when he got into trouble. "We had made a clubhouse using haystacks for furniture in one of the old barracks buildings. Since the room had been painted blue, we called it the blue room."

It was blue in more ways than one. "We went up after supper one night and proceeded to do our normal bullshit session," Richard says. "New guys always had great stories and jokes to tell. So we were up in this room taking turns talking. Every other word usually comes out a cuss word, you know; the normal when adults aren't around."

The blue room may also have gotten its nickname from the haze of cigarette smoke produced there. Although smoking was not permitted, the boys sometimes found a way. "Our meeting in the blue room was an opportunity to smoke," Richard says. "I was one of the few who didn't. After probably fifteen to twenty minutes, one of the boys said something to the effect of, 'Wouldn't it be funny if Vic Crow (our cottage-parent) was standing outside the window listening to us?' And we all laughed. About that time, this big booming voice comes through the window,

Richard in 1961.

'Well, as a matter of fact, I am standing outside the window!' You never saw such scrambling, putting out lit cigarettes, and hiding the rest. Vic came in and chewed us out. I forget what our punishment was. But it was still funny!"

Richard does remember the punishment he received on another occasion. Suspended from school for a week after accidentally soaking the bus driver with a squirt gun on the school bus, Richard faced further consequences back on the Ranch. "Somebody had donated a commercial stove to the Ranch," Richard says. "Big. Gunk on it like you wouldn't believe. You know what my project was? 'Here's your Brillo pad. Here's your scraper. This ain't no country club!'"

There were times when he and the other boys would grumble, feeding off each other's complaints. Richard lowers his voice in imitation of his grouchy adolescent self and growls, "They're treating us really bad." And then he laughs. "I had a friend, one of the first boys there. He used to fix me up with girls. He was the real looker. Suave. Had the lines like you wouldn't believe. We decided to run away."

Richard describes the Great Escape, not too difficult since the Ranch had an open campus. "We made it down to the auction barn outside of La Junta and were waiting for the train. We're looking down to where the train should be coming, and we see these red lights and sirens making a beeline for us. The cop gets out. He was not one of our favorites. He drew his gun and started chasing us around a stack of wood. We finally stopped. He throws us in the back of the car and took us down to the county jail."

At the jail, Richard and his friend enjoyed the big picture window in their cell where they could sit and watch the girls go by on the sidewalk outside. They were in no hurry to go back to the Ranch. "Dick Jones was the one-eyed sheriff in La Junta," Richard remembers. "He had a patch over one eye. He was a pretty good, decent guy, and a good friend to the Boys Ranch. He was trying to talk us into going back. But we said, 'No, we'd rather go to the reformatory in Golden.' This is how our attitude was." About that time, Richard and his friend started singing, which, he says, "drove the jail keeper nuts." Apparently their singing was the last straw. "Finally," Richard says, "Sheriff Jones said, 'I'm taking you back to the Ranch, regardless.'"

Richard and some friends flew the coop once more. This time their flight ended after a few days, when their money ran out. Returning to the roost, the boys were called in to an administrator's office. As Richard puts it, "The administrator wasn't there. He had a trip to go on, which he decided was more important than staying and talking to us. So," Richard chuckles and shakes his head in disbelief, "he had tape-recorded his lecture, and we had to sit and listen to it on the machine." Perhaps not the most effective administrative action in the history of the Ranch, this method of reprimand just made the boys mad. Says Richard, "It rubbed us the wrong way. We went up and got horses and took them into town, the back way, of course. We went trotting down the street. Nobody turned us in. We came back later with the horses. We never got busted for that." That particular administrator didn't stay long at the Ranch.

Richard, center, in plaid, with other fellow Colorado Boys Ranchers, 1967.

Despite his "jailbreaks," it is the freedom on the Ranch that Richard remembers now. "They gave me the time and freedom to actually develop," he says. "To be able to think by myself and not be harried by anybody else." And, in spite of his escapades, Richard did develop into a successful young man. He was the first Boys Rancher to be awarded a gold ring for grade point average, conduct, cooperation, and attitude. He was chosen by the La Junta American Legion post to represent them at Boys State. At La Junta High School, he excelled in football and wrestling, despite the loss of his thumb. He also excelled academically and was a member of the National Honor Society. Richard received a scholarship for college from First Federal Savings and Loan of La Junta.

When Richard had graduated from high school and was leaving CBR for college, he wrote a letter of thanks to Colorado Boys Ranch. He said in part, "I can still remember that first day when I arrived, five years ago, mixed up and kind of scared, but full of curiosity. CBR has shown me the way to stand tall and set an example for other young boys. People can see that there is hope for the mixed-up kids of our generation. I want to thank each and every person who has contributed in any way, from the bottom of my heart. It has set me on the right track and will keep me there. May God bless each and every one of you."

After two years at Otero Junior College in La Junta, Richard was not quite a fully fledged adult and needed another fatherly nudge before he could spread his wings. Unsure what to do with his life, Richard was considering quitting college when another CBR board member stepped in to give him some guidance. "Charlie Williams, who owned Williams Chevrolet, said, 'No, no, no,'" Richard remembers. "He helped me get the paperwork done to transfer to the University of Colorado in Boulder." Richard transferred to the university and went on to earn two bachelor's degrees.

As a computer consultant, Richard has received kudos for his organizational and communication ability, skills for which he credits the Ranch. "Every business environment that I get into is almost an extension of the Boys Ranch," Richard says. "You don't go down the normal operational lines in terms of 'This one reports to this one.'" The real world, as Richard found it, turned out to be like the Ranch, where "nothing was set in stone." "You're accommodating all kinds of kids in all kinds of different ways and orchestrating how many activities?" Richard asks. "It's an environment where you get a lot done, but it's because of the familiarity and the freedom that you have within the system."

His clients at large corporations call him "self-motivated, results oriented, easy to work with, and very well liked," accolades for which he deserves the credit. When they say he "handles himself with coolness and professionalism," Richard may have John May's boxing lessons to thank.

A few years after he left the Ranch, Richard's ability to keep a cool head literally saved the lives of two small children. Richard was driving home to La Junta from the university in Boulder. It was night. As Richard drove around a curve outside Pueblo, he witnessed an accident in which a car rolled and burst into flames. "I just happened to be the first one there. I stopped my car and ran over. I got a couple kids out of the car and I was trying to reach in again, but it was too hot. I actually had to keep the kids from trying to go back in," he says. "They watched their mother and a couple of their siblings burn up. It was tragic."

Instead of congratulating himself on the lives he saved, Richard continues to worry about how he might have saved more. "I thought, 'You really need to carry an extinguisher, some heavy gloves, if it ever happens again.'" Yet he acknowledges that he risked his own life by saving the two children. "I thought later, 'What if the car blew up? Where would you be?' But, at the time," he says, "you don't even think of those kinds of things."

After college, Richard married and had three children of his own. Although the marriage ended in divorce, he speaks of his children with obvious affection and concern for their inter-ests. He is involved in their lives and is busy helping them as they grow into young adulthood. He uses the word *nurture* repeatedly as he talks about the awesome responsibility of fatherhood.

Before he became a father in his own right, Richard got his first taste of that responsibility after college when he returned to Colorado Boys Ranch to work as a teacher. Although he was only twenty-two at the time, in the eyes of the boys at the Ranch, Richard made the transition from big brother to father figure. He remembers, "I didn't watch the clock when I was teaching. I usu-ally stayed out afterwards and ate dinner at the Ranch and then went home." Richard got to know the boys well. Those boys who knew their fathers usually had harsh memories of them or felt disconnected from them. Richard recalls the backgrounds of these boys, so similar to his own before coming to the Ranch.

"Yeah, they had a roof over their head," Richard says, "but they were wild, free-roaming."

Rooftops still figure prominently in Richard's memory. During his years as a teacher at Colorado Boys Ranch, a rooftop was the setting for a scene that he will never forget.

"Around Christmas, I was up on top of first cottage, putting the lights up," Richard says, "and this one boy was up there helping me, and, out of the blue, it came out.

"'Gee, Rich,' he said, 'I really wish I'd had you for a dad.'

"I didn't even really know what to say. I told him, 'Your dad should have treated you halfway decent.'"

Hours have passed while Richard has told his story. The restaurant is nearly empty. Richard's ice cream has melted, and he has hardly touched his dessert.

—CQL

# CHAPTER TWO

# The Early Days

## Founding of Colorado Boys Ranch

*The many fatherless and troubled boys who have passed
through the gates of Colorado Boys Ranch have a group
of dedicated men to thank for their second chance in life.
Those early founders sacrificed their own time and
treasure to rescue boys who were on a slippery slope, a
slope that for many would have ended in prison. To
understand the dedication of these men to a cause that
others might consider hopeless, it is necessary to travel
back to an earlier time.*

In the late 1930s, Colorado Boys Ranch was not even a gleam in
the eyes of the city fathers of La Junta. Another area landmark,
Bent's Fort, had lain in ruins for nearly a century, no longer the
proud trading post it had once been. But in the late 1930s, the
town of La Junta, tucked along the banks of the Arkansas River in
southeastern Colorado, was alive and well.

Despite tough times during the Great Depression, the
farming, ranching, and railroading community of La Junta,

Colorado, had plenty of homegrown pride. In 1938, the town published a brochure extolling the features of their Arkansas Valley community. Next to photos of sugar beet fields, the Santa Fe Railroad yards, and the Kit Carson Hotel, the town's brochure boasted a snapshot of the boyhood home of La Junta's favorite son, Everette Marshall.

The reigning world heavyweight wrestling champion from 1936 until 1939, Marshall was busy in those days crisscrossing America and Europe on wrestling tours. Known far and wide as "The Blond Bear of the Rockies," Marshall was beloved of sports-writers and sports fans throughout the country. When he returned to his hometown, Marshall used his winnings to build a successful farming and ranching spread across the road from his father's ranch.

Two decades later, in 1959, Everette Marshall was asked to join with Dr. Richard Davis and other bighearted citizens from up and down the Arkansas Valley to create Colorado Boys Ranch, a haven for "little boys with big problems." Over the years, Colorado Boys Ranch evolved into CBR YouthConnect.

It is fitting that CBR YouthConnect, a place where the efforts of many caring professionals and dedicated supporters unite to

Original CBR board of directors. *Back row, left to right,* Doyle Davidson, John May, James Myers, Everette Marshall, and Elias Candell. *Front row, left to right,* S. O. Jeffers, Robert Cody, Richard Davis, Milton Richert, and Carl Shafer.

heal emotionally scarred youth, should have, by happy circumstance, a town named La Junta as its address. La Junta is, as they say, the place "where it all comes together." The town's slogan refers chiefly to the definition of the word of Spanish origin, pronounced "la hunta," meaning "junction or meeting place." Not only is La Junta the place where railroad lines came together around the time of the city's incorporation, in 1881, but it was also, a half century earlier, the meeting place of trails and trappers.

This meeting place, Bent's Fort, located six miles east of present-day La Junta, was an important trade center at the junction (la junta) of the Taos and Santa Fe trails. The brothers Charles and William Bent and their partner, Ceran St. Vrain, built the fort in 1833. The site they chose was on the north bank of the Arkansas River at a place where travelers from St. Louis crossed the river, bound for Santa Fe.

The National Park Service notes, "For much of its sixteen-year history, the fort was the only major permanent white settlement on the Santa Fe Trail between Missouri and the Mexican settlements." And, according to *Colorado: A History of the Centennial State*, Bent's Fort was the first semipermanent European settlement in Colorado.

Information about Bent's Fort figures prominently in a time line display at the Colorado History Museum in Denver. Visitors are informed that this fort was "the most powerful outpost on the high plains, serving both the fur trade and the Santa Fe Trail. During its heyday, the fort was the commercial hub of an empire stretching from the Central Rockies to St. Louis. Trade was brisk. From the mountains came trappers with pelts, and from the plains came Indians with their goods (chiefly buffalo robes brought by the Southern Cheyenne and Arapaho Indians), which they traded for items from as far away as Britain and France."

Because the trading post was located on the northern banks of the Arkansas River, "the tense international boundary separating the United States and Mexico," the museum time line goes on to say that "because it was deep in Indian Country, it was also built for defense." In later years, the adobe fort became a staging area for Colonel Stephen W. Kearny's Army of the West, which marched from Bent's Fort into New Mexico during the war with Mexico in 1846. By that time, the buffalo trade was in decline. A few years later, in 1849, the fort was abandoned and burned to the ground.

A century later, war on an even bigger scale brought another military post to the area. When World War II exploded around the world, even remote rural communities were affected. Just north of La Junta and a few miles from the ruins of Bent's Fort, an area of open grassland was commissioned to become an army air base. The waters of the Arkansas River, which had drawn trappers, traders, farmers, and soldiers, had little to do with La Junta being chosen as the site for the base. Rather, the endless blue skies that envelop the area made it a good place to train pilots. Just as Kearny's troops had been sent out a century before, these airmen were sent off to fight for their country in foreign lands.

A housing area for families of civilian workers at the base was built across the highway and christened "La Junta Village." When World War II ended, the military moved out of the base. The town of La Junta, with a population of about 10,000, continued to thrive. But the civilian housing area of La Junta Village, which had been constructed at a cost of more than a half million dollars, was abandoned. Tumbleweeds and dust blew in, covering the remains of the houses, much as they had done following the abandonment of Bent's Fort a hundred years before.

By the late 1950s, "the land and the fifty-one cinder block buildings of La Junta Village had been neglected and unused for some fifteen years," reports Dr. Davis, a La Junta physician at that time. In a history of Colorado Boys Ranch, Dr. Davis writes, "Roofs had caved in, streets had disappeared, weeds covered the area, and trees had died for lack of water. The area was used as a dump."

But like the early pioneers who first came to the area, a handful of men with foresight looked at these inhospitable surroundings and saw potential. "Late in 1958, at a State-wide meeting of the Colorado County Judges Association held in Redstone, Colorado," Dr. Davis writes, "the decision was made that a place was needed to care for near or predelinquent boys. The county judges had jurisdiction over juveniles. The thirty-five judges present were concerned that each year 4,000 Colorado boys had to be called delinquent by the courts. These judges were especially bothered because there was no place for the boys who needed control but did not need to be sent to the reformatory. The idea of a boys ranch that could be called home was backed enthusiastically by the judges." The judges envisioned a home, not a jail, away from the pressure of the big city that would not only protect these abused and abandoned boys, but would also help and heal them. But where could such a home be organized and how would it be financed?

After the meeting in Redstone, Judge Howard Ashton of Boulder County called Otero County judge Hal Chapman and

The ravages of time, weather, and vandalism took a toll on La Junta Village, later to become the Colorado Boys Ranch.

asked about the old wartime housing area. Dr. Davis writes, "Judge Chapman of Rocky Ford became so excited about the possibility of a Boys Ranch at La Junta Village that he promoted a meeting of the La Junta Chamber of Commerce and all interested persons, including Tom Russell, City Manager, and other La Junta city officials.

"The meeting was held in the Kit Carson Hotel in La Junta in January of 1959. A committee of local businessmen was appointed to determine the feasibility of such a project. Dr. Richard L. Davis was the chairman of the committee, which also included Seldon O. Jeffers, pharmacist; Jim Myers, manager of the REA Corporation; Carl Shafer, lumber company manager; John May, car dealer; and Milton Richert, attorney and banker."

That same day, with the informal but industrious "let's get down to brass tacks" approach typical of the Arkansas Valley, the first meeting of this committee was held immediately on the sidewalk outside the Kit Carson Hotel. It was decided that some investigation of the concept of a boys ranch needed to be done. "The best way was to visit Cal Farley's Boys Ranch in Amarillo, Texas," Dr. Davis writes. With a telephone call and a gracious invitation, the group made the trip the following week.

"After a complete indoctrination and tour of the ranch," Dr. Davis writes, "we were informed that, without good financial backing, a dedicated group of people, suffering through government rules and regulations, an enormous amount of volunteer help, obtaining a superintendent, house parents, sound policies, and a first class program, the project would be next to impossible to implement. We were also told that such a mission, as we were on, was one of several hundred visitations from other groups wanting to start a boys ranch. The success of these groups was less than ten percent. We weren't exactly being discouraged, because of the enormous need, but we should know what we were getting into. Truthfully, it was a long ride home."

The long journey from Amarillo offered little in the way of scenery but plenty of scope for the mind's eye. When the committee returned to La Junta, another meeting was called of the original group. A report was given. The decision: "Let's give it a try."

Like Bent's Fort, the Boys Ranch would be a first for Colorado. The job ahead was daunting. "Windows framed in jagged fringes of glass; chimneys jutting in asymmetrical decay; and head high patches of weeds and windblown rubble painted a distorted pattern in realism," says Dolores Stark in an article she wrote for *The Gasser*, the official publication of Colorado Interstate Gas, when CBR was in its infancy. "Inside, sinks had been smashed, bathrooms were dismantled, walls and ceiling had been ripped and slashed until, finally, only the village's gaping remains were left on the windswept prairie. Remains resembling a skeleton with its bones picked clean, and cloaked in faded tatters."

To continue in Ms. Stark's vivid prose, an immeasurable amount of volunteer blood, sweat, and tears went into the back-breaking work of resurrecting that skeleton. Dr. Davis's history lists pages upon pages of individuals and organizations that contributed money, time, and labor to get the Boys Ranch off the ground. The ground itself was the first order of business.

The federal government, which still owned La Junta Village, created a local housing authority to take title. The city of La Junta then deeded the thirty-seven and a half acres of land and the buildings to Colorado Boys Ranch Foundation for the princely sum of one dollar. Otero County donated another 160 acres to the Ranch. Brothers Olin, Milton, and John Richert purchased the rest of the half section of land surrounding the Ranch and donated this land to the foundation in memory of their father, John.

Dr. Davis was elected president of the board of trustees. The board also included the five other original committee members. In addition, as Dr. Davis writes, "We added Everette Marshall, former world heavyweight wrestling champion, now rancher-cattleman, Bob Cody, savings and loan firm, Elias Candell, attorney from Lakewood, Earl Brubaker, large cement products owner and manager, and Doyle Davidson, travel promotion official. City Manager, Tom Russell, was executive secretary [at that time]. Olin Richert and J. H. McDonald, both bankers, were trust officers."

Soon after the first board was developed, as Dr. Davis writes, "Two outstanding men were asked to join and both accepted with enthusiasm. These men were also considered founders of CBR. District Judge 'Mitch' Johns of Denver twisted arms of well-known and well-to-do citizens of Denver and helped tremendously in aiding John May's program for wills to remember CBR Foundation. District Judge George Doll of Fort Morgan (with a smaller, less wealthy population to beseech) was interested in livestock and was responsible for many donations from the north country. When Judge Doll performed marriages," Dr. Davis writes, "he refused to charge a fee, but told the couples he would accept a donation for CBR."

By the spring of 1961, the nonprofit, nonsectarian foundation was ready to receive its first boys with open arms. "The only paid employees at the Boys Ranch," says Dr. Davis, "were executive secretary, John May; his secretary, Mrs. Grace Rhodes; ranch manager and house parents, Mr. and Mrs. Estelle Robinson; and Mrs. Mary Watters, the cook." Sadly, Dr. Davis reports, "Mr. Russell, the City Manager, did not live to see the fruits of his labors come true. He died the day the first boys arrived." But because of the caring of those thirty-five county judges and the contributions of many hundreds of citizens, a home had been created that has since sheltered thousands of boys.

Ever since the first boys arrived at Colorado Boys Ranch, immersed in the hard work of reforming their own lives, they have also been giving back to the Ranch and the local community. In a striking symmetry, the effort that local citizens bestowed to resurrect and transform the dilapidated housing area made it possible for transformed youth from Colorado Boys Ranch to help in construction projects on and off campus. Some Boys Ranchers helped with restoration work on Bent's Fort that took place in the 1970s. Now a living-history museum in the National Park Service, Bent's Fort draws visitors from around the world. Most recently, the Boys Ranchers have used their skills to help build a two-story library for their own use on campus.

CBR has received national attention for its innovative treatment program and services. It has been featured on *NBC Nightly News*, PBS's *Nature* series, The History Channel, A&E, and *Animal Planet*. Stories about the Boys Ranch have been published in *Chicken Soup for the Pet Lover's Soul*, *Boy's Life*, and numerous national and regional newspapers. CBR has received honors and awards, including the El Pomar Foundation Award for Excellence in Youth Development. Recently, the medical director of CBR and the director of clinical affairs traveled to Asia and Eastern Europe, respectively, where they had been invited to share CBR's success story with their professional counterparts on the other side of the world.

In 2004, CBR received an outstanding evaluation from The Joint Commission on Accreditation of Healthcare Organizations (JCAHO). CBR had been getting excellent reviews from JCAHO for many years, important credentialing as a psychiatric residential treatment center. This year, the reviewer commented, "I have to tell you, in all honesty, you are one of the best residential treatment facilities I have surveyed over the last thirteen plus years. You folks have a tremendous amount to be proud of here. I don't say that lightly. We probably survey, collectively, my peers and I, several hundred residential treatment centers in the country each year. By far, in my experience, this is one of the excellent facilities in the country. And who would think it would be out in the middle of southern Colorado? But it is."

Given the history of the area, it is perhaps not surprising that La Junta has again become a national, and even international, crossroads. Colorado Boys Ranch, now known as CBR YouthConnect, is today the living and breathing junction where troubled boys, not just from Colorado but from across the country, come to reconstruct their lives. And it is the place from which experienced professionals go out to share their knowledge with the world.

—CQL

# The Blond Bear of
the Rockies

## Everette Marshall

*Everette Marshall began life as a small-town-Colorado farm boy, but went on to become one of the most famous wrestlers in the United States. Beloved as "The Blond Bear of the Rockies" by fans and sportswriters across the country, Marshall was the undisputed world heavyweight wrestling champion from 1936 until 1939. Marshall achieved success in a second arena by becoming a champion farmer in Colorado's Arkansas Valley. He built the largest cattle-feeding operation in the area and was dubbed by various publications as the nation's "Cantaloupe King." But for the champ, as for many who rise to the peak of their professions, there eventually came a fall.*

*"Marshall was everybody's friend," editor Al Burtis of the* La Junta Tribune-Democrat *said. "Even to the extent of being a soft touch. But because of that, almost no one envied his steady climb to fame; when he was on top no one grudged him the spotlight, and when business reverses overtook him, everyone was quick to explain, 'He was too good.'"*

*Marshall was truly a champion, both as a wrestler and as a farmer, but perhaps most enduringly, and endearingly, he was a champion for youth.*

✦ ✦ ✦

"My father really did care about people," says Ann Marshall Schomburg. "Maybe because he had help himself as a boy. I know that my grandmother (actually my stepgrandmother) was the kind who would inspire him."

Ann, a physical therapy professor at Regis University in Denver, was born the year that her father earned the world wrestling title. She grew up with her brother, Robert, and her parents, Everette and Harriet Marshall, on a farm outside La Junta,

across the road from Everette's father and stepmother. Of these folks, only Ann survives to carry the memories of the Marshall family saga.

"Dad was born on November 5, 1905, on his father's farm," Ann says. "He had a younger sister who died by eating matches when she was four years old. I know that because we decorated her grave with flowers on Memorial Day each year.

"When my father was a boy of thirteen or so, his parents divorced, and

Everette Marshall.

his mother left," Ann reveals. "My mother told me the story, but my father never talked about those kind of things. A very unpleasant situation. It must have been messy. Who knows what happened there? After the divorce, my dad's mother moved out to San Francisco and married a longshoreman. She was out of the picture. She was sort of the black sheep."

"I have a feeling that was an awful time in my father's life," Ann says. "I don't think he had an easy time growing up. I think his experience as a teenager must have been something else. In 1919, right after World War I, he ran away and joined the marines. He was only fourteen years old. But when they found out his true age, they sent him home."

"My grandfather, Henry Claude Marshall, was a good farmer, but very quiet, much more of an introvert," Ann says. "I think my dad was around fifteen when his father remarried. He wed a wonderful woman, Cora Pearl. I always considered her my real grandmother."

"Before marrying my grandfather, Cora was a spinster schoolteacher who never let the sun touch her skin," Ann recalls. "She wore smocks that came down to her wrists and gloves and a bonnet when she worked in her garden. It was a beautiful garden; I cannot tell you how beautiful it was. My grandmother was a fantastic woman," Ann continues, "very articulate and literate, and very much an educator. She was the superintendent of one of the rural schools. She got Dad back into high school after he had run away. I think she was the one who brought Dad through that period. You need that. She was a very strong woman."

Strength was a gift bestowed on Everette at birth, a boon renewed by his stepmother's care, and a quality he cultivated himself throughout life. Nine pounds when he was born, he was a whopping twenty-one pounds at only three months of age. When Everette was ten years old, a farmhand told the strapping young boy he could become the strongest man in the world. "Yea, he could become the greatest of bone crushers—the champion of all wrestlers, that is, if he wanted to *be* a champ," or so it was written in *Rocky Mountain Life*. The 1948 article, with the rather bewildering title "The Wrestler and the Cantaloupe," describes Marshall's dual success as both wrestler and farmer and goes on to say, "Probably thousands of other kids have been fed the same bunkhouse line. But Everette believed it. Not that he was gullible, but because he had faith in himself."

As a youth, Everette put his muscles to the test in daily workouts. In addition to the physically arduous chores of a farm boy—heaving 100-pound sacks of grain over his head, for example—Marshall built his strength and agility with an exercise routine of acrobatic feats. He would climb hand over hand up a haystacker rope forty feet from the ground and then across another thirty feet, three times a day. He would walk on his hands from the farmhouse to the barn, a distance over a city block in length. And every day he ended his calisthenics with a four-mile run.

When fourteen-year-old Marshall was sent home to La Junta from his failed attempt to join the marines, all that energy did not go to waste. A local wrestler who worked for the Santa Fe Railroad noticed the youth's exceptional strength and drive. "Pete Jordan took a shine to the jug-shaped young Marshall and spent hours teaching him the lore of plain and fancy brawling as known best to railroaders," the *La Junta Tribune-Democrat* reported. Eventually, Marshall claimed to know more than 1,000 wrestling holds, but he credited Jordan with teaching him the airplane spin for which Marshall was to become famous.

In those days, there were few illegal holds in wrestling. Marshall described the airplane spin in an interview: "Well, it takes great arm and shoulder strength and a little noodle work. In the 'spin' I lured a fellow into laxness, grabbed him by the wrist or arm or leg and gave him a quick jerk while my other hand was getting a crotch hold. The head was down and by spinning the hoisted opponent around six or seven times, by merely pivoting on my heels, I made the blood rush to his head, got him dizzy, then hurled him to the floor. It seldom failed." In another interview, Marshall pointed out, "I was always careful to throw them on their shoulders, not their heads."

When he wasn't doing his farm chores or practicing his wrestling moves, Marshall was playing high school football. He made the All-State team and helped the La Junta Tigers win the state championship in 1925. In college, he wrestled at the University of Denver under the famed coach Granville "Granny" Johnson, and he learned more wrestling techniques at the University of Iowa from the renowned coach Mike Howard.

When heavyweight-wrestling partners were hard to come by at home in La Junta, young Marshall turned to the animal kingdom. On a trip to a carnival in Manitou Springs, Marshall bought a bear cub to use as a training partner. He named the bear "Gotch" after the illustrious wrestler Frank Gotch. According to *The Denver Post*, although the animal had all his teeth and claws, "in a normal wrestling match the bear simply exerted great pushing strength. In other words, a fair match for the man."

According to *Rocky Mountain Life*, Gotch enjoyed the workouts: "The bear would amble into the middle of the mat, roll over on his back, and wait for the challenger." But when Gotch finally matured, weighing in at 425 pounds, the bear was sometimes too much for even Marshall to handle. When his wrestling career required him to spend more time on the road, Marshall gave the bear to a zoo, but not before sportswriters, always ready to come up with a catchy handle, dubbed Marshall "The Blond Bear of the Rockies." The nickname stuck.

Everette chose the partner for his life's journey well. Harriet Dunham, a striking brunette he had met in high school and married in 1929, went everywhere with her husband, supporting him in all his endeavors. Like Everette's grandmother, the "spinster schoolteacher" who persuaded Everette to go back to high school, Harriet was a strong and gracious woman. "I don't think my father would have been able to do all the things he did without her," says their daughter, Ann.

Together, Everette and Harriet chalked up over 300,000 miles as they crisscrossed the country on the professional-wrestling circuit, making friends wherever they went. Sometimes the couple took trains, but often they would drive. One article reported, "Night after night they would leave after the main event. Harriet would drive for 200 miles while Everette slept. Then Everette would drive. Flats? They fixed them together. 'We could make a tire change at night on a dirt road in six minutes flat,' said Everette." The couple's two children, Robert and Ann, were born during these barnstorming years.

In 1936, Marshall earned the world heavyweight wrestling title by pinning the defender from Detroit, Ali Baba, otherwise known as the "Terrible Turk." Despite the colorful nicknames, this was a time when professional wrestling was, according to Frank Haraway of *The Denver Post*, "a serious bruising game ... before it was invaded by histrionic weirdoes and monsters."

Still, "The Blond Bear of the Rockies" made for plenty of colorful copy during the Depression years. When Marshall was inducted into the Colorado Sports Hall of Fame in 1967, Haraway wrote, "Except for Jack Dempsey, who preceded Marshall into the Colorado Sports Hall of Fame, two years ago, no Colorado sports great has ever commanded the miles of newspaper copy that followed Marshall on his coast-to-coast mat travels."

Movie star handsome, with thick blond hair and a Kirk Douglas cleft chin, Marshall was a favorite of the crowds. But he did not trade on his good looks. Instead, he sculpted a remarkably strong physique and combined that with scientific wrestling knowledge to take on all comers.

Marshall with Jack Dempsey.

In more than 2,000 contests in a professional wrestling career spanning eighteen years, Marshall's matches grossed more than $2.5 million and drew crowds of up to 23,000. It was reported that Marshall never lost a match on falls and was pinned only a half dozen times. Marshall always went into the ring to win and managed to achieve victory 99.8 percent of the time. "That's better than Ivory soap for purity," boasted Marshall.

The tongue-in-cheek Ivory soap reference was a fitting analogy. Marshall took justifiable pride in maintaining his credo of hard work and clean living. "The nicest thing ever written about me was by Ed Cochran of the Hearst newspapers," Everette once said. "He wrote that of the thousands of amateur and professional athletes he had known through the years, Everette Marshall was the hardest training, cleanest-living, and best-conditioned athlete he had ever known. I carried that clipping till it just wore out."

There were plenty of other flattering clippings from which Marshall could have chosen. In 1941, the *Rocky Mountain News* reported, "Mr. Marshall, at least outside the ring, is a mild-mannered, very gentlemanly, modest youth. He neither drinks, smokes, nor curses, and, between mauling and being mauled, is a regular attendant of the Methodist Church. He has never had a bone broken but has had some tendons pulled. The only outward sign of his professional activities is a slight cauliflower that marks the spot where Strangler Lewis took off the tip of his right ear by a hammerlock in 1930."

The disfigurement to his ear didn't much bother the Blond Bear. "Mr. Marshall thought about having the resulting excrescence modified by a plastic surgeon," the *Rocky Mountain News* article went on to say, "but found the operation would cost $300, which he preferred to invest in a dairy cow."

What Marshall lacked in vanity he made up for in good sense. As smart about farming as he was about wrestling, he chose to plow his earnings from the ring into farmland back in his hometown. He and Harriet bought property surrounding his father's farm near La Junta and built up quite a spread. Before long, Marshall was at the top of his game in two quite diverse occupations.

Marshall's accomplishments at farming were no surprise to his wrestling competitors. They often watched when he opened his traveling bag in the dressing room before a match. "Out fell a collection of farm magazines," said *Rocky Mountain Life*. "It wasn't just a come-on to give the boys the idea that he was a yokel from the sticks. He studied those journals. On the train and plane hops he read about farming. In the larger cities he showed up at dawn in the wholesale markets to talk about methods of handling produce." In 1947, the year he finally retired from the ring, Marshall shipped about 75 percent of all the fine Rocky Ford, Colorado, cantaloupes, under the name of his two children, "Robert Ann." Marshall's cattle-feeding operation became quite large, with feedlots equipped to hold 10,000 head of cattle. "Success in wrestling is like success in business," Marshall once said. "To get ahead you must have drive—the urge to win."

Marshall certainly had that urge, but for the champ there was more to life than winning. "How many professional matches he had during his career or how much money he made from them, I don't know, and I question whether he himself knew," wrote Ed Orazem of the Pueblo *Star Journal*. Among the many sportswriters who knew and loved the Blond Bear, Orazem was proud to call himself one of Everette's closest friends. "This I do know," Orazem continued, "if he made a million or two million dollars, he must have given away at least half. If he was asked to appear on a benefit card, he not only donated his entire purse, but he also refused to accept payment for the expenses he incurred for appearing on the card."

Orazem recounted a typical example of the wrestler's generosity. "I'll never forget the night Everette was on a program at the KC gymnasium," he wrote. "A young miner from Florence suffered a broken leg in a preliminary match. Everette was quick to realize that the miner could not afford to be hospitalized or to lose his wages while incapacitated. So when Everette stepped onto the ring for the main event, he announced to the crowd he would donate his purse to the ill-fated miner and asked the fans to make whatever donations their consciences dictated. The miner never knew who paid his hospital bill, but when he was ready to go home, he owed nothing." Everette had taken care of it.

Bigheartedness was a trademark that lasted throughout Marshall's wrestling career. "It was typical of Marshall that $20,000 of the gate from his first championship match with Gus Sonnenberg went to a boys home in Los Angeles," wrote Haraway in *The Denver Post*. "And it was just as typical that in the match in which Everette lost his title, that $18,700 of the gate went to a crippled children's home."

Even after Marshall retired from the ring, his generous habits continued. Ann recalls how her father once drove a tractor four miles through snowdrifts just to pick up a load of groceries and newspapers for his workers who couldn't get into town. "My dad made sure he did the best he could by all the hired hands," Ann says. "He had hardly any turnover. We had really wonderful families of farmworkers. My father would always go and check on them. One family would have a new baby every year, and the husband always called my dad first before they called the doctor."

In addition to his farming and ranching work, Marshall found time to become involved in a variety of community projects involving youth. Many of these involved athletics. Of the region's youth, Marshall, ever the astute farmer, said, "These kids are the best crop we've got."

In the 1960s, long after the Blond Bear had gone gray, Marshall found his true calling. "My father really found out what he could do for people through the Colorado Boys Ranch," says Ann. His friend Ed Orazem wrote, "[The] Boys Ranch in La Junta is a monument to the man."

"Lots of people made Colorado Boys Ranch go," Ann is careful to point out. "I want to be sure to give credit to the founders who brought my father into it. Dr. Davis did as much of a favor for my father by inviting him to join the board as my father did for the Boys Ranch."

Everette became an emissary for CBR, using his connections as a wrestler and a rancher to solicit financial support for the nonprofit endeavor. "He had friends all over Colorado," says Ann. "He had that kind of personality." A superintendent at Colorado Boys Ranch said, "Without the fame attached to Marshall's name, the Ranch never would have been a reality."

Not only did Marshall offer his celebrity to help CBR, but he also gave thousands of dollars in cash and truckloads of produce to the facility for boys. In addition, he tendered his loyal crew of laborers, along with heavy equipment from his farm, to clean up the Ranch before the first boys arrived. Organizing gangs of community volunteers to help with the cleanup, Marshall bestowed his own still-significant brawn to help with the arduous work.

Most importantly, over the years the ex-champ gave his time to the boys on the Ranch spending many hours with them. Marshall was an impressive yet friendly figure to the young boys.

"We used to have a tug-of-war every time he came out to the Boys Ranch," recalls Richard, the first boy who came to CBR. Richard, now a successful computer expert, has fond memories of those mock battles with his boyhood hero. "At first it wasn't too bad, maybe four, five, six kids on one end of the rope and Everette on the other," says Richard. "But as time went by and more boys arrived on the Ranch, it was sixteen, twenty-five, thirty. It still didn't make any difference. He still pulled every one of us."

Richard also recalls visits out to the Marshall property with the other boys. "He took us up to his barn where he used to practice for wrestling," Richard says. "He had this empty bear cage out front, but his gym was inside and still had all the weights. He let us use them."

Ann saw firsthand how Colorado Boys Ranch became a special passion for her father. "When Colorado Boys Ranch opened in 1961," Ann recalls, "Dad took every bridle, every saddle, all of

Harriet and Everette Marshall with their children, Ann and Robert.

those kinds of things, out to the Boys Ranch. He gave everything that he had that was not tacked down, everything that he thought the boys would enjoy. I knew that Dad really cared about that Boys Ranch when he said, 'Ann, I hope you don't mind. Your saddle is gone.'" Already a gracious young woman at that time, she was happy to oblige.

Ann herself had benefited from the rural way of life and the values her father instilled. "He really did do everything he could as far as giving my brother and me a healthy place to grow up," she says. She recalls helping her mother earn pin money by feeding chickens, and she has fond memories of going out at dusk with her dad to make sure water was flowing in the irrigation ditches. "I get emotional thinking about my family and that farm," Ann said in an interview about her father in *The Denver Post*. "It was a wonderful life in many ways."

But despite the firm grasp that Everette had on so many things, the rural way of life that his farming and cattle-feeding business sustained finally slipped through his fingers. "I think my father truly loved his farm," Ann says. "He truly loved it. And to have it go the way it did was really a shame. It was really hard."

Marshall lost his farm and his home to bankruptcy in the mid-1960s. Everette and Harriet were forced to move into town, leaving the land they loved. They each took up jobs for a time in La Junta, and a few years later moved to Fort Collins to be near their son. In a strange piece of irony, during the same week in 1967 that *The Denver Post* reported Marshall had lost his bankruptcy appeal, the paper also ran a feature-length story with the banner headline "Hall of Fame Taps Everette Marshall." Marshall later presented the scroll he received from the Colorado Sports Hall of Fame to Colorado Boys Ranch. The Blond Bear died a few years later, on February 10, 1973, at age sixty-seven.

Three decades after his death, Marshall was still worthy of significant newspaper coverage. On July 28, 2002, a feature about

Everette Marshall appeared in *The Denver Post* as one in a series of articles about Colorado's small-town sports heroes. In that piece, Mike Burrows described the cause of Marshall's bankruptcy by explaining that the former wrestler "thought he was erasing debt and solidifying income for his permanent retirement in September 1963, when he sold his land and everything on it to investors from Arizona, California, and Montana who claimed to have big bucks. They turned out to be swindlers. They told Marshall they would assume his debt as a down payment, then ignored the obligation while selling his cattle and machinery."

In an interview for that article, Ann said that when creditors took control of her father's farm, his spirit and savings evaporated. "He was trustworthy to a fault," Ann said, "and he ended up losing just about everything."

Despite the downturn in her father's financial situation, Ann says, "He still had lots of good memories, and he left a legacy. He touched lives that we don't even know about. And the one thing he was most proud of was Colorado Boys Ranch."

Time and misfortune could not diminish the world champion. When Marshall was a young man he stood nearly six feet tall, weighed 220 pounds, had an eighteen-and-a-half-inch bicep, a fifteen-and-a-half-inch forearm, a waist of only thirty-two inches, and a chest circumference of forty-seven inches, fifty when expanded. For a time, Marshall's weight went over 300 pounds and, in later years, his chest measurement increased to sixty inches. Those are impressive figures. But it is the strength and size of Marshall's compassion, especially for troubled youth, that defies calculation and continues to outlive the champ. Even at the end, when the increasing magnitude of his chest expansion couldn't help him put a stranglehold on his dwindling personal fortune, Everette Oldham Marshall, "The Blond Bear of the Rockies," always remained one bighearted bear of a man.

—CQL

# A Rock-and-Roll
# Kind of Guy

## David Quicksall

*When people at CBR say, "Caring Brings Results," I know
from experience that it is true. When I met Dave in 1978,
we were both in our twenties. I soon learned he was a
former resident of Colorado Boys Ranch. Coming to care
for this young man was the turning point in my life's
journey.*

*Perhaps I should have been wary of getting involved
with someone with Dave's background. On our first date,
he told me his mother had been institutionalized all her
adult life because of schizophrenia. He had never known
his father.*

*But Dave assured me that the love he received from
his grandparents had given him a firm foundation. When
he lost them at age thirteen, he told me, the caring he
received at Colorado Boys Ranch kept him whole. I know
that CBR was the home that made Dave's life successful,
and my life with him possible.*

Seven years after I met Dave, I sat in the doctor's waiting room, nervously tapping my feet and watching for Dave to arrive. It was the summer of 1985. Dave and I had been married for six years, and our daughters, Sarah and Rachel, ages three and one, were at home with a babysitter. The waiting room was empty. Even the receptionist had left for the day. "Why would the doctor want us to meet him after all the other patients have gone?" I wondered.

In the last few weeks, Dave had begun to wake up frequently in the middle of the night drenched in sweat. He had lost fifteen pounds and looked pale. Most worrisome to me, Dave, a hard-working young trial attorney, had begun coming home from work in the afternoons to nap. That wasn't like him. As I waited anxiously for Dave to arrive at his doctor's office, my arms began to tingle. I realized I was hyperventilating, and I tried to "rebreathe" into my cupped hands the way I had learned in nursing school and practiced when I was pregnant while attending Lamaze classes with Dave.

"I shouldn't be worried," I thought. "If there were a problem, I'm sure Dave could handle it." His life was already a success story. Like many of the boys who had lived at Colorado Boys Ranch in the early 1960s, Dave was an orphan of sorts. But blessed with a brilliant mind, Dave had graduated in the top ten of his high school class in La Junta. He had put himself through the Colorado School of Mines and graduated magna cum laude from the University of Colorado School of Law.

My first introduction to Colorado Boys Ranch came a few months after we met, when Dave asked me to accompany him to his tenth high school reunion in La Junta. He was excited to show me the town where he grew up, but in particular he wanted me to see Colorado Boys Ranch, where he had lived for four years.

On our way to the reunion, we passed through farming towns along the Arkansas River east of Pueblo and stopped at roadside stands to buy melons and pinyon nuts. When we arrived at Colorado Boys Ranch, Dave pointed out the cottages, the dining hall, the classrooms, the administration building, the chapel, the corrals, and the mesa. He beamed with delight at the improvements that had occurred since his days as a Boys Rancher. I looked hard, squinting in the bright sunlight, trying to see the Ranch the way Dave saw it. To him, Colorado Boys Ranch was home.

By 1985, Dave was a partner in a small, close-knit law firm and a valued member of the Colorado Boys Ranch board of trustees. That summer, the CBR Foundation had given Dave the Everette Marshall Distinguished Service Award for his work helping CBR transition from the orphanage for troubled boys that it was in his day to a full-fledged psychiatric residential treatment facility for boys. He was, by any measure, a successful young man. Life was good.

But the doctor's insistence that Dave and I both come to talk to him after normal office hours seemed ominous. When Dave finally arrived, the doctor came out of his office and ushered us both inside. "We have the results of the blood test," he said. Dave held my hand as we sat facing the physician across his desk. Accustomed to waiting for a judge or jury to announce trial results for his client, Dave now waited for his own verdict. The doctor looked at Dave and said, "You have leukemia."

A bone marrow test a few days later confirmed that Dave's symptoms were due to ALL, acute lymphocytic leukemia. Immature white blood cells were growing out of control, squeezing out room for healthy red blood cells, causing his pallor and fatigue. Why Dave? Perhaps his exposures to benzene during college summers working in an oil refinery plant and on an off-shore oil rig while pursuing his undergraduate degree in chemical and petroleum refining engineering were a cause. More commonly found and frequently curable in children, Dave's form of ALL is often fatal within two years in adults.

Dave was thirty-five years old. Being handed a more pessimistic prognosis because he had acquired this "childhood illness" as an adult seemed ironic. He adopted a new favorite joke. It went like this: A doctor comes into a hospital room and tells the patient, "I've got good news and bad news. The good news is you've only got twenty-four hours to live. The bad news is I forgot to tell you yesterday."

It was typical of Dave to smile at fate. The ups and downs of Dave's fortunes could have filled a Dickens novel. But, although he loved the legal meanderings in Charles Dickens's *Bleak House*, Dave's wry sense of humor more closely matched his favorite book, Joseph Heller's offbeat World War II story, *Catch-22*.

Dave didn't go home and wait for the end to come. Together we researched the medical literature and found a new treatment protocol with better odds than the oncologist had given him. Dave fought his disease with the same intelligence and tenacity he used at trial.

Dave also drew strength from his childhood memories, many of those connected to the Boys Ranch. Just before his illness, Dave had written down some of these recollections. One page recalled his recent travels, driving to La Junta to attend board meetings at Colorado Boys Ranch. He wrote:

> Most often now I cross the canal about five o'clock. I drive the two-lane highway past the limestone bluffs, and the landscape quickly turns to sagebrush and flat desert. It is that time when the backlighted prairie fades to dusk then dark. The cars and pickups turn on their headlights.
>
> To the right is a junkyard of car hulks stretching from 1946 to a place where they disappear to the east in a gully. A little further ahead is a long tin building with a peaked roof that—like the junkyard—is a survivor. I

remember when, as a young man illegally drunk on beer and Jack Daniels, my friends and I made fools of ourselves playing country homilies there, late at night, to a crowd, which would have swayed without our music. The place did an eight-year stint as a 3.2 beer rock 'n' roll joint and has now settled into existence as a skating rink.

To the left is the silhouette of the Boys Ranch. I will be forever bound to remember John when I view that scene. John. Fourteen. And how, over twenty years ago, when he was transported down this same road in a ducktail haircut and short sleeve shirt with rolled sleeves, he looked over to the left of the road, spotted the Boys Ranch, and asked if they were approaching a turkey farm. He was quickly and officiously told that, no, he was approaching his residence of the next six years.

The scene is one of stillness with a facade of emptiness. I say that because, really, there is a stark constancy about this stretch of road and its solitude that is lacking in the city. This is a place that evokes the companionship of old images with near clarity. I can almost remember what it was like all those years ago. The feeling can come back here in the same way that a scent on a spring day brings back memories of childhood.

The long tin building that Dave describes as a rock 'n' roll joint turned skating rink has by the turn of the new millennium been reborn again as a church. It bears an old and faded sign on which the words *New Hope* can just barely be discerned. Although it is not a part of Colorado Boys Ranch, the tin church with its message of hope is still the last building one sees east of the highway before turning the corner west into CBR's campus. And, although the sign on the church has faded, the hope around the corner hasn't grown old.

Did Dave, like his friend John, feel some apprehension as he approached Colorado Boys Ranch for the first time in 1964, or did he feel a sense of hope? Maybe some of both. After all, he had been a "town boy" in La Junta and had heard rumors about the Ranch, some good, some bad.

The same could be said about his early childhood: Some good. Some bad. Dave was born to Lois Wilson at the Florence Crittenton Home for Unwed Mothers in Denver in 1950. All Dave knew about his father was that he was from Montreal, Canada, and that he, too, was named David.

After giving birth, Lois took her infant son back to La Junta to raise him with the help of her parents. Lois captured many smiling expressions on Dave's face with her Brownie camera in dozens of black-and-white photos during his toddler years. A few years later, Lois married a local man whose last name was Quicksall. The three lived in one half of a small duplex. Lois's parents lived in the other half.

Before long, Lois began to show signs of psychosis. Her husband divorced her and moved out. She was diagnosed as schizophrenic and was sent to live at the State Hospital in Pueblo. Four-year-old Dave was left with his grandparents. Lois was institutionalized for the rest of her life.

Dave's grandfather often traveled with his work, painting boxcars for the Santa Fe Railroad, and, in the summers, Dave and his grandparents lived in a boxcar in Clovis, New Mexico. When they were home in La Junta, Dave's grandfather often had his morning coffee at the kitchen table with Dave, who sat across from him sipping milk laced with coffee from an oversized mug. After coffee, they would head to the river to go fishing.

Dave worshipped his grandmother, Pansy Anna, despite the fact that when he was a toddler, the only way she could get him to take a nap was to pin him down with her arm across his body. A bustling, cheerful woman, Pansy Anna often told

Dave he was the most wonderful boy in the world.

Sometimes Dave's mother would come home for a visit and not want to go back to the mental institution. Dave's grandparents had to trick their daughter to get her into the car for the return ride to the State Hospital by pretending they were just going to get ice cream. Still, Dave's childhood memories were mainly of the happy times: playing with his cousins in the ravine behind his grandparents' home; building a go-cart with his friend Jesse; going to Saturday matinees.

By the time Dave reached junior high, he was already fine-tuning his sense of humor. His idea of a good joke in seventh grade was bristling his flattop at people and spraying them with the snow that had accumulated on his hair while he rode his bike to school. It was an innocent time. Dave later worried, as many grown children do, that his boyish high jinks might have caused his grandmother worry. The old photos of Pansy Anna, smiling mischievously behind round spectacles and drying her hands on her apron, indicate that she enjoyed the challenge of raising this young boy.

Dave was just thirteen and engrossed in a matinee in La Junta with his friends Jesse and Terry when the local

Dave with his grandparents.

Baptist minister tapped him on the shoulder. The other boys gawked, knowing something unusual must have happened for the minister to be searching for Dave on a Saturday afternoon at the Fox Theater. Quietly, the minister took Dave aside and told him the news that Pansy Anna had died. Dave was stunned. He had not been prepared for his grandmother's death. No one had told him how serious her recent illness had been.

When Pansy Anna died, Dave's widowed grandfather still had to travel with his railroad job. For a time, Dave slept on the couch at his great-grandmother's apartment, but she was just too old to care for him. Dave's grandfather decided to relinquish Dave to the custody of the state. Wise souls suggested Dave could benefit from the environment available just three miles north of La Junta at the relatively new Colorado Boys Ranch.

While at CBR, David became an accomplished guitar player. A budding songwriter as well, he wrote his own tribute to his grandmother, who had traveled from Oklahoma to La Junta during the Great Depression:

## Pansy Anna

Some people try to tell you that Enid Oklahoma,
Sits on the back road to glory,
That might be that bitter country's only claim to fame,
Except for a girl that was born there,
On the back road to Glory
And has now gone back the way she came.

She wasn't any fine-bred lady
Of a respected social class
She knew calluses and bruises by their names,
But she held life like a flower and was happy
When it bloomed
And weeded out the thorns as they came.

I knew her when I was quite young
And she raised me up her way
I'd ask what she was thinking
And she'd say real plain and clear
I'd give her sass and trouble every hour of her day
And now I wish I could make it up to her.

Pansy Anna, Pansy Anna
I'd give you roses if I had my way
I love you more
than words
can say.

During the years Dave lived at CBR, he formed close relationships with the adults who cared for him. He was given time
and support to deal with his anguish at the loss of his grandmother and the virtual loss of his mother, father, and grandfather.
Despite his grief, Dave quickly adjusted to the Boys Ranch and
was soon acknowledged as a leader. His responsible actions
earned him the respect of the staff and a great deal of freedom.

It was the sixties. John Lennon was Dave's idol. Dave, who
now realized that bristling his flattop was no longer cool, spent
hours carefully combing his hair down across his forehead in the
popular surfer style. He made many persuasive trips to the office
of the Boys Ranch administrator, Mr. Stieff, a retired military
officer, requesting approval for longer hairstyles. Dave took
special care that his clothes always looked sharp. He picked out
crewneck sweaters and turtlenecks that matched those of his
friends at the Ranch, John and Steve. He took out a loan from Mr.
Stieff to buy his first guitar and paid it off by working after school
cleaning typewriters at Fawcett Office Supply in La Junta.

While at the Ranch, Dave was asked to join some friends
from town in local rock-and-roll bands. He sang and played

Dave (right) with his band the Kritters.

rhythm and lead guitar. One group he was in, The Kritters, was hired to play at high school dances up and down the Arkansas Valley.

Like the Boys State leader he was, and like the engineer and attorney he was to become, Dave handled the business affairs of his band in a meticulous and professional manner. I have seen the copy of a letter he wrote and filed away for posterity:

> Dear Mrs. Brothern:
>
> I regret that I must cancel our dance at South Canon Hall on August 6. One member of our band found out last night that he would be out of town on a business trip on that weekend. Without him it would be impossible for us to play.
>
> > Sincerely yours,
> > David Quicksall
> > "The Kritters"

It's hard to say what kind of "out of town business trip" a sixteen-year-old might need to attend. Nevertheless, Dave always took his obligations seriously. The Boys Ranch administrator and the board trusted Dave to the extent that he was allowed to buy a car and go on overnight trips to play at dances as far away as Goodland, Kansas.

Dave participated in other activities that the Ranch had to offer at that time. In 4-H, he took over raising George, a sweet-natured but huge Black Angus bull that had worn out his other handlers. He prized his cowboy boots. He went on horseback rides and long walks around the mesa behind the Ranch with his roommate, John, talking about girls and sports. He was an Eagle Scout and loved to backpack and do camp crafts. But CBR encouraged him to be who he was, and Dave was always a rock-and-roll kind of guy.

Dave claimed he survived law school in large part because of the fun he had playing the guitar music of Jackson Browne with his law school friend David Douglas. Although Dave did not become a professional musician, his experiences at CBR affected the choices he made in his career in other ways. When he graduated from law school, Dave returned to La Junta as an assistant district attorney, but soon switched sides to work for the state public defender's office. He identified with the little guy, and continued throughout his public and private practice to fight for the underdog.

Dave's determination to give back to the community was, according to a former administrator of the Ranch, what made Dave a real success after he left CBR. As an attorney, as well as in private life, Dave's remarkable ability was most aptly defined by the term *counselor*. I think it was some-thing he learned at the Boys Ranch that made Dave such a good lis-tener, wise adviser, and loyal friend. Judges and other attorneys respected Dave for his brilliant legal mind and high ethical standards as a trial lawyer.

Dave's sense of humor, too, worked

Dave (top left) and his cottagemates in 1964.

Everette Marshall congratulates Dave on good grades in 1967.

well for him even in the courtroom. He made an impression on our first date by telling me the story of how he outwitted a witch in a La Junta trial.

Dave was defending a man accused of murder. His client was too terrified to testify in his own defense because a codefendant had hired the witch, whose purpose was to scare him into silence. It was working. The witch accomplished her intimidation by sitting in the front row of the courtroom, holding a shoe box full of voodoo trinkets, and giving Dave's client the evil eye. Dave, in his soft Arkansas Valley drawl, later referred to her as the "hit witch."

Dave's solution was to ask the local priest to come into the courtroom and stare ominously at the witch. With good grace, the priest agreed, and, in frustration, the hit witch left the courtroom. Dave's client was able to testify and was later acquitted.

Dave used that same humor and determination to battle his illness. Greg Klein, a close friend and bandmate from high school, asked Dave as he was undergoing treatment for leukemia what had allowed him to triumph in a challenging life. Dave shrugged and smiled. "Rock and roll," he said.

Dave receives the Everette Marshall Distinguished Service Award from Harriet Marshall in 1985.

The chemotherapy and radiation that he underwent for his "zookemia," as our small daughters called it, allowed Dave to continue working and living a relatively normal life for three years. One week before Christmas of 1988, just after Dave had completed his three-year regimen of chemotherapy, the leukemia came raging back. Dave, the girls, and I flew immediately to Seattle so he could have a bone marrow transplant.

Dave was admitted to Fred Hutchinson Cancer Research Center. Using his own marrow, since no donor match could be found, Dave endured a harrowing bone marrow transplant procedure, which included several months in isolation in a sterile room.

After massive doses of chemotherapy and radiation, Dave's lungs began to shut down. He was struggling to breathe, but his platelets were so low he could not be put on a respirator. The doctors feared that the trauma of intubation would cause him to bleed into his lungs. Without enough platelets for clotting, he would drown in his own blood. They were sure he was going to die within hours. A nurse asked me to put on scrub clothes and go inside the sterile area to tell Dave their dire prediction.

Dressed as if for surgery in a gown, surgical mask, cap, and sterile gloves, I went into the room. I leaned over Dave and asked if he wanted to talk about dying. Between labored gasps of breath, he said, "No. Jesus is here." By faith and sheer inner strength, Dave survived the crisis and became known by the nurses on the floor as "the miracle man." The transplant gave Dave another three years of remission.

Throughout his life, Dave's belief in God was unwavering, though not unquestioning. He had been raised as a Southern Baptist by Pansy Anna and had walked forward in church to be saved at age twelve.

In his twenties, he wrote a poem about childlike faith and innocence in which a sandbox is the central metaphor. Ten years later, Dave quipped in his journal, "Last night we read some terrific poetry by that insightful, irreverent poet, David Quicksall. Thinking of childhood (and sandboxes) and seeing the joy of fatherhood, I will close, thinking that we must always be aware of our tendency to complacency and knowing that my inquisitiveness has survived another year."

He later added, on a more solemn note, "Now I realize that most of us will spend our lives with our feet in that sand—stretching and pushing for salvation and for understanding."

After four months in Seattle, we returned to Colorado and Dave slowly recovered and eventually returned to work. In 1991, three years after the transplant, the leukemia came back again. With our two little girls and me to care for, Dave would go to any lengths to survive—even endure another bone marrow transplant. But he could not use his own marrow a second time, so we stepped up our search for a marrow donor. Neither the girls nor I were a match. A blood relative, his mother or father, would be the best hope.

Sadly, his mother's mental illness had ended in suicide one year before Dave's first transplant. With this second relapse, Dave was compelled to look for the father he had never met. We went to our friend Troy Zook, a private investigator whom Dave knew from his days as a public defender. Troy's search uncovered some ironic twists of fate.

Dave's mother had once told me that when Dave was a newborn she had taken him by train to Montreal to find his father. She said that she had been turned away at the front door by Dave's paternal grandmother. I had dismissed this story as unlikely, since I assumed Lois's mental illness would have made her incapable of a transcontinental journey. Troy discovered that Lois's story was true.

Lois had gone to Montreal in 1950, with the infant Dave in her arms. She knocked on the door of what she thought was Dave's father's boyhood home. The elderly woman who answered was shocked and said she did have a grown son by that name, but this child could not be his. She sent the bewildered Lois, and her baby, packing.

Nevertheless, Troy revealed that Lois was close to the truth. Dave's father had lived in Montreal. He was a Canadian who had been an RAF pilot during World War II. After the war, Dave's father met Lois at the soda fountain where she worked, near the University of Denver, where he was a student. Shortly after this young man recorded a date with Lois Wilson in his diary in 1949, he returned to Montreal.

But, almost diabolically, it turned out that Dave's father had a cousin who also lived in Montreal and who had the same name. It was the home of this cousin that Lois had found. And it was this cousin's mother who Lois had beseeched with the infant Dave in her arms. Because Lois had gone to the wrong house in Montreal, Dave's real father may never have known of his son's existence. Lois never knew she had knocked on the wrong door.

Other aspects of Dave's history unfolded like a Dickens novel. Dave had been forced to make his own way through life. But now we learned from our private detective friend that Dave's father had received an MBA from Harvard, had been a successful Canadian businessman, and had flown a small plane around the world to promote Montreal's Expo '67. Tragically, we learned that Dave's father had died when his small plane crashed. He was just forty-one at the time of the accident, and Dave only sixteen and still a boy at CBR. But we also learned that Dave's father had another son and two daughters. These half siblings, now grown, agreed to an introduction. Dave flew to New York to meet them.

The two sisters and one brother were immediately charmed by Dave's intelligence, humor, and dark-haired good looks, which they shared. Musical talent also ran in their genes. Dave, who had been raised as a Southern Baptist but had become a Catholic after our marriage, now learned that his father and half siblings were Jewish. Dave joked that his Southern Baptist grandmother, Pansy Anna, would be rolling over in her grave. Dave, however, was simply pleased to know more about his father, including his religious heritage.

During the weekend that Dave spent in New York, his brother let him sleep on the couch in the living room of his Manhattan apartment. As Dave was drifting off to sleep, he heard his brother call out from the bedroom, "Good night, bro."

Although they would gladly have been donors, Dave's half siblings were not tissue matches. A bone marrow donor was never found. Dave died in 1991. He was forty-one, the same age at which his father had died. Dave's courage and perseverance had stretched his life six and a half years beyond his diagnosis. Our daughters were seven and ten at the time of Dave's death. They had experienced their father's love and were now old enough to remember him.

Just before he died, Sarah and Rachel came to the ICU to kiss their father good-bye. Because of the chemotherapy, he was bald and jaundiced. With his wire-rimmed glasses, he looked like Gandhi. Dave's face and forehead were still covered in the pink and red lipstick kisses his two half sisters had left when they came from back East to say good-bye. His half brother was distraught to have so recently discovered in Dave an older brother whom he greatly admired, only to lose him within a year.

Dave's funeral was held in a large church across the street from the hospital where he died. Not surprisingly, the church was packed. Friends from Colorado Boys Ranch, from high school and law school, from the courthouse, from the auto shop where Dave took his car to be repaired, from the hospital, and from every part of Dave's life were in attendance.

John, his roommate from Colorado Boys Ranch, was present at the funeral. David Douglas, his guitar-playing friend from law school, read from the New Testament. Greg Klein, Dave's high school friend and bandmate, gave the eulogy, recalling Dave's sense of humor, his courage, and, most of all, his love for his family.

For someone who had been orphaned in adolescence, Dave had found his place in an amazingly large extended family by the time of his death. Dave's family now included dozens of friends, many of whom considered Dave their brother. This was not only a credit to Dave, but also a great comfort to our daughters and to me. Our children were the nucleus that gave his adult life meaning. My family loved Dave as their own son, brother, cousin, nephew. But Colorado Boys Ranch had remained the significant family of his childhood. And true to the deepest purpose of the Ranch, Dave returned the love he was given as a young boy at CBR into the community, manyfold.

Some people might see Dave as a tragic hero. His natural gifts of a keen intelligence and wry sense of humor were two of his saving graces. His steadfast faith was another. And he would add to that his supportive, nurturing, and stable years at Colorado Boys Ranch—his real home. Dave would never accept that his life was tragic, nor, though his friends would argue otherwise, would he admit that he had lived, or died, a hero.

In literary terms, a tragic hero is defined as one who is brought to ruin or suffers extreme sorrow as a result of a tragic flaw, a moral weakness, or a failure, despite supreme struggle to overcome unfavorable circumstances. Leukemia was the fatal flaw in Dave's blood. But there were no flaws in his character. He never blamed anyone for the hardships he suffered. He just went on with his life. Dave's struggles made him morally strong, determined to conquer whatever befell him, and convinced that life was good.

In the years since they stood and spoke without faltering at their father's funeral, little girls in ivory dresses, Sarah and Rachel have grown into wonderful young ladies, diligent in their studies and dedicated to community service. They, too, are advocates for the underdogs of this world.

Several years after Dave died, I remarried and was fortunate to have another child. At the time of this writing, Sam is six years old and adores his father, Bill. Sam also knows about Sarah and Rachel's father, Dave, and how he grew up at Colorado Boys Ranch. Somehow, Sam feels a connection to this man he never met. He sometimes stumbles around in Dave's old cowboy boots. The tan boots come up to Sam's knees. They are only size nine, but they are big shoes to fill. Every time I hug Sam and tell him he is the most wonderful boy in the world, I think about the boys at Colorado Boys Ranch. How many were told they were the most wonderful boys in the world when they were six years old? How many were abused or neglected instead?

A year after Dave's death, CBR dedicated a new building in his honor, one that welcomes new boys as they arrive on campus. The building is one that Dave helped plan as Colorado Boys Ranch was transitioning into a psychiatric residential treatment facility for troubled boys. CBR named their new diagnostic unit the Quicksall Center. Inside, on the wall, there is a plaque with Dave's picture and the inscription:

## David L. Quicksall

CBR Rancher 1964 to 1968

CBR Board of Directors 1979 to 1985

In Honor and Loving Memory of David

This special care facility is named

Quicksall Center

David's life exemplified HOPE, COURAGE and ACCOMPLISHMENT ...

Our wish for all youth who reside at Quicksall Center.

Boys who come to CBR YouthConnect today will not meet Dave. But when they are welcomed into the Quicksall Center, they will meet the same kind of caring people and be given the same kind of love that Dave received as a boy at CBR forty years ago. They may even learn to play the guitar in the music room that now exists on campus, thanks in part to the gift of Dave's law school friend. Perhaps Dave's story, as well as the remarkable success stories of other boys and their supporters included in this book, will help to inspire sad and troubled boys and the adults who care for them to strive to do good things and to give back the love they receive. That is all that most parents really wish for their children.

In the 1980s, Dave wrote a song that still speaks to the boys at CBR, and to any of us who seek hope and strength in living and in dying:

Starlight is just an afterglow

Of a light that shone

That we could not know

Your light is clearer than the starlight's hue

And the moon is a mirror of the love in you.

Reflection shows the way we must turn
There are no answers but the ones we learn
There are no questions but the ones we choose
And no greater lesson than the love in you.

They say we're forever,
Well that may be true
But one thing everlasting
Is the love in you.

—CQL

CHAPTER
FIVE

# Water Gravy

## Eldon Warren

*Many people take photographs to chronicle their lives and share with others. Photographs are objective, accurate, and revealing. But for Eldon Warren, a professional artist and a former Boys Rancher, paintings make a much more expressive visual record. Ever since he was a small boy, Eldon has recorded his life through his artwork. "My paintings are like my diary," he says. "I can look at any one of them and tell you when it was, where it was, and what I was doing at the time." Yet Eldon has only pencil drawings from his early childhood. There was no money for paint. There wasn't even enough money for food.*

"Have you ever heard of water gravy?" asks Eldon. "I ate a ton of it. It is a mixture of flour, lard, and water. We browned the lard-and-flour mixture in a skillet and then added the water. After a bit, you have gravy. You pour it over homemade bread and serve it hot. The lard containers were turned into lunch buckets, and we carried bread and water gravy to school for lunch."

Since this water gravy was made back in the 1960s, at a time when there were no microwave ovens in school lunchrooms, the lunchtime gravy on those slices of bread had to be eaten cold. But the rest of Eldon's life was heating up, and it was hard for the slight thirteen-year-old de facto head of the household to know what to do.

Then one day, it was out of Eldon's hands. A social worker appeared at the screen door of his mother's small frame house in a tiny agricultural town in northeastern Colorado. Eldon's life, the lives of his four siblings, and that of his disabled, arthritic mother were about to change forever. It was 1966. After making numerous routine visits to this welfare family, which was trying to get by on $165 a month, the social worker was ready to intervene. As Eldon says, "She thought we were headed for trouble. I guess if you see a bunch of unsupervised kids running around kind of wild, then that is what you might think."

The now fifty-year-old Eldon is philosophical about that day; the young Eldon was not. He was angry, and, as he puts it, "I had plenty to be angry about. And I was defenseless as well."

Remembering the day the social worker showed up at the screen door, Eldon paints the picture with words. "I remember the social worker coming to the house and delivering the news," he says. "I remember that I felt anger laced with dread. It wasn't rage, but sometimes a person gets angry enough that a heat runs up the back of his neck. I had a sick feeling in the pit of my stomach, and I knew that I had no choices and no amount of trying would change anything. I remember trying to explain it to my little sister, but I didn't have much luck. So after I had her totally confused, my mom told me to leave my sister alone. I'm sure my sister got the picture not long after, though."

If Eldon had actually painted that day, the picture he rendered might have tried to capture a voiceless scream. "I was initially very bent out of shape," Eldon says. "I had one life, and all of a sudden I had a different life, and there was nothing I could do about it. Like it or not."

Drawing, perhaps begun as an attempt to express his feelings, perhaps just to imitate an older brother's passion for drawing cars, became an obsession for Eldon. As a budding artist, Eldon did not have art lessons or fancy supplies, but if he could find a piece of typing paper and a pencil, he would draw.

"From the time I was very small, I have been fascinated by light and the differences between light and shadow," Eldon says. "Even now, if I am driving down the road looking for something to paint, it is the light that will get to me."

The light of the northeastern Colorado plains, where Eldon grew up, can be glaring. But there were other, harsher elements in Eldon's early life from which he might have wished to shield his eyes. Eldon guards those reminiscences of his childhood with the words "That's another story." Nearly all the references to his father are tempered with that aside.

Eldon's father abandoned his crippled wife and five small children. However, even before he left the family, he was giving his expensive coon-hunting dogs more attention and a larger share of the resources than he gave to his kids. He even pocketed the money that the oldest son earned selling bait. So, although Eldon suggests that his father might have given him an artistic gene or two, he leaves his indebtedness to his father at that.

Life was hard when you were ten years old and had a small sister to look after, school to attend, groceries to help buy, food to help cook, and a wringer washing machine to help operate. "There were hand-me-downs and shoes with holes in the bottom," Eldon remembers. "The few bucks we had to live on bought flour, lard by the bucket, and potatoes. There was surely more than that, but those were what I remember the most. Sometimes, in those early days when Dad was still around, we had a coon," Eldon recalls. "Very greasy."

Eldon describes the area where he played as a child: "Our backyard was the same as our front yard. Dirt. There was an alley and an old wooden shed." The artist in Eldon cannot help but describe the shed's features: "Not a speck of paint on it, so the wood was weathered and gray. In front of the shed lay an old pickup truck box someone had left years before. My brother and I played in and around that rusty thing and spent a lot of time up and down the alley."

Eldon's mother was not well. "Mom spent most of her time in bed," Eldon says. "She had the front corner room. She could still get around some then, but I think she just kind of quit and gave up trying to stay ahead of her arthritis. She lay around and, as time went on, got worse and worse. There was no nursing care for her until she went to a nursing home."

So even though Eldon was angry that day in 1966, he knows now what his world must have looked like to the social worker. A nearly bedridden mother and five undersupervised children did not look good. And it was probably a recipe for trouble.

Eldon's mother was put in a nursing home where she could be cared for adequately. His little sister was placed in a home in Denver. His two older brothers went into foster care. Eldon and his younger brother were sent to Colorado Boys Ranch.

Eldon describes his first moments at the Ranch: "I remember it was dark when the social worker dropped us off and drove away. I was standing out in front of the office and my mom was crying."

But Eldon took on his new challenge and, even today, downplays his loss. "Well, you know, when you are thirteen or fourteen, it's easier to take. It was the same there for everyone. You adjust."

This was February, late in his freshman year of high school. As was customary at the Ranch, Eldon was quickly integrated into daily life. That included being outfitted with clothes, enrolling in public school, earning his allowance with daily chores, and, as

Eldon forcefully points out, having "shoes without holes, a warm place to sleep, and three squares a day." No water gravy.

For boys at Colorado Boys Ranch, the *Ranch* part of its name was operative. Most boys participated in ranch-related activities, such as caring for horses or cutting hay. Not Eldon. He does remember once riding out on the mesa and regularly feeding the ranch dogs to earn his 75-cents-a-week allowance. But what did Eldon really do at the Ranch? He painted.

Bonna Hammond, now an energetic eighty-year-old working artist and a vital member of her local arts league, was Eldon's art teacher at La Junta High School. She remembers Eldon as one of her favorite students. "When I first met him, he needed lots of help," Bonna recalls. "They all do. But he was very willing. He wanted to learn new things. He was creative, and he wasn't afraid to make a mistake. Eldon was always willing to try again, which is what I want in an art student. Mistakes don't count. Not doing it does. He took every art class he could."

Eldon never stopped studying art. "You have to study all your life," reflects Mrs. Hammond. "And that's what I liked about Eldon." And although Mrs. Hammond taught and guided her students in subtle ways—or, as she wryly says, "snuck her lessons under their hides"—Eldon seemed to learn them well.

At the end of every school day, Eldon hopped on the bus and went home to the Ranch, not to be a range rider or cow roper, but to continue to develop his artistic talent. "I don't think they tried to steer us in any one direction," Eldon says, no pun intended. "There was one kid there who had a pretty good singing voice, and the Ranch administrator's wife, Mrs. Stieff, made sure he had singing lessons. When she saw something special, then that was the direction she took a kid, but she didn't push."

Mrs. Stieff took Eldon's art seriously. "Mrs. Stieff bought the first painting I ever sold," Eldon remembers. "It was all orange and yellow and red. Like flowers. Pretty abstract. She actually hung it on her wall, not on her wall at the office either. It was in her home." Eldon does not have any of the paintings from that time in his life, because he gave most of them away. But he remembers that orange painting and how it made him feel.

Mrs. Stieff gave him access to the tools he needed: blank purchase orders to the art supply store in town. "I never bought much, but I had everything I needed," Eldon recalls. And he had a place to work. "They set me up in fifth cottage. There was a little attic up over the cottage-parents' living quarters. I used it for a studio. I had to climb a ladder to get to it. I did what I had to do at the Ranch, but mostly I painted."

Eldon says the Myers-Briggs personality test determined that he is "as much of a wallflower as anyone can get." His life, however, seems to tell a different story. He not only "mostly painted" in La Junta, he also met a girl there, and their romance became quite serious.

The Ranch administrator reacted to this romance with dismay, as many parents of a young teenager might. "Mr. Stieff did not like the fact that I was involved with this girl," Eldon says. "One summer he sent me and a friend from the Ranch to Alamosa to build fences. We built fences from sunup to sundown for eight dollars a day, but the real reason we think we were there was because the Ranch didn't like our women."

The Boys Ranch attempted to enroll Eldon in a commercial art school in Denver, even taking him on a seven-hour round-trip visit. But at the time, he saw this as another ploy to move him away from his girlfriend. Eldon was not persuaded, and he ran away from the Ranch at age seventeen to marry, with his mother's permission, the eighteen-year-old girl from La Junta. They lived in a tiny twelve-dollar-a-week basement apartment while Eldon completed his senior year in high school. Poverty had a familiar face, and Eldon says that as a young couple they often had "only fifty cents to our name."

Eldon's oil painting *Storm Over the Picketwire*, a La Junta area canyon.

Eldon's first marriage lasted twenty-four years. While it did not last a lifetime, it gave him his beloved daughter and her family, including two "wonderful grandkids." And, while the Ranch was not able to dissuade Eldon from his teenage romance, it had more than encouraged him in his life's passion, art.

"I have thought about this a lot," Eldon says. "If I hadn't gone to the Ranch, I would have been doing the same thing my brothers are doing: laying irrigation pipe. I would have a farmer's tan, and, I can almost guarantee, I'd be living out in Yuma in some three-bedroom farmhouse somewhere, probably doodling, drawing a bit. There is no doubt in my mind that none of this would exist," he says, gesturing to the gallerylike art-filled walls of his Denver home. "I'd probably have a stack of typing paper drawings this tall. But in those tiny agricultural towns, you pretty much lived the same kind of life you started until you finished it."

He completes that thought with "You know, if I had been discouraged in any way at the Ranch, maybe even the smallest way, I'm not sure it would have turned out like this."

Although Eldon turned down art school and has earned his living mainly as a welder, he says, "I can't stop painting anymore than I can stop eating." Painting for the last thirty-five years, primarily in two media, watercolor and oils, has been the major and defining force in his life.

"I painted all those early years of our marriage," Eldon says. "Sometimes the only place I had to paint was on the kitchen table. If the painting slowed down, it was most likely because the cash wasn't flowing so well. Sometimes I'd get upset with my work and I would stop. But in a very short time, I found I needed a painting fix, and back I'd go."

Although it has been years since he lived in the area, the spare big sky and wide-open horizon of the Arkansas Valley landscape around La Junta inspires Eldon's work even today. He says it is his favorite place to paint. A recent painting captures those endless prairies of his youth. In that painting, the bright blue Colorado sky haloes several scrubby green trees. In the foreground, a small abandoned adobe building is surrounded by the warm golden colors of the dried prairie grasses at the end of the summer season.

"My favorite place to paint is southeastern Colorado," Eldon remarks. "To look at it, one might get the idea that there is nothing there but a bunch of sagebrush, cactus, and dirt." But Eldon sees so very much more: rich wildlife, recent and prehistoric artifacts, and, most importantly, its own special beauty.

He explains, "It never changes. There is no place I'd rather be. But to really experience the prairie, I have to be quiet. I have to listen to the heat and the flies buzzing. I have to accept it as it is, and I think when I do that, I can begin to see it the way it is. It is a place to think. The spaces are so wide and the horizons so far that one can lose himself pretty easily. And when a person is alone in those wide-open spaces, it can be pretty humbling. I don't judge it, and it doesn't judge me. And I think, 'She's beautiful.'"

"I do the majority of my work out in the open, plein air," Eldon says. "What motivates me is a desire to let others know where I've been, what I've seen, and how I felt about it. Sometimes that isn't easy. But I think I always manage to reach the viewer in some way. I am most drawn to scenes that are filled with bright sunlight and long dark shadows. In this part of the country, that isn't hard to find."

Each time Eldon picks up a brush, it is a brand-new experience. "I know that tomorrow or the next day, I am going to paint the best painting of my life," he says. And each time Eldon picks up his brush, he wonders whether this is the day.

Sometimes he gets stuck. "I can always tell when I have a problem," Eldon says. "I constantly look at art, and I constantly compare. Why isn't my work as good as that piece? And then I will study. I will find a book and sit with it for three weeks, and if it can teach me something, I will buy it."

When he gets unstuck, "It can be such a thrill," Eldon says. "Like when you're thirteen or fourteen and you have a crush on a girl and you get this feeling inside," he says, pointing to his chest. "And that's the way it still is with me and painting."

Eldon's love affair with art, begun in his youth, continues to this day. He has won numerous awards in nationally juried shows, and his work hangs on the walls of admirers from coast to coast, and even in Japan. Galleries across the country carry Eldon's work. He has helped organize shows in his capacity as president and vice president of a local art league. He has a new, happy marriage, and he is mentoring his artistic stepson.

Eldon grows daily as he explores the endless possibilities of his newest artistic path: impressionistic landscapes. Eldon participated in the juried "Painting the Parks, Estes Park Plein Air 2003" event. He won one of the very prestigious top-three show awards with his oil painting titled *Brainard Lake*. He has recently been judged to be in the top 100 of the Arts for the Parks show, sponsored by the National Park Service. He was chosen from among 2,500 paintings for that distinction. Colorado Boys Ranch has bought several of his works.

Eldon has kept in touch with the Ranch and has returned to give inspirational talks to the boys. Despite the fact that he never claimed to be a cowboy during his time at the Ranch, Eldon's advice to the boys is phrased in western lingo. "Take it by the horns and do it," he says, "whatever it is you want to do."

"It's amazing how going back and experiencing the Ranch again can bring back the feelings I felt in those days," Eldon says. "Some good, some not so good. I think what came back the strongest was that feeling of being singular. For as many other boys and staff that were around, I think most of the guys still felt pretty much by themselves. I think we all had a hole to fill up somewhere inside us. Some managed to find a way to fill it, and some just managed."

Eldon is no longer making water gravy, but he still remembers the physical and emotional hunger of his youth. In his typical fashion, he uses a visual illustration to explain. "There is an old movie," Eldon says, "where a couple of small, dirty boys are looking through the restaurant window at the people inside. They eventually get shooed away, of course, but there is a hungry look in their eyes that I see in the old images. A sadness that tells you that they know they are on the outside and they are looking hard for a way in."

Eldon Warren found his way in through his art. Perhaps he paints his life because, at one crucial time in his unsettled youth, he was encouraged to be the person he really was. But mostly he paints for that feeling it gives him inside. Just for the sheer joy of it.

—JP

# Foxhole Prayers

# Bill Files

*Bill Files survived some of the fiercest battles of World War II because he didn't close his eyes when horror was all around. Half a world away, during that monumental conflict at Iwo Jima, he looked death in the eye. When it was over, he came home to southern Colorado glad, and lucky, to be alive.*

*But even in peacetime, the former reconnaissance sergeant kept his eyes open. And when he saw a new kind of horror, in the stories of abandoned, abused, and troubled boys coming to Colorado Boys Ranch, he didn't flinch. For more than four decades, Bill has served as a volunteer for Colorado Boys Ranch, fighting for these boys. His lessons of courage, learned long ago in battle, turned into the positive action of helping boys at Colorado Boys Ranch who face their own fears. Bill Files is a man of keen sense, ready in battle. He is also a man of unusual sensitivity, steadfast in love.*

✦ ✦ ✦

Bill is a marine's marine. At six feet, three inches and near his "summer weight" of 200 pounds, he makes an impressive figure. Tall, straight, and broad of shoulder, even into his eighth decade Bill could still pose for a Marine Corps recruiting poster. Famous for the ability to spin a yarn, his own story is straightforward.

"My name is Willie Manley Files," he says, "That's my true given name. But I go by Bill. I was born in Savoy, Texas. My dad passed away when I was ten, leaving six of us. I don't know how my mother turned us all out, but she was a pretty religious little gal. We were two girls and four boys. And we were farmers. I had kind of a religious beginning with my family. We rode our wagons to church."

Leaving Texas and the wagons behind, Bill moved to Colorado in 1939. By 1942, he had joined the United States Marines and was soon fighting, and praying, in Guam, Guadalcanal, Bougainville, and Iwo Jima. "I carried a rifle as a reconnaissance sergeant," Bill says of his time with the 9th Regiment Weapons Company, 3rd Marine Division. "I was the person that reconnoiters routes."

In the midst of the war, Bill did not forget those wagon rides to church. But churchgoing was different in the rugged island terrain of the Asiatic Pacific. "We had a kind of quasi-religious experience," Bill says. "We built our own chapels out of palm fronds. We tried to dignify it. It got ecumenical back in those days in the Marine Corps," he says. "Very seldom would you ask the guy on the right or the left what his religion was, as long as he had sworn to take an oath, like you did, to die for our country. That meant you took care of your buddies because they were going to take care of you."

For decades after the war, Bill continued to take care of his war buddies, volunteering to drive injured veterans to the Fort Lyons Veterans Hospital. Many of the veterans that Bill helped had psychological as well as physical wounds. Although he counts himself lucky, Bill is not without his own scars from the war. On Iwo Jima, he took a bullet that tore off a piece of one of his vertebrae. More than fifty years later, he avoids watching war movies and, like many veterans, is reluctant to talk about his war experiences. He still has nightmares. "My wife says I almost kicked her out of bed one night," Bill says. "Thank God all that has been dreams. Some guys go into real live action."

To combat the nightmares, Bill has devoted countless waking hours to organizations such as the Marine Corps League, American Legion, Fraternal Order of the Eagles, Easter Seals, and Disabled American Veterans. For his wounds at Iwo Jima, Bill earned a Purple Heart and, along with his comrades, was given the Presidential Unit Citation. His dogged altruism after the war has earned him many community awards, but the one he cherishes most is the Files Volunteer Service Award, established in his honor at Colorado Boys Ranch. The 100-year plaque, with Bill's name at the top of a growing list of outstanding volunteers, hangs in the dining hall at Colorado Boys Ranch to the left of the stage, next to the United States flag.

Long past his own mustering-out date, this former marine continues to shoulder the cares of others. The reason is simple, according to Bill. "At Iwo Jima and Guadalcanal, I made a lot of promises," he explains, "a lot of foxhole prayers."

When pressed, he will tell you some details of those wartime prayer vigils. "But I would never be able to tell you about the living conditions," he says. "Jungle rot. Malaria. Elephantiasis. The casualties in many cases were more from the environment than from bullets. We'd get acute malaria for three or four days. About four of those mosquitoes could lift you off the ground," he says with a wink.

His last battle is the most vivid in his mind. "In Iwo Jima, we lost so many," Bill says, the smile leaving his face. "We hit there in February of '45. The island was eight square miles, with very little camouflage and no trees. So we were exposed. The Japanese had annihilated one particular company. We knew very few of the people that were in our company, because they were drawn from other units. We formed a line replacing about 260 men with 40 men. In the tactics that you use placing men at the front, you dig foxholes fairly close together, fifteen to twenty yards apart. But with 40 people replacing 260 men, there were a lot of empty foxholes. I don't know how far apart we were."

Bill cannot forget the nighttime banzai attacks by the Japanese. "It was getting dark," he recalls. "The flares that the Japanese used to light up the island were a kind of a high yellow, and ours were phosphorus white. It wouldn't take too many flares to light up those eight square miles of land like daylight.

"The first night and the second night there was a banzai charge," Bill says. "As soon as we saw the Japanese come over this little hill in front of our foxhole, I hollered, 'Halt!' One was already at the foxhole. He shot the dirt pile, which we called a parapet, in front of our foxhole. That threw dust all over my face. But we got him, and here came the others. I don't know how many men came after us.

"I had an M-1 Garand .30-caliber rifle, and on the end of it we had a rocket grenade," Bill says. "You could only fire one round, then you had to manually reload. My weapon jammed. I don't even remember what my buddy was doing, to tell you the truth, but I started pulling pins out of grenades and throwing them. There was machine-gun fire to my right, rifle fire to my left. And it was quite a ways away. The next morning, they were stacked up in front of us like cordwood. The body count was not as important then as it is now. I really couldn't tell you. There was piles of them out there."

More than 6,000 U.S. Marines were killed on the volcanic soil of Iwo Jima. Bill was one of the lucky ones. He was hit by a bullet but lived. "I was wounded with a .31-caliber Japanese rifle,"

Bill says. "The bullet penetrated through the hip and ricocheted off my back. If it had been a modern-day weapon, I would have been killed."

Bill's injured body was taken up by some of his Marine Corps buddies. "Two guys with a gurney came and picked me up," Bill says. "The Japanese were still shelling. There were mortars coming. The two guys carrying me jumped into a shell crater and left me up on top of the ground," he says. He can shake his head and laugh about it now. "Finally," he says, "they got out, picked me up, and took me back to an aid station. They checked me out and gave me morphine. The next day they were loading cargo ships. I was lucky. I got on the hospital ship and I came home."

After Bill recuperated, he was reassigned as a drill instructor in San Diego. He met his wife there, and, after he was discharged, Bill returned to his job at CF&I Steel in Pueblo. The Pueblo newspaper, *The Chieftain*, interviewed Bill on the fortieth anniversary of the U.S. invasion of Iwo Jima. In that article he recalled, "I came back and worked at the steel mill two years, real hard physical labor. It was the best therapy I could have had. I had no time on my hands to think of what had happened to my buddies or what could have happened to me. Sometimes the bitterness comes back, because you think of all the guys you knew and were close to," he said. "But once you get as old as I am, you see it differently. I don't hate anymore."

Indeed, far from hating, Bill is the founder of "The Hug Club." Instead of a rifle, he now carries hug coupons signed by him and his wife that say, "Good for one hug from someone who likes you just the way you are." On the back of the coupon, Bill has printed the Colorado Boys Ranch motto, "It is easier to build a boy than to mend a man." Bill gives a coupon and a hug to anyone who will take one. But, speaking like a former marine— or perhaps mocking the tough-guy image—he cautions, "I don't hug men. I shake their hands." He gets a big grin on his face when he mentions that he once got a hug from First Lady Barbara Bush.

It was during Bill's long civil service career as chief of security police at the Pueblo Army Depot that he first became acquainted with Colorado Boys Ranch. "It was on September 9, 1961, a Saturday," Bill says. His memory of the event is crystal clear. "Everette Marshall had called me and asked if he could bring some boys from Colorado Boys Ranch to a barbeque I was hosting for the Sportsmen's Club at the Army Depot. He came, and the boys, five or six of them, came with a sack of onions, and that was a promotion for the Boys Ranch.

"I knew Everette Marshall, but he didn't know me," Bill says of the famous wrestler. "I saw Marshall wrestle at Pueblo Junior College. He became a professional, but he quit the wrestling when they started the clowning bit. And Everette Marshall and John May, the executive secretary for Colorado Boys Ranch, thought, because of this barbeque, that I was some kind of a big wheel, which I wasn't. I was just helping.

"They wanted me to come down and see the Ranch," Bill recalls. "I went down with a buddy to see. They gave us a tour. All the buildings were broken down, windows broken, doors off, trees in the middle of the street. Have you ever seen these blinders they put on mules so they can't see?" Bill asks. He laughs. "I wanted to get some of those and put them on myself and get out of there.

"But here came one of the boys," Bill says. "I called him Arthur Godfrey. He had a snake in his hand. John May was driving. John stopped and rolled down his window, and this kid stuck this snake under his nose. The boy said, 'What kind of snake is this?' And John jumped back. Then the boy went around to Everette Marshall's window and put it under his nose, and, lucky for all of us, it was a bull snake. So I kind of took the blinders about half off."

Bill began bringing donations down to the Ranch from Pueblo. "I got some donations from my dentist, who was retiring. My pickup was loaded. That dental chair weighed a lot." Soon Bill was hauling boys in the other direction, taking them from the Boys Ranch in La Junta to the state fair in Pueblo.

It wasn't VJ day, but it must have seemed like some kind of victory celebration to the boys from the Ranch when Bill arranged for their bus to receive a police escort, with sirens wailing, down the main boulevard of Pueblo on their way to the state fair. Bill also arranged for the boys to receive special attention from famous Western stars. The boys felt like big shots when they had their pictures taken with *Gunsmoke* star Ken Curtis (Festus Haggen), Rex Allen, Roy Rogers, and Dale Evans.

Bill was asked by the Colorado Boys Ranch board of directors to found an advisory board, and he put a great deal of work into organizing that statewide group. He wrote many letters seeking support for Colorado Boys Ranch. In 1998, Bill, who had been widowed, remarried. He and his new wife, Lois, were invited

Boys Ranchers with Milburn Stone (Doc Adams) and Ken Curtis (Festus Haggen) of TV's *Gunsmoke* series.

to have their wedding at Arlington Chapel on the grounds of Colorado Boys Ranch. Boys Ranchers were in attendance for the Easter sunrise wedding service. Colorado Boys Ranch President Chuck Thompson said of their wedding, "For our boys to witness the love and commitment of these two longtime Boys Ranch supporters was very special."

Love and commitment are the medals of honor in Bill's well-lived life. He never really put on the blinders that he wished for that day he first saw the dilapidated early Boys Ranch. Instead, he kept his eyes, and his heart, wide open.

—CQL

# CHAPTER SEVEN

# Tank Officer
# in a Santa Suit

## Doyle Davidson

*One would never suspect that the gentle soul who has played Santa Claus at Christmas dinners at the Colorado Boys Ranch for four decades was once a tank officer with General Patton at the Battle of the Bulge. Doyle Davidson, now eighty-one years old, is still the tall and handsome man he was as an officer and a gentleman in World War II. When the war ended, Doyle also ended his career as an army officer. Yet he has truly remained a "gentle" man. Through him, generations of boys at Colorado Boys Ranch have known the kindness and generosity of Father Christmas.*

This year, for the first time in more than forty years, Doyle did not don the Santa suit for Christmas dinner at Colorado Boys Ranch. His wife, Peggy, is seriously ill, and because he is suffering speech problems of his own, Doyle decided it was time to pass the Santa suit on. At six feet and 160 pounds, the slim Doyle never did meet the girth requirements for Santa. But if the measure of a man is the size of his heart, then Doyle more than fills the bill.

Doyle grew up during the Depression on a farm in south-east Colorado. Although he says, "I'm eighty-one and I get kind of mixed up with my memory sometimes," Doyle cannot forget the day he first spotted his wife. "I saw Peggy walking down the street in Lamar with my girl cousin," he says, "and I said to myself, 'Boy, that's the cutest girl I've seen.'" Even as a boy, Doyle had the keen vision he would later need as a forward observer in the army. He looked into the distance and began making plans. "I'm going to marry that girl," he said to himself.

It took diligent reconnaissance and quite a few years for Doyle to accomplish his mission. "Peggy's folks had a little grocery store in those days," Doyle says. "All the farmers would come into town on the weekend. Every Sunday, my dad and I would go to that store in Lamar to pick up *The Denver Post*. Everybody likes the funny papers. I'd see Peggy running around there. And I just kind of followed her around."

Doyle kept Peggy in his sights as he completed high school and college, where he was in ROTC. Upon graduation from Colorado State University, Doyle was commissioned in the United States Army. Peggy had one more year of nurses training to complete, but they didn't want to wait any longer. D day was approaching. In April of 1944, Doyle and Peggy were married. One week later, Doyle shipped overseas.

Fifty-eight years have passed. Peggy and Doyle welcome a visitor, one of many over the years, to the La Junta home where they raised their two children. Due to a lung condition, Peggy stays tethered to oxygen via a long tube. The tube winds from the kitchen, where Peggy sits at the table, up the stairs to the master bedroom, where it connects to the oxygen tank. In addition to the oxygen tank, Doyle divulges, there is another unusual feature upstairs in the master bedroom: a big photo of General Patton.

Not many folks have a picture of General Patton hanging on their bedroom wall, but like Peggy and her oxygen tank, Doyle is unusually attached. "Patton was the greatest general I've ever seen," Doyle says. "When he wanted to do something, he did it. He was right in front. He wasn't sitting back pushing. He was up there leading." Not all of Doyle's recollections are pleasant by any means. "General Patton got a little piece of my butt a few times," Doyle says. He chuckles as he recalls being chewed out by "Old Blood and Guts."

"I saw him three times during the Battle of the Bulge," Doyle says. "The first time was in a theater building in Belgium. I was a first lieutenant, a tank officer in the 274th Armored Artillery Battalion. I was a forward observer. I went out with infantry and tank crew, and when they needed artillery, it was my job to map it out and get artillery firing in that area. General Patton called all his officers in from his corps into this theater. It was pretty well full, and every one of us was kind of shaking, you know, thinking, 'What's going on? This man is a warrior.'

"All of a sudden, somebody says, 'Attention!' Boy, up we stood out of our seats," Doyle recalls. "And in he comes, in a big old trench coat and a helmet. He had a swagger stick in his hand and two ivory handles on his hips: a Smith & Wesson .357 and that old Colt .45 that he had. And he just stood on the stage for about three minutes and didn't say a damn thing. Just looked. And then he says, 'I'll tell you what. I want you sons of bitches to fire ten more rounds of artillery where you're firing one. You shoot that many rounds and most of you will go home. We can get more ammunition, but we can't get more good soldiers.' That was about all he said. Then he turned and walked off.

"The next time I saw Patton," Doyle recalls, "two army units were in the way of where he wanted to go. It was all jammed up. He was standing up on his jeep getting the tanks out of the way. I drove right past him to go into the Battle of the Bulge."

Doyle's third and final meeting with Patton was face to face. "We were about two miles out of Bastogne," Doyle recalls. "We got our tanks off to the side so they couldn't shoot us down the road. We had been firing, and we were getting ready to shoot a few more when all of a sudden the big boy comes up in a jeep. Just a jeep. All the rest of us had armor. And Patton says, 'Who's the son of a bitch who's supposed to be our forward up here?' And I say, 'Yes sir, that's me.' Patton growls, 'Get some shells on those so-and-sos up there.' Well it so happened that I had already relayed back to battalion giving them a target on the map and ordered a fire mission. Our shells started coming over our heads just as Patton was speaking. So Patton says, 'Good going, lieutenant! Keep it up! See you later.' I was scared to death."

Doyle's awe of Patton at the Battle of the Bulge still looms large in his mind. Despite that kind of fear, or maybe because of it, Doyle made it from D day plus twenty-three, when he landed at Omaha Beach, through the Battle of the Bulge and all the way to Hitler's Eagle's Nest in Berchtesgaden. But years later, in peacetime, Doyle feared for his life one more time.

It was 1960. Doyle was looking into the crazed eyes of a desperate man. Facing him outside the door of his Harrah's Club hotel room was a man Doyle knew, but only vaguely. The desperate man was a fund-raiser, recently hired by Colorado Boys Ranch. Unbeknownst to the newly fledged ranch, or to Doyle, who was a founding board member, the fund-raiser was a gambler. He was looking for cash, but he wasn't planning to give it to Colorado Boys Ranch.

Doyle recalls how the tense situation came about. "Back in La Junta, the Colorado Boys Ranch board had been discussing how we needed some funding," Doyle says. "The wives of the board members were having coffee klatches in their homes and charging a dollar a cup for the coffee to raise money for the Ranch. It started out that way. It really was a nickel-and-dime operation. We needed money to refurbish the old civilian housing area near the La Junta air base, which had been abandoned after World War II. This was going to become the Boys Ranch. In the fifteen years since the war, the doors of those duplexes had been blown off. Russian thistles had blown in. We hadn't opened the doors yet. We didn't have any boys. We didn't even have letterhead or a telephone. Dr. Davis, one of the original board members, pulled his checkbook out of his hip pocket and wrote out a check for $1,000 and said, 'Let's get going.'

"But we needed more help," Doyle recalls. "So this professional fund-raiser came in and talked to the board. He said he would like to take on the deal of bringing all the funds in, and we would not have to pay him until the money started to come in. We discussed all this and thought it would be a pretty good idea. So the fund-raiser came aboard. But I wasn't expecting to see him in Lake Tahoe.

"I was working at that time for the National Highway 50 Federation," Doyle says. "It was a traveling job putting together a strong organization to advertise the coast-to-coast highway. We were trying to bring travelers back to towns like La Junta, because the new interstate freeways had siphoned them off. I was doing volunteer work with the CBR board, as much as I could work it in, along with my Highway 50 job. This trip was to meet with the president of the Highway 50 organization, John Gianotti, who was also the public relations man for Harrah's gambling casino in Lake Tahoe.

"After dinner I had gone down to the casino from my room. And I'm not a gambler," Doyle says. "I just walked around and looked at the tables. All of a sudden I see this fellow. We were eye to eye. It was this fund-raiser. The fund-raiser from Colorado is out there shooting craps. I hadn't expected to see him there, but I didn't think anything about it. I said, 'Oh, it's good to see you.'

"I went up to my room, and about 10:30 P.M. there was a knock come on my door," Doyle recalls. "I opened up the door, and it was this fund-raiser standing right there. He had these piercing eyes. And he looked at me and he said, 'I bet you carry a lot of money on you when you're out traveling like this.' All of a sudden, I knew what was going to happen. I did have about $500 in my pocket, but I didn't tell him that. I said, 'No, I don't carry a lot of money, because these people along the road give me hospitality.' He just looked daggers through me, really wild in the face. I thought he was going to hit me. All of a sudden, he stomped his foot, turned around, and took off. I closed and bolted the door as fast as I could.

"That fund-raiser just scared the 'H' out of me," the gentle Doyle says. "I didn't want to call my wife and get her upset, so I called Milt Richert, the banker on our board for Colorado Boys Ranch. I said, 'Milt, don't call my wife and scare her, but I want you and the Boys Ranch board to know what your fund-raiser is doing. He might come back and possibly harm me, forcing me to give him some money. I want somebody to know about this confrontation in case I get bumped off.' I didn't sleep well that night.

"The next morning," Doyle continues, "I left a note in my room, in case anything happened to me, and went down to the dining room to have breakfast with Gianotti. He was reading a newspaper with a three-column banner headline: 'Suicide in the Desert.'

"Oh, that headline shook me," Doyle says. "A cold sweat came over me as I read the article. It was that fellow who was going to be our fund-raiser for CBR and who was wanting money from me. I know, undoubtedly, he got too strong into Harrah's Club and he took off. They found his car and a pistol and him with a bullet in his head. I lost my appetite. John Gianotti was a card-carrying member of the local sheriff's posse, and he told me that they felt it was a closed case as a suicide."

"That stuck in my mind, and I can see that fund-raiser's face to this day," Doyle says.

But Bob Cody, another original Colorado Boys Ranch board member, recalls the story slightly differently. "The fund-raiser did get money from us," Bob says. "We gave him $25,000 up front. We had to cosign notes. Here I was, an insurance salesman with four or five kids at the time. And we had to cover that loss. Personally. That was one of our biggest starting mistakes. I think it proves that even though we had pretty good businessmen on the board, we were really novices. We tried to find our way."

Doyle agrees on that point. "It's just one of those things. God had to direct us. Really, it's a miracle we started the Boys Ranch at all."

But Colorado Boys Ranch did finally open its doors, now back on their hinges, and the first boys began arriving in the early sixties. Doyle was struck by the story of one boy in particular. "John May, the first administrator of Colorado Boys Ranch, was going to Denver to get this boy who had been referred to us," Doyle recalls. "Since I was in Denver for a meeting, he asked me to meet him at the boy's house. The boy lived on Larimer Street. That was the honky-tonk street of Denver.

"So we were standing in front of this little house at ten in the morning, and we see this little boy playing out in the yard," Doyle recalls. "We had the note from the judge to take custody of the boy. The parents had been notified and agreed and knew we were coming. John said to the boy, 'Can we talk with your father?' And the boy said, 'Oh, yeah, he's right down here. Follow me.' The little boy started running down the street. About a block and a half from where he lived, he ran into a tavern. So we followed him. There was only the bartender and one other man in the bar.

"That was the boy's father," Doyle says, "sitting on a bar stool slumped over the bar with a glass of whiskey in front of his face. Passed out. We asked his name, but he couldn't do anything but grunt. So we looked at the boy and said, 'Is your mother home?' And he said, 'Sure, she's home.'

"We went back to his house," Doyle says. "That little boy picked up a big old two-by-four and went around to the side of the house. He started beating on the house beneath a window with his two-by-four. Pretty soon this scratchy female voice said, 'What do you want?' And the boy said, 'Mother, there's some men here to see you.'

"So she comes to the door about ten minutes later," Doyle says, "all ruffled, filthy dirty. We told her what our mission was and showed her the documents. She didn't say anything. She just handed out an old tattered suitcase full of her son's possessions and shut the door. We were taking her son, but she didn't say anything to him.

"When we told the little boy we were taking him to a ranch, he was nice about it," Doyle remembers. "He just got in the car and went with us. We found out later his mother worked in that tavern until midnight and from midnight on she was a prostitute. And that's what this little boy was living with, a prostitute and an alcoholic. That was one hell hole."

Doyle didn't let these rough experiences scare him away from Colorado Boys Ranch. He has worked for over forty years as both a volunteer and later as a part-time employee for the Ranch. Doyle has coordinated special events such as auctions at the state fair and annual golf tournaments to raise money for the boys. He speaks to service clubs and the Colorado Cattlemen's Association on behalf of these boys. Recently he has been on the road again, visiting hundreds of donors in the southern Colorado area to thank them for their donations to CBR. And, of course, for forty-three years on the Ranch, he has been Santa.

Christmastime has always been poignant at the Ranch, especially for those boys who have no homes to return to for the holidays. That touched Doyle's heart, so he and his wife, Peggy, began inviting one of the Boys Ranchers to come to their home in La Junta for dinner on Christmas Eve. Doyle recalls, "One Christmas Eve this boy showed up from the Ranch at our door, and he

Doyle Davidson as the CBR Santa.

had this poinsettia. It was kind of stripped down and sorry looking, and we wondered where he got it. One of our neighbors about three houses down from us had a lot of poinsettias on her porch. We found out later that the boy had asked to be dropped off at the corner so he could walk the rest of the way. He must have gone up there and swiped one of those to give to my wife. But we knew that his heart was in the right place. He wanted to bring a present to my wife for having him in for Christmas Eve dinner."

In addition to hosting individual boys at their home on Christmas Eve, Doyle and Peggy always attended the Christmas dinner at the Ranch, where Doyle played Father Christmas. The dinner was especially poignant for Doyle the December of 2002. He sat at a table in the back of the dining hall next to Bob Cody, the only other surviving member of the original CBR board. Peggy, who once worked as a nurse for CBR, was not well enough to join them. Two former Boys Ranchers, now in their fifties, sat with their own wives, looking on from another table. Current Boys Ranchers got up on the stage and performed skits, sang songs, and recited the "Cowboy's Prayer." One of those former

Boys Ranchers said of the Christmas program, "It was all so unpolished that you had to love it."

At the end of the evening, a big fellow in a belted coat with pants tucked into tall black boots came out onto the stage. With a costume like that, it could have been General Patton. But this man's uniform was bright red, not olive drab, and in his hand he held a bag of presents, not a swagger stick. But for the first time in forty-three years, the man standing on the stage in the Santa suit was not Doyle. A new Santa inhabited the crimson clothing and the white beard. Boys Ranchers and children of staff members bunched around the stage, but Doyle, his blue eyes twinkling, remained at his table in the back of the room. Dressed in civilian clothes, he wore a simple gray suit, a black tie, and a wide grin.

—CQL

# Joyriding

## Steve

*Not unexpectedly, Steve's appearance has altered a bit in the thirty-five years since he was a Boys Rancher. Among other changes, he grew a moustache and has cultivated it for decades. On the morning he was to be interviewed about his days at Colorado Boys Ranch, Steve went into the bathroom to shave. As he stared into the bathroom mirror, he got so lost in reverie about his days as a boy at CBR that he unintentionally shaved off half his moustache. There was nothing to do but smile and shave off the other half.*

When Steve was thirteen years old, he did not have a mustache, but he did have a paper route, a bicycle, and an eye for fine automobiles. While delivering newspapers in suburban Denver one day in 1963, weaving his bicycle in and out of the cars parked along his street, a 1960 four-door Chevrolet Biscayne caught his eye. Steve was too young for a driver's license, but he was old enough to know the make and model of most cars on the road. The most interesting feature of the Biscayne was that the keys were sticking out of the driver's side door. Steve looked around. There was nobody in sight.

"I took the keys, I guess," Steve says. "Or I told somebody, and they took them." Some details have faded over the course of forty years. "The next night, three of us snuck out of our houses. We met at the car and pushed it down to the end of the block. Then we all got in, and away we went." Taking the car was Steve's first trip outside the law. "We didn't actually steal it," he explains, describing their thinking at the time. "We went joyriding."

Taking turns behind the wheel, the boys laughed and joked as they careened out of Denver, up the highway to Red Rocks, and into the mountains near Evergreen. "We drove around until about five thirty in the morning," Steve says. But the joyride had to come to an end. "It was getting light out," Steve explains, "and we had to be home in time to do our paper routes."

Squinting into the glare of the early morning sun, they drove back down the mountain into Denver. "We stashed the car in a parking lot," Steve says, "but we were stupid. When we finished delivering our papers, we decided to get back in the car and go sporting around some more." Steve shakes his head and says, "We pulled out of the parking lot and came to a traffic light and made the turn. There was a cop right behind us. Needless to say, we got busted. That was my life of crime."

Steve went to court and was put on probation for a year. All might have been well except that physically, Steve was not well at all. His stomach began to give him a rough ride. "I had ulcers," Steve explains. "And nobody at school would believe me."

He missed a lot of classes. "My stomach would get to churning, and sometimes I felt sick to my stomach when I'd been in school all day. Or even in the morning before I went to school. I guess it was just anticipation," he says. "It might have been teenage stress, living with my grandparents and mother and two brothers. And the fact, I guess, of not having a father around.

"I never knew my father," Steve says. "I finally met him when I was about ten years old, but it meant nothing to me. When Mother divorced, she took us back to live with her parents. All three of them, my mother and my grandparents, raised us kids. So basically, I had three bosses. It put a great strain on me, as I think it would anybody. I always respected them, but, unfortunately, I was probably pushing my limits." Steve admits, "I had a very bad attitude towards authority."

After Steve's joyride, the new authority figure in his life was a probation officer who didn't believe a boy Steve's age could have an ulcer. Despite a week of tests at Porter Hospital confirming that Steve indeed did have a bad ulcer, his "truancy" brought him in front of a judge for a second time.

The final destination of Steve's joyride, he learned, might be the state reformatory for boys in Golden. He says, "I couldn't figure it out. What in the heck did I do? I was never a good student. I just did not want to go to school. Why would they send me to jail?"

Colorado's county judges believed strongly that boys like Steve who had gotten into minor scrapes with the law needed care and counseling, not prison. Their pleas for an alternative to state penal institutions had spurred the private citizens of the Arkansas Valley to create Colorado Boys Ranch in La Junta. The judge in Steve's case recommended that Steve be placed there for one year. Steve and his mother agreed, but, he recalls, "It was a great shock, and I was very mad at the time."

The night before he was to leave for the Boys Ranch, Steve and his friends snuck out for one final joyride. This time Steve took his mom's car, a 1959 Chevrolet Impala. "We drove around a while and I backed her car into a pole. The pole smashed the center section of the bumper right where you put the gas in. So I went home and faced the music. What were they going to do?" he smiles. "Send me away?

"The next morning, Mom took the car down to the local service station," Steve recalls. "They removed the center part of the bumper so we could put gas in. Needless to say, I was at the Boys Ranch that afternoon."

Steve, his mother, and his grandparents all made the trip to Colorado Boys Ranch in the family car. It was a warm winter Sunday in February of 1964. The journey was a return, of sorts, for Steve's grandparents. Along the Arkansas River just east of Pueblo, they passed through Avondale, where Steve's grandparents had been born and raised around the turn of the century. "My grandparents both came from families of twelve children, and they still had people in Ordway," Steve recalls, referring to another small farming community in the Arkansas Valley. Steve, however, had been born and raised in Denver. Unlike his grandparents, Steve was a big-city boy.

Steve remembers being driven through the main gate of Colorado Boys Ranch and crossing the cattle guard. "Back then, all the roads were dirt," Steve recalls. "I saw all those open fields, run-down buildings, and I thought to myself, "What in the hell have I gotten myself into now?"

After Steve was deposited at the Ranch, the family car headed back out the main gate. He narrowed his eyes as dust from the rear tires swirled into the dry air. Steve was already counting the 365 days until he would be leaving the Boys Ranch in that car. He began to size up his situation. There were fewer than twenty boys on the Ranch at that time. "I met my roommates, Richard and Johnny. Richard was two years older but about my same size. There wasn't anybody else bigger than Richard and me, and so we put on the gloves. I think Richard was trying to see who was the toughest. He was going to prove that he was the meanest dude on the planet. We went a few rounds, and he nailed the side of my face. It hurt pretty good. I didn't let him know it hurt. I just said, 'That's enough.' I think he was trying to make sure I had my place."

Steve's place, it turned out, was with Mr. Homer Walker. "Homer was an old cowhand," Steve says. "He was about sixty years old and a big man, about 250 pounds. He had salt-and-pepper hair, a ruddy complexion, and red cheeks and nose. I guessed he must have farmed and ranched for quite some time. Homer was the cowboy and the ranch hand for the Boys Ranch at that time. His wife was a great lady there too. They were my cottage-parents. He was talkative, and we got along very well. I don't see how I couldn't, being with him all day."

Instead of climbing into the school bus with the other boys each morning, Steve climbed into the front passenger seat of an old Chevy truck, riding "shotgun" with Homer as they ran errands for the Boys Ranch. Academic testing had shown that Steve wasn't ready to join the ninth grade in La Junta, and the school recommended he wait until fall. Since missing school had been the reason he was sent to Colorado Boys Ranch in the first place, it seemed odd to Steve that he was kept out of school for a semester. But he didn't object. He received a different kind of education that spring.

"Basically, my days consisted of going with Homer," Steve says. "Every morning I'd get up and go over to the kitchen for breakfast. The other kids would eat and then go off to school. Homer and me would relax for a little while. Then we'd get in the truck.

"We had an old Chevrolet pickup with a stock rack on the back," Steve recalls. "Every morning we'd drive the truck into La Junta to one of the feed and grain places that gave feed to the Boys Ranch. We'd back the truck in there, and they'd pour down a big old truckload of silage. We'd check the cattle and make sure the water was working properly. We'd clean up the corral. Homer and me went on many a journey to pick up cattle. One time we went all the way up towards Limon and picked up a big Charolais heifer that a woman had given to the Ranch.

"Homer taught me how to ride and how to throw a rope too. And I learned to castrate the cattle. That was the first time in my life I ever bulldogged a calf and sat there and watched the operation get done. I thought, 'Oh, jeez!' I couldn't believe you just sort of grab them and 'chung' and slash some pine tar on 'em and there they go. I never did it myself. All I did was bulldog the calf and stretch its legs out so Homer could get down there and do his thing. We had a little fire there for the branding irons, and we branded them at the same time. I did do that a couple times. I can still smell the burning hide and hair.

"Homer Walker and I became very good friends," Steve says. "I started to have a lot better respect for my elders. That was Mr. and Mrs. Walker's doing, I think, because they were very, well, I wouldn't say strict, but you knew when they told you to do something you best do it."

One day that spring, Homer told Steve to put Bay Rum into the horse trailer. Bay Rum was the horse Steve always rode, one he had broken himself at the Boys Ranch. He didn't know what Homer had in mind, but he knew he best do it.

"Bay Rum was a little bay horse, a kind of reddish brown mare quarter horse that I had put my dibs on," Steve says. "Frank, another boy at the Ranch, had his dibs on an old gelding, a strawberry roan. Neither one was broke, so we sort of challenged each other to break these horses. When Frank got home from school in the afternoons, we would get up on the corral fence and climb on these things. We just got aboard there, and they'd buck a little, and piss and moan, and we'd stay right there in the saddle."

When Steve put his horse in the trailer that spring day, he didn't ask any questions. But he couldn't help noticing the large Morgan horse, which dwarfed Bay Rum, already in the trailer. The Morgan belonged to Ward, another cottage-parent at the Boys Ranch. Ward would be going along on this trip.

"Ward was a local rancher and rodeo buff, sixty years old, tall, and very fit for his age," Steve says. "He rolled his own cigarettes and always wore his boots, jeans, and a scarf around his neck. He had been to Madison Square Garden to do double team roping. Ward and Homer were both very good men," Steve says. "I can say I'm very proud to have known them both.

"I got in the truck with Homer and Ward, and we drove down to Ward's ranch near Walsenburg. I got my horse, Bay Rum, out of the trailer, and Ward got his horse out.

"I said, 'Okay, what do you want me to do?'

"'Well, there's eight or ten head of cattle in the valley down there. I need them up here,' Ward said. So I started to get on my little horse, Bay Rum, but Ward said, 'Here, why don't you take mine?'

"Ward's horse was named Big John," Steve recalls. "He was a great big sixteen- or seventeen-hand Morgan horse that Ward used for roping and cutting and even to pull his pickup truck. He was a big son of a gun.

"I thought, 'My God.' I was scared to death.

"'It's no big deal,' Ward said. 'You can ride him. No problem.'

"So I said, 'Okay.'

"He told me to go down this gully," Steve says. "It's a good couple miles down. 'There's eight or ten head of cattle down there,' Ward said. 'Just herd them up and bring them back and I'll put them in this other pasture.'

"So I got up on this big old horse," Steve says, "and I didn't know where in the hell I was going. But Ward pointed me in the right direction. By George, I got down there. It seemed like forever to me. I saw the cows down there and I started moving towards them and, boy, this horse just amazed me. I didn't have to do much of anything. That horse was so smart; all you had to do was use your knees. I barely had to rein him, and he just got those cattle all in a bunch and got behind them. That horse just

Steve bulldogs a calf at the ranch.

knew what he was doing and herded them back up there. And the cattle were probably smart too. I'm sure it wasn't all my doing. It took me an hour or something like that, I imagine, or better. And I come back up, and Homer and Ward are just sitting there waiting for me. And I think they were pretty surprised that I did what I did. And I was damned surprised too," Steve laughs.

"Now that I think of it," Steve says, "I think the only reason they went was to do it for me. That's why they made that trip, I think. They wanted to see what I could do.

"It was a very good experience," Steve says. "I had never done anything like that before, but they trusted me. I didn't even know if I was going in the right direction. And, by God, I got back up there with all those cattle. That was probably one of the biggest days I ever had in my life, as far as that goes. That was a good time."

When Steve let his mom know he was roping and ranching, she sent him a pair of boots and a jean jacket. After supper most evenings, Steve and his buddy Frank would ask Homer if they could take their horses to the rodeo arena across the highway from the Boys Ranch to practice roping. "He'd say, 'Sure. Just be back by eight o'clock,'" Steve recalls. "Frank was pretty good at roping," Steve says, "but I was never any good at it. Anyway, we'd go over and the ol' boys were over there practicing roping the steers for the Arkansas Valley Fair. They'd bring the steers over to us and say, 'Do you want to ride these?' And we'd say, 'Sure.'

"They'd put them in the squeeze chute and me and Frank would hop up on them and we didn't have a rope or anything else," Steve recalls. "They'd just open the gate, like they would with a bull. We'd ride as far as we could, maybe fifteen feet and a couple jumps, and we'd be on our butts, sitting looking around. It was a lot of fun."

Steve worked up the nerve to enter a rodeo at the arena. "I had this big old white horse that was an ex-barrel racer that somebody had donated to the Ranch," Steve says. "He was the fastest son of a gun you ever saw in your life. He was an older horse, had to be fifteen or twenty years old, but, boy, that son of a gun would run. And he definitely knew his steps still. I entered the pole-bending event and won first place. That was a great experience too."

At the end of the summer, Steve and Frank went to the rodeo in Brighton with Homer. "We went up on a Friday afternoon, and Rex Allen Sr. was there," Steve recalls. "Me and Frank slept in the back of the truck, and the next day we went out and rode some very large steers, and naturally got the crap beat out of us."

When fall came, Steve started riding the bus to school with the other boys. He remembers singing New Christy Minstrels folk songs in the back of the bus with his cottagemates, Dave, Johnny, and Richard. Steve was happy to be able to see some girls again and make some friends, but not so thrilled to be in school.

His friend Dave, a straight-A student, tried to help him with his work, but "I was never scholastic at all," says Steve. School continued to be a struggle. When his year was up, Steve was anxious to go back to Denver. There was a girl waiting for him there. Not long after Steve returned to Denver, his girlfriend got pregnant. At age seventeen, Steve dropped out of high school to marry her and support his new family. "That's something I do not regret in any way, shape, or form," Steve says. "I thought the day my son was born was the best day of my life."

Steve got a job shagging cars at a Chevrolet dealership, and, by the time his son was born, he had worked his way up to writing service orders. "I was the guy who meets you and asks what's wrong with your car. I'd write up the order and make sure everything got done, and I'd call you back and give you the estimate or give you the bad news that now you've got some serious problem. I became a service manager. For thirty-five years. That was basically what I did with my life was work for an automobile dealership."

Steve says, "When we stole that car that time, that was the most criminal thing I ever did. But if I hadn't gone to the Boys Ranch, I would have gotten into some more trouble, I can guarantee you that. If I'd gone to the reformatory instead of the Boys Ranch, I would have gotten into the wrong crowd, and I guarantee I would have been in prison many times by now, or possibly dead. Who knows?"

Steve felt his year at Colorado Boys Ranch was an awakening experience. "I'm glad to say that year was one of the best experiences of my life," Steve says. "I'll never be ashamed to say I was a Boys Rancher. It was just for a short time, but I had a very good experience at the Boys Ranch, and I wouldn't give it up. It was a great way to grow up and look at the world in a different way. I came back from the Ranch and my attitude went around the circle 100 percent. I was a lot smarter. I guess I got an appreciation that life was not a free ride. You had to get up and go for the gusto."

Life, for Steve, was not always a joyride after his year at Colorado Boys Ranch. He has faced many bumps along the road, but has managed to keep his hands on the wheel. "Life," says Steve, "is a big give-and-take situation."

Now retired, Steve has moved back down to the Arkansas Valley. He still has an eye for automobiles. "When I lived in San Diego, I purchased a 1967 Chevy Malibu. I put in a 350-horsepower engine, a 350 turbo hydromatic three-speed transmission, tires, wheels. It was very fast. The car I'm trying to buy now, if I can find a way to finance it, is a 1948 Chevrolet Stylemaster coupe. I'd like to drive it in parades here in town. It's a beauty," Steve says. "I hope I can find a way to get it."

—CQL

# CHAPTER NINE

# Wellspring

## Vic and Joyce Crow

*Ranching is in Vic Crow's blood, in his sweat, and in his tears. Although at age seventy-six, Vic's toil on the land is over, his tears still lie close to the surface. As he tells the story of how his father's homestead ranch was lost and how he and his wife, Joyce, became early cottage-parents at Colorado Boys Ranch, tears well up. Struggles long held underground are tapped and bubble up afresh, like water from an artesian well.*

Ranching goes way back in Vic Crow's family. "I was born in the San Luis Valley of Colorado," Vic begins. "My father came to Colorado in 1918 and homesteaded on a ranch adjoining what is now the Sand Dunes National Park. His father, my grandfather, had two large ranches in the area of Enid, Oklahoma, and Oklahoma City. When it comes to ranching," Vic says, "we go all the way back."

But at the beginning, there was trouble. "My father was born in 1900 in the Cherokee Nation," Vic says, describing the territory that was later to become Oklahoma. "He left there as a young man. What bothers me about that ... what comes to my mind ... " He stops. "The way the white people treated the Indians," Vic says, and he stops again. Tears spill over and his voice catches. "My father said he actually saw them catch an Indian and skin him alive," he gasps. Vic reaches into a pocket and pulls out a handkerchief. He wipes his face. "My father said he didn't want nothing to do with what was going on there with the Indians. I really don't know the story that well," he says, "but my father ran away; he left his father."

Vic composes himself and begins again. "My father came to Colorado and started homesteading in Saguache County, and, of course, that's an Indian area right next to the sand dunes. My father built fences and he drilled wells and he done things and he put together quite a ranch," Vic says proudly. "He owned close to 30,000 acres of land when he died, and he didn't owe one dollar on it."

But tracing his mother's branch of the family tree, Vic explains there was no history of ranching and no great love for it. "My mother came from New York City," Vic says. "She married my father in Denver, and he took her to the San Luis Valley to homestead next to the sand dunes. And she never did like it," Vic says. "The sand."

Vic's mother's journey to the San Luis Valley was very different from his father's. "My mother came to Denver as a young girl on the orphan train. And if you want to get into that story, it will take a little while," Vic warns.

"My grandmother came from Czechoslovakia to New York and couldn't speak the language," Vic says. "She had three little kids. My mother was the youngest of the three. But my grandfather abandoned them. Then the children were taken from her. My grandmother worked hard for years. She got a job as a maid at the Waldorf Astoria. She then married a man who worked on the Holland Tunnel, but he died from the gases. My grandmother learned seven languages fluently, and eventually she worked where they came into the Statue of Liberty. She then married an attorney, and they looked for her three children for years but could never find them. They had lost all track of each other. That's the end of the story there," Vic says.

"But to come on down there a little ways," Vic says, as he sits back in his chair, "if you want to come a little further, which you need to," he continues with a smile, "because once I start on that story, I've got to finish it." He grins.

"It's an odd thing. During World War II, one of those three children, my mother's brother, joined the service, and he went back to New York to get his birth certificate to prove he was a citizen," Vic says. "And lo and behold, during the war my grandmother decided to see if that had happened. And sure enough, it had. Through that, she made contact with all three of her children. She found my mother, who was in Colorado, of all things. My grandmother made that contact with us in the San Luis Valley, during World War II," Vic concludes, "when I was in high school."

The subject of World War II wipes the smile from Vic's face and takes him down another lane of memories. "Another kind of a strange thing," Vic says, "I never did go into the service. I graduated in '44, so I was ready to go. I did go to Denver on the old train and took my examination. I was 1-A. That means you're ready to go. You're a fit man. Nothing wrong with you serving. Well," he says, "I never went."

"He was physically fit," Vic's wife, Joyce, interjects. "He was a football player in high school in Mosca."

Up until now, Joyce has been sitting quietly by Vic's side as he talks in the living room of their Cañon City home. Vic and Joyce were high school sweethearts. Joyce was the daughter of a sheep shearer on an adjoining ranch. They have been married for fifty-six years.

As Vic talks, Joyce jots things down in a notebook. She also refers to old entries in her notebook to jog her memory, which has been failing in recent years. "Give Joyce a date, and she can look in that notebook and tell you what happened on any given day," Vic says. "I'm just bragging on Joyce a little bit," Vic says as he smiles, "but she's got to be bragged on. At one time she was a walking encyclopedia." He looks at her fondly, then his thoughts return to the war.

"I didn't go," Vic says. "What happened, the War Board got a hold of my ... " Vic's voice breaks and he cries quietly as the memories flood back.

Joyce looks down at her notebook and says, "It's okay."

"I'll be all right," Vic says. "I always have trouble with that. I don't know why," he whispers.

"I was ready to go," Vic starts again in a hoarse voice, "but my father owned the ranch, and he had 300 head of cattle, Herefords, and every year he sent ten to fifteen train cars to Swift Packing Company in Denver," Vic says. "The War Board asked my father to not let me go. They would keep me out."

"His friends and the ones his age did go," Joyce explains.

"And some of them didn't come back," Vic says. He sobs.

Joyce reaches over and covers Vic's hand with her own. He takes a deep breath. He has reached the source of his struggle. "My father said to me, and I can remember it, he said, 'If you want to go, you go,' he says, 'but we'll sell the ranch immediately.'

"My father could not run the ranch by himself," Vic explains. "He had hurt himself pretty bad on a horse. A saddle horn injured his heart. My father could not ride a horse anymore."

Vic leans forward and continues, "My father said to me, 'If you want to stay, I've got enough points to keep three men out of the service. If you want to stay, you'll never be bothered. You'll get some slack from people.' So he let me make the decision. And

I said, 'If I go, you'll sell the ranch?' He said, 'I have to. The ranch is for sale the minute you get on the train.'

"So," Vic says, "I stayed on. And I became a slave to my father on the ranch. We had a winter headquarters and a summer headquarters, some of it in the dry lakes country. Sometimes he'd take me in the old pickup with a horse and drop me off eighteen miles from home at the end of the Ranch. It was that long to get to the other pasture near the sand dunes. And I would hit every well and count the cattle. We had ten to fifteen pump wells and twenty-one artesian wells. Wherever there was a well, there was a post about so big around, went into the air about fifteen feet, with a rubber tire on it so you could see it from far off. That told the guys on horses working that area that there was a well there.

"There was ninety-nine miles of fence on my dad's ranch," Vic says. "And I'd work on the fences. That's what I did. During the war it was work, work, work," Vic makes clear as he slaps the back of his hand on his palm. "I became a workaholic. But my dad made sure I stayed active in the community. He wasn't a hard man, but he was a driven man, because he knew what that ranch meant to the war effort. And the reason I break down every time ... " Vic pauses in his explanation.

Vic breathes deeply. It is clearly difficult for Vic to dredge up these memories, but he seems determined to bring them to the surface. "The reason I break down is because I became the boy whose father was so rich he can keep his son out of the war," Vic says. He pauses. "It's not true," he says, "but I felt it."

Vic recalls the days right after the war ended. "The war had taken an awful toll on everybody. Then the service boys were coming home and finding that their girlfriends, and even their wives. ... There was one guy on the ranch that came home and found out his wife had turned into a terrible person while he was gone. There were heartbreaks," Vic says. "Heartbreaks, you know?"

But Vic and Joyce never suffered that kind of heartbreak. "We got married pretty soon after we met," Joyce says with a smile, recalling their wedding in 1946.

"We went together for almost a year, honey," Vic replies. "We were awful young and awful ignorant, but we were in love."

Their marriage was strong, the work on his father's ranch was good, and Vic and Joyce were blessed with children. But there was another kind of heartbreak in store for them. In 1951, Vic's father died, and everything changed.

"After my father died, my mother took over the ranch," Vic says, "and she was no rancher. She never was and still wasn't. Instead of keeping the ranch in the family, she traded it off. It's too bad what happened. And that's another complete story."

Vic is reluctant to talk about why his mother sold the family ranch, but her brother's gambling debts were at least part of her motivation. "I guess gambling takes ahold like alcohol or anything else," Vic says. "These facts are facts, but they're not very nice facts. My uncle lost my mother's ranch," Vic says. "It all went to Las Vegas. And not one dollar was owed on the ranch. Not one dime. It was hard."

Vic and his father's hard work had helped the war effort and preserved the family ranch. But now, just a few years later, Vic was forced to watch all of their efforts evaporate, like salty sweat into the dry Colorado air.

"It came to this," Vic says. "I became so bitter over what happened with my father's ranch that I lost contact with my mother almost completely. She moved to California and lived in a house near the beach. I went to see her every two years, just because I thought I should, and she would say, 'Oh, I'm so glad to see you.' And I'd do the same. But it was the phoniest situation you'd ever seen.

"I had a special friend who was a pastor in Arizona," Vic says. "When we'd go to see my mother, we'd always stop and see him on the way. He told me one time, he said, 'I know the background, Vic. You know, I'm going to tell you something. You have got to ask your mother for forgiveness for your attitude.' I said, 'But pastor, she's the one that lost the ranch. It would be worth millions now.'

Vic and Joyce left the pastor and continued on through the night toward California, but the idea of apologizing to his mother grated on Vic with every mile. "I told myself that she done it," Vic says. "I didn't have nothing to do with it. Why should I apologize?" This led to a heated argument between him and Joyce. Conjuring up an old-time appellation for the Devil, Vic says, "The Old Adversary, he got after Joyce and I. And Joyce and I had a problem. I shouted at her, 'I want to go home.' And Joyce said, 'No, we have to go on. You have to do what the pastor told you.'

"Well, anyhow, it wasn't a very pleasant trip," Vic recalls. "And as I went across the desert that night, I became so distraught over the happenings and so forth that I pulled the car off the side of the highway and got out and slammed the door and started walking across the desert. Well, now, a lot of men will understand what I'm going to say, and probably a lot of them have experienced it. But the further I walked, the slower I went, hoping that Joyce would catch me. Does it make sense? And she did, God bless her.

"So I came back to the car," Vic continues, "and we drove on that night and we got to the seashore. You could see the water from the little house my mother was in. Joyce and I went in, and as usual I said, 'Mother, hello. How are you?' And I loved her and squeezed her a little and I sat down over there. And I was fine and she was fine and we started talking. And I thought, 'Vic, you came down here for a purpose, now do it.' And I got up and went over and knelt on my knees in front of my mother and took her hands and tears came into my eyes. I said, 'Mother, I need forgiveness for the hatred that I've carried for what happened with the family ranch over all these years.' And she got up out of her chair and took me by the hands and lifted me up and she looked me straight in the eyes and said, 'Son, it is I who should ask forgiveness for what happened to your father's ranch after you'd gone through the war effort and all.' And we fell into each others arms."

To Vic, that moment of reconciliation was worth everything. "Things were already gone then," Vic says, "but I had begun to put the ranch back together. I had 800 acres in a little old place that didn't amount to nothing compared to my father's ranch. But it's still 800 acres. Well, it amounted to something later, because Joyce and I went to work on it. We got some old pastureland, and we leveled it and built a new home. We had ourselves a little herd of cattle, and we had 2,000 head of sheep and a high-range permit. We never did put all the ranch back together, but we put 7,000 or 8,000 acres together, and Joyce and I were doing pretty good."

But Vic and Joyce were not content. "Well," Vic says, "that was a spiritual thing. We were doing real good at that time. We had three little girls. We had our ranch, a contracting business, and an apartment-house business in Denver. But we hungered, and we didn't know what we were a hungering for. But we know now, it was the Spirit we was a hungering for.

"In 1961, Joyce and I went to Larkspur and stayed overnight for a meeting," Vic says. "I don't know what it was about, somebody preaching or something. And at that meeting they handed out a little old brochure, not any bigger than that," and he shows the palm of his hand. "It was just a flimsy piece of paper. And it told about Colorado Boys Ranch and its struggles. There were just a few boys there at that time. And when we left the meeting, I said, 'Joyce, let's take a ride.'"

Joyce lights up as she remembers the trip. "We went clear out through Punkin Center," Joyce says, "through Sugar City, and into La Junta. We found our way out north and drove in."

"That's what it looked like," Vic says as he points to a picture of dilapidated buildings on the early Boys Ranch. "It was a tangled-up mess. We saw a couple of the kids. We drove out of there, and we talked about it all the way home, and we said, 'You know, that's really a challenge, isn't it?'"

Vic and Joyce weren't strangers to the challenge of taking care of troubled boys. They had already been foster parents and had taken in many troubled or abandoned youth. And, Vic had grown up with some. "That's the kind of kids my dad had out on our ranch," Vic says. "We used to build fence together. My father took kids in that Judge Black in Denver would send to him. And we had two Indian boys, Benny and Ferdinand, who came off of the reservation, out of Taos. So I was raised with these kids."

When Vic and Joyce heard the call for help from Colorado Boys Ranch in 1961, it had been open for less than a year. The first cottage-parents were leaving, and there were concerns about whether CBR would stay afloat. Vic remembers those days as

Vic and Joyce Crow welcome a new boy to the ranch, 1963.

"teeter-tottery times for Colorado Boys Ranch." Dr. Davis, the board president, told Vic that if he and Joyce weren't coming, the Boys Ranch might have to fold.

"Doc Davis was a gentle, gentle person," Vic says. Although the Boys Ranch desperately needed new cottage-parents, Dr. Davis expressed concern about the Crows' three girls living at the Ranch. But Vic and Joyce were persistent. "I don't know what I said, but we convinced Doc that we were serious," Vic remembers. "In the end, Doc said, 'How quick can you come?' and I said, 'You name it.' We were there by the first of the year. We put three businesses aside in less than two months and went over there and drove in, and there we were."

Vic pulls out a metal strongbox where he still keeps the records of the ranching business he did for Colorado Boys Ranch forty years ago. In the den of his Cañon City home, Vic places the strongbox on a table near the fireplace. A huge pair of long horns hangs above the fireplace. The horns were a going-away present from the San Luis Valley community when Vic and Joyce left to go to Colorado Boys Ranch in 1962.

"These are the cattle counts," Vic explains as he opens the strongbox. Slips of paper, yellowed with age, record gifts of cattle, individual cows given to Colorado Boys Ranch in name but raised

Vic teaches boys about fence building.

on various private ranches throughout the state. Vic explains how Colorado ranchers then gave proceeds of the sale of these cattle to the Boys Ranch.

"See, Everette Marshall and I put together quite a deal,

a herd of cattle scattered around the state," Vic says. "This idea was not mine. It was Everette Marshall's," Vic says, referring to the world champion wrestler and Boys Ranch supporter. "I don't want to take any credit. Everette started it, and he knew I was an old cowboy and kind of understood the ranching. I traveled the country in a Plymouth station wagon. I met an awful lot of cattlemen across the state. Some of the cattle come out of San Luis Valley, some come out of Pagosa Springs, the Western Slope, North Park, South Park, and all of that. We scattered all over the state of Colorado. And Everette Marshall knew everybody. There was no stranger to Everette Marshall. He was all heart. As big as he was, you could never offend him. I could probably still have been offended in those days," Vic says and laughs. "In fact, I was a few times. I was only human. But Everette was a little older." And wiser, Vic implies.

While Vic traveled a good deal soliciting these livestock donations for Colorado Boys Ranch, he also spent a good deal of time building corrals and planting trees with the boys on the Ranch itself. But he gives Joyce the credit for running things on the Boys Ranch during those years. "She was more important than I was, really," Vic says. "She could tell you the names of those kids, their birthdays, when they hit the Ranch and what they got for Christmas, all of them, any of them. She went to the schools almost every day and made sure the boys got their homework done.

"A lot of the time I had to go and sit in the classroom beside them to make sure the work was carried out," Joyce says. "They didn't mind that, and I guess I liked it too," she giggles.

But there was some resistance in the community. "Yes," Vic says, "there were problems and there was resentment. Some said we had no right to bring a bunch of sorry kids into that community and into that school system to mix with the other kids. I didn't pay no attention to it. I knew what I was doing," Vic asserts and Joyce concurs. "I believed in it," says Joyce, "and I would stand up for them."

Vic and Joyce needed the strength of their convictions. "We had some real discouragements a few times. You know, you're bound to have," Vic says. But they soldiered on. "We didn't have rules as such," Vic says. "I guess I thought it up as I went." But Vic and Joyce did seek professional advice, even in those early years, for the boys on the Ranch. "A team of psychologists came down to help us know what kids need," Vic says. "I remember one of them coined this phrase and I used it: 'A boy doesn't care how much you know until he knows how much you care.'"

Vic and Joyce's devotion to each other, to the land, and to needy boys has not diminished, despite the passage of time. After a few years, they returned to their own ranch and the businesses they had set aside. The Crows were not the first cottage-parents at Colorado Boys Ranch, nor were they the last. In subsequent decades, many other cottage-parents, psychologists, social workers, and ranch managers have made their way to Colorado Boys Ranch. And thousands of boys have come to know how much all these people cared.

Vic is dry-eyed as he finishes his story. It is a drought year in Colorado. Like the desiccated ranchland in the eastern part of the state, Vic's dreams of holding on to his father's homestead have long since dried up and turned to dust. But that doesn't matter to Vic. He knows that he and Joyce were part of the wellspring of love and caring a different kind of ranch. And that's something he can hold on to.

—CQL

CHAPTER
TEN

# The Pilgrimage
## Arlington Chapel

*Journeys require faith, a belief in a goal worth achieving.*
*Heroic journeys require tremendous effort and perseverance*
*and are impressive in length and scope. The boys who*
*come to CBR make a significant physical journey just to*
*arrive at this out-of-the-way geographical location, but*
*their emotional journey, past psychological demons to new*
*and stable terrain, is very often of heroic proportions. It is*
*fitting that the little white chapel that sits foursquare and*
*full of faith atop a knoll at Colorado Boys Ranch has*
*made a journey of its own to match and inspire the jour-*
*neys of the boys.*

If faith can move mountains, then it may not be surprising that
a fifty-year-old wooden church could be moved across twenty-
seven miles of open prairie, through pastures of grazing cattle,
and over two irrigation canals without a single pane of glass
breaking. But that journey required more than the horsepower of
the truck that pulled the 1,400-square-foot church, intact and
complete with a bell tower, on the back of a trailer from its home

in Arlington, Colorado, to the Boys Ranch in 1967. Like much of what is accomplished at CBR, it required the help of the local community and the strong faith of a few.

Although CBR has been nonsectarian throughout its history, the spiritual needs of the boys have always been addressed. Because there was no chapel on the Ranch property in the 1960s, every Sunday the boys were taken into town, where they could attend the church of their choice. Administrators said they felt an obligation to "teach the boys a set of moral and spiritual values that would help them to realize the importance of religion in their everyday lives."

Colorado Boys Ranch had fifty-one boys attending eleven churches in La Junta in those days. Because staffing was limited on Sunday mornings, boys were often dropped off at their churches and were on their own. Not too surprisingly, instead of sitting in rapt attention listening to the minister or priest, many boys went in the front door and out the back, running around town until it was time to be picked up. They frequently ended up at a diner they dubbed "Patty's Cathedral."

Downtown La Junta was not exactly a den of iniquity on Sunday mornings, but the need for a place of worship on the Ranch grounds was becoming evident. An interfaith chapel would not only solve the Sunday supervision problem, it would also give the boys a spiritual haven available any day of the week.

An appeal letter was sent out to the churches of Colorado in the winter of 1967 asking for contributions to build an inter-denominational chapel at Colorado Boys Ranch. Instead of money, a different kind of offer came their way. The Evangelical United Brethren of the little community of Arlington, a bend in the road thirty miles northeast of La Junta, wanted to donate their church to the Boys Ranch.

Built for $2,500 in 1917 and dedicated by several Kansas families who had moved to Colorado's eastern plains to homestead, the church had served the Arlington community for fifty years. Among the founders, the Andersons were an important family. Mary Anderson Ruthart, one of the last two students to graduate from Arlington's school, in 1944, grew up hearing stories of how her grandfather, Nen Anderson, her father, Clair Anderson, and two uncles helped dig the basement for the church. In a history of the church, she writes as if it were happening today: "On March 10, 1916, you'll find horses pulling a large metal scoop with a wooden handle on either side. As teams of horses pull, two handles are lifted by a man walking behind driving his team. As the scoop moves, a sharp front edge cuts into the ground. The slip fills, is pulled out of the hole, and dumped. The horses and men strain under the weight as they trudge in and out of the hollow, filling and dumping load after load of the yellow adobe soil."

The determination of those early homesteaders to dig a deep foundation for their church was matched by that of their descendants to maintain the church as a beacon of faith on the prairie. Helen Crowe, aged ninety-three and a longtime supporter of Colorado Boys Ranch, remembers riding her horse toward that beacon as a young girl: "In 1919, when I was eight years old, I would jump on a horse and ride eight miles, by myself, through fences and straight across dryland prairie, to spend a weekend with my friend Glenna and attend the little church in Arlington," she recalls. "On Sundays, there would be a fellowship supper in the church basement. We had to import a preacher from Haswell, ten miles to the north. After the covered-dish supper, the minister would preach a sermon," Helen recollects. "He'd eat first," she is careful to point out. His was not the patient faith of the woman who, telling the tale with a pious twinkle, always declined second helpings at dinner, "in hopes," she murmurs, "of the sweet hereafter."

The faith of Arlington's community, however, was steadfast. It did not diminish with time, even though the congregation began to shrink in size. The membership had never been large, varying from thirty-two to sixty, but it had been active in supporting its church-sponsored colleges and missions. With the population of the area dwindling in the decades after World War II, it seemed inevitable that the church would eventually shut its doors. In February of 1967, following a fellowship supper like those of the early part of the century, the local conference of the church voted unanimously to discontinue services and to offer their church to Colorado Boys Ranch. *If* it could be moved.

Moving the congregation to donate their church proved easier than moving the church to the Boys Ranch. An article in a local newspaper describes some of the problems: "8/31/67: The Arlington church building was standing on the north bank of the Fort Lyon storage canal Wednesday, some 20 miles from La Junta. There were two reasons for the holdup. Contractor Cecil Tombleson of Lamar said the rain had slicked the roads too much to make moving safe. Further, a cat was needed to fill in the Fort Lyons storage canal so the 14-foot wide wheels could cross the canal. After the rig crosses, the cat will reopen the canal. Although the rigging and wheels under the church are only 14 feet wide, the entire structure is a 40-foot span and the church stands some 40 feet high. This has presented recurring problems even though much of the country between CBR and Arlington is open prairie. Any sort of overhead line had to be cut and repaired after the church had passed through."

Like the journey of each boy at Colorado Boys Ranch, the church took its own time to arrive at its new foundation. Inching along at four miles per day, slower than a man would walk but perhaps the distance a man could travel on his knees in one day, the church made its way across the prairie. The slow pilgrimage of the clapboard chapel lumbering across pasture and prairie gave the local whiteface cattle plenty of time to mosey out of the way. But the large white structure, looming like a giant prairie schooner before the dark gray thunderclouds of late August, drew long, quizzical looks from the cows as it sailed slowly by. After a seven-day voyage, the chapel finally came to anchor, facing east on its new foundation at Colorado Boys Ranch.

Before the chapel began its odyssey, a final service had been held in Arlington on May 14, 1967. It must have been bittersweet when during the service, the deed was handed over by Mary Anderson Ruthart's father, Clair Anderson, chairman of the board of trustees of the church, to Earl Brubaker, president of the board of directors of Colorado Boys Ranch. Boys from the Ranch sat next to church members who, although sad to say good-bye to their church, were delighted that their old building would live on through these young people. The closing sermon of that final service was fittingly titled "The Tie That Binds."

On December 3, 1967, another service was held to dedicate the now interdenominational chapel at its new location at Colorado Boys Ranch. The bells in the tower pealed out as the

On wheels, Arlington Chapel is almost "home" at CBR after traveling twenty-seven miles across the prairie.

entire Arlington congregation joined the boys on the Ranch for the service. The building was bursting at the seams with Boys Ranch staff, boys, former congregants, and townspeople from La Junta, totaling more than 300 in all. One Boys Rancher read the twenty-third psalm. Another said a prayer of dedication. The Boys Ranch choir of more than forty voices sang, "The Lord is My Shepherd." There was no public address system, but the acoustics were good. Mrs. Gantt, a cottage-parent known to the boys affectionately as "Granny," sang the Lord's Prayer. The overflow crowd in the basement could hear her soulful voice as clearly as those sitting in the front pew. There wasn't a dry eye in the house.

Reverend Woelfe, former pastor of the church, noted that the chapel had been built when riders on horseback came to worship in the middle of the prairie and it was still standing strong in the space age, ready to serve these young boys. Appropriately, and according to custom, the service was preceded by a lunch for the honored guests in the Ranch dining hall. For years afterward, remaining members of the original Brethren congregation returned to Colorado Boys Ranch every May to celebrate the anniversary of their gift. Arlington Day at the Ranch included a special service in the chapel and, of course, a meal in the Ranch dining hall, *before* the service.

Over the years that the little white chapel has rested on the grounds of Colorado Boys Ranch, it has been the site of some special services. "Granny" Gantt's daughter, Cheryl, was married there. Bill Files and his wife were married there at an Easter sunrise service. And several former Boys Ranchers have returned to the Ranch to be married in Arlington Chapel as well. In the 1970s, when a former Boys Rancher married his La Junta High School sweetheart in Arlington Chapel, the local paper reported the fashion of the day: "Escorted to the altar by her father, the lovely bride was dressed in a long-sleeved afternoon-length gown of white double knit, accented at the neckline, wrists, and empire waistline with narrow gold braid. A western love ballad entitled 'I Love You Because' was sung by Darlene Blair, a secretary at the Boys Ranch."

Church attendance at Colorado Boys Ranch is no longer mandatory, as it was in the late 1960s when boys were required to roll out of bed, put on a tie, and slick back their hair for Sunday morning service on the Ranch. But the chapel is still available for boys who wish to voluntarily attend weekly services, and as a safe haven where boys can go to receive spiritual guidance or just spend some time alone in contemplation. The vast open space of the plains may seem a little overwhelming to some of the boys who come to Colorado Boys Ranch from big cities. Many find comfort and a sense of serenity inside the little chapel.

The chapel has lived up to the dreams of the CBR board president who asked in his 1967 letter of appeal for a chapel, "a haven of comfort to all boys who will call the Boys Ranch their home in future years." The faith, hope, and charity of the Arlington community provided that haven for many troubled boys.

Administrators have changed over the years, but the values of Colorado Boys Ranch remain remarkably the

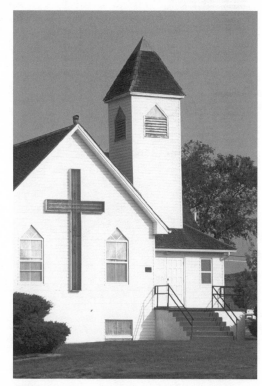

Arlington Chapel at home on the Colorado Boys Ranch campus.

same. Thirty years after the chapel was moved, Chuck Thompson, president of Colorado Boys Ranch, remarked: "The philosophy of the Colorado Boys Ranch is to provide access and exposure to every possible source of support and strength to our youth for their journey through life. The Ranch believes that youth need the opportunity to develop a personal sense of hope and comfort on which to build a future. We believe that spiritual growth and development can help a youth build the strength and character necessary to become hopeful and productive citizens."

Most of Arlington's Brethren congregants have passed on, and only a handful of buildings are still standing in Arlington these days. The place where the church once stood is now just an empty slab. But the empty space that existed in the hearts of many of the boys who come to Colorado Boys Ranch is being filled with love and hope.

Far out on the eastern plains of Colorado, mountains themselves might be considered a matter of faith, since they cannot be seen. But whether or not faith can move mountains, it plainly can move chapels. Even though the building hasn't budged in more than four decades, the chapel and its founders continue to be a part of the hero's journey for many of today's troubled boys.

—CQL

# CHAPTER ELEVEN

# The Best-Laid Plan

# Three Boys and a Horse

*The plan would go into effect that night, after lights-out. The three boys had already scouted out an old mare and a well-worn saddle. But they didn't think to get hold of a compass. They knew their direction was toward the mountains, beyond the mesa that shouldered Colorado Boys Ranch to the west.*

Shadows around the Ranch were growing long. The setting sun struck the tall open gate to Colorado Boys Ranch and cast a long horseshoe shape across the prairie to the east. But the boys didn't think about the approaching dark. They didn't think about how hard it would be to steer a horse west toward the mountains in the middle of the night. They had their plan. Grab a horse, swipe a saddle, and ride west. It wasn't much of a plan. But it was their plan.

A chilly breeze brushed their cheeks. But it didn't catch the boys' attention. And they didn't think about how cold it could get in November after the sun went down.

While the tack room was still unlocked, the boys snatched the saddle and hid it outside, behind a shed. It didn't occur to them what a tight squeeze one saddle would be for three boys. And they didn't really think about how the horse would like it.

They just thought about the plan.

After they stashed the saddle, they heard Patty ringing the big porch bell for supper. Food was something they did think about. Their stomachs needed filling. They joined the other boys crowding into the dining hall. As they filed past, Patty tussled their hair. They didn't think about that. They had their plan.

✦ ✦ ✦

Patty didn't know about the plan, but she was accustomed to the pranks that boys could think up. Her first day of work at Colorado Boys Ranch, in 1964, had been spent in the administrator's office in the haze of a stink bomb. Instead of typing or filing, Patty had spent the day opening up windows and airing things out. She never did discover the culprit. Patty knew that the boys got such a kick out of it that they would all have gladly taken the blame. She figured they were jealous of whoever thought it up.

Patty's baptism of fire prepared her to greet most of the boys' mischief with a grin. Years had passed since the stink bomb incident, and Patty had become the interim administrator at the Ranch. She was well liked by many of the boys, but she could be strict. When a boy named Kenneth got into trouble, Patty punished him by taking away Popo, the old Appaloosa she had assigned to him. Kenneth dearly loved that horse. The next morning, Patty came into work and found a sympathy card on her desk. Curious about why she would be getting a sympathy card, Patty opened it up. Inside it said, "I'll do anything. I'll move the sun to get Popo back. In deepest sympathy, Kenneth." Patty couldn't help but laugh. Kenneth and Popo were eventually reunited.

The night of the plan, Patty was at home. She lived a few miles down the road from the Boys Ranch with her widowed mother. The weather had turned bitter cold, and, after a long day at the Ranch, Patty was glad to get under the covers and catch some shut-eye.

It was hard to sleep some nights thinking about the situation of the boys on the Ranch. Patty had recently accepted an eight-year-old boy whose well-groomed and well-dressed mother had brought him out to the Ranch. The woman had said, "I'll leave him here on one condition: that I never see him again. I'm not a mother. I don't have a mother's bone in me."

"We'll take him," Patty replied.

As she drifted off to sleep that night, Patty thought about that woman. "My mom would have fought a grizzly bear for any of us," Patty thought. "But maybe it's better to acknowledge that you can't do it."

About 3:00 A.M., the phone rang. It was the sheriff.

It wasn't the first time Patty had received a late-night phone call concerning the boys. On an earlier occasion, a local law enforcement officer had phoned her in the middle of the night to ask if any of the boys were missing.

"Why do you ask?" Patty said.

"Well, there's a car been stolen in town, and I thought maybe a Boys Rancher had took it," he said.

"Have you called every other home in La Junta and checked on their children?" Patty asked.

"Well, no," said the officer.

"Well, when you've done that, then you call me back," Patty said, and hung up the phone.

But the fact was, sometimes the sheriff's suspicions were correct, and this was one of them. Patty picked up the phone that freezing November night and listened to the sheriff's concern. It seemed that some quilts had gone missing from a clothesline near Swink.

The plan had gone awry. The boys did manage to sneak out after their cottage-parents had fallen asleep. They did manage to swing the saddle up on the old mare and climb aboard. And they did manage to head west across the mesa.

The cold night air bit into them as they and their horse stumbled across the frozen, uneven ground in the dark. But the mountains were too far off and the sky too black to make out the western horizon. They could at least see a few lights in the neighboring town of Swink, and they headed there.

The plan was beginning to lose its luster. It no longer seemed like the brightest idea they had ever had. Things weren't so bad at the Ranch. They weren't really mad at anybody. They just liked the idea of the plan. Now they were freezing and wondering what they should do.

They saw the quilts on a farmer's clothesline. They took them.

Patty listened on the phone as the sheriff told her the rest of the story. After the farmer's wife had called to report her missing quilts, the sheriff had driven out to Swink to check things out. Something made him go out to the old barn. Wind whistled through the broken boards. He found the boys inside the barn. They were freezing cold. Their bodies were shivering, their lips were blue, and their teeth were chattering. But the horse was fine. The boys had used all the stolen quilts to cover that old mare and saved none for themselves. They were found with their arms around the horse, saying sweet things and trying to keep her warm.

—CQL

CHAPTER
TWELVE

# A Tough Old Bird

## Betty and a Wiley Rooster

*Unlike Patty, Betty had always been a city girl. Before taking a job as the editor of "The Rancher," the newsletter for Colorado Boys Ranch, she had never set foot on a ranch or a farm. On a blistering hot summer day in 1972, Betty came to work at the Ranch, clothed as usual in a dress, nylons, and high-heeled shoes. Around noon that day, she grabbed her camera and stepped out of the office, planning to shoot some pictures for the next Boys Ranch publication. Little did she know a mean old cuss was outside itching for a fight. Scratching his feet in the packed clay, the dirty, lowdown, two-legged varmint raised his eyes and drew a bead on his opponent.*

Betty's last name was Wiley, but that was, in fact, a name more fitting for her adversary, an overly large, extremely aggressive, and cunning rooster. A fighting cock in his former life, the aging contender was in retirement at Colorado Boys Ranch, spending his golden years creating chaos wherever he went. The tough old bird ruled the roost, frequently escaped from his enclosure, and didn't take kindly to strangers.

Betty wasn't looking for a fight. She knew the rooster's reputation and didn't want to cross his path. But busy with her photo assignment, Betty forgot about the cantankerous bird. The rooster spied Betty as she wandered into the corral unawares. Now he had the drop on her. Armed only with the 35-mm camera slung around her neck, Betty was cornered. There was no one else in sight. The giant rooster clawed the earth one more time, and then suddenly he made his attack. She was hit. Hit hard.

Betty yelled, "Schultzy!" But the ever-present maintenance man was nowhere in sight. Bleeding and hurt, she scrambled onto the corral fence. His head cocked, the rooster held his ground and eyed her with a sideways glare.

Feeling he had made his point, the rooster moved away, strutting. Betty jumped down and hightailed it to the administration building. She limped into the office, one shoe off, her hair in disarray. Her legs were bloody where she had been struck. Her nylon stockings, miraculously, were not torn. They didn't even have a run.

"What in the world happened to you?" her boss asked, horrified at Betty's appearance.

"You've got a rooster out there that needs his neck wrung," Betty replied.

This wasn't the first time Betty had gotten crosswise with one of the animals on the Ranch. Her first nemesis had been a tiny honey bear named Bunky. This cute, furry little animal from South America is also known as a kinkajou. In the 1970s, the permanent shelter for the menagerie of small animals that live at

Colorado Boys Ranch had not yet been built. Consequently, Bunky bunked in the administration building.

Although he had a cage, the little kinkajou was an escape artist who frequently broke out to search and destroy. Being nocturnal, Bunky often went on night missions. When Betty came to work in the morning, she knew instantly if the furry paper shredder had been in operation the night before. Papers would be torn up and scattered from one end of the office to the other.

Nothing was safe from Bunky. Two new red vinyl chairs sat in the waiting area of the administration building, a gift of Seldon Jeffers, local pharmacist and member of the board of trustees. Something about those chairs irritated the little honey bear, and they soon felt the wrath of Bunky's claws. Every time Mr. Jeffers came by the office at the Boys Ranch for a visit, Betty had to make sure someone was sitting on the chairs, nonchalantly hiding the holes that Bunky had torn in the vinyl cushions. Finally, Betty had had enough.

She said to her boss, "It's me or Bunky. Either you get him to a zoo, or you hand me my walking papers."

Although the folks at Colorado Boys Ranch firmly believe that no boy is a hopeless case, no matter how troubled, they had to admit that once in a while, they came across an incorrigible specimen in the animal kingdom. Neither Bunky nor the rooster was long for the Ranch.

Betty, meanwhile, nursed her wounds. She wore those miraculous nylons for quite a while and continued working on the Ranch for twenty-five years. She wrote hundreds of articles for the Boys Ranch and helped to spread their message far and wide. She became familiar enough with ranching and farming to broadcast the Colorado Boys Ranch haying report on the local radio station. And she was a friend to many boys who came through the Ranch's doors.

With the demise of the rooster, it could be said that a tough old bird left one tough old broad in its place. But Betty was soft-hearted, at least when it came to the boys. As the years went by, nobody seemed to miss the rooster, but many of the former Boys Ranchers who had known Betty in the early days returned in later years to say hello to the straight shooter in the front office.

—CQL

CHAPTER
THIRTEEN

# All in the Family

# Jack

*Jack smiles wryly as the youngest of his three daughters enters the room to use the electric pencil sharpener. She may really need to sharpen her pencil, or, perhaps, like her two sisters, who have already made the trip, she is just curious about the interview going on in the kitchen.*

"Be quick, honey," Jack says as he waits for the grinding noise to cease for the third time during the interview. He rolls his eyes as the tape recorder is restarted, but there seems to be no real annoyance in Jack's small facial gesture. After all, those three blond daughters are doing homework in the next room with their mother, and everyone knows how much faster the work goes when the tools are sharp.

The fourth interruption to shut off the tape recorder is a call from Korea. It is an army lieutenant colonel who needs to consult with Jack about an event that is to occur the next day. The information is given, the call ends, and the tape recorder is turned back on.

With army fatigues tucked into polished black boots, a precision haircut, a well-groomed mustache, and a tall, fit frame, Jack is a striking figure. In his mid-thirties, he is a chief warrant officer 4, with technical duties in the U.S. Army Space and Missile Defense Command. Jack travels all over the world for his job. He is one of those servicemen who keep the defensive satellite systems running for the United States so we know immediately when a missile is fired anywhere in the world.

When Jack was fifteen, he didn't know anything about missile systems, army careers, or being a dad. However, he did know that his own family life was in disarray. It was 1977 and the spring of his freshman year in high school. Jack may have wished then that he could control his life the way he would later manage satellite computer systems. In his home, no missiles were being fired, but lots of damage was being done, and Jack seemed to be the cause.

Jack says that coming to CBR was a last resort. When asked what would have been the alternative, he says, "I'm not sure. I don't even know how my parents heard about the Ranch. I just know that they made it sound as if I didn't have any other options."

Jack had lived with one parent, his mother, from age two until age twelve. That was when his mother discovered that having an adolescent boy in the home was a challenge that was becoming unmanageable. He had been getting into some trouble. As Jack puts it, "I was a kid getting into things I shouldn't have been: a bit of shoplifting, throwing eggs from the roof, cutting school, and just generally being a pain." Not big trouble, but his mother had had enough.

Jack went to live with his father and stepmother. "I lived there from sixth through ninth grade, and, as I got older, my folks became more and more concerned," Jack says. Even though Jack kept up with school, he found things to do after school that made for problems. Before he had a driver's license, he drove a car that belonged to a friend. He had an accident and promised to fix it on his own. He didn't. He lied about his whereabouts. Jack explains that there was nothing "hard core" about his behavior, but his problems pushed the family too hard. They even tried a mental hospital. It was not a solution. As someone who would later work with Jack at the Ranch said, "There was a 'closeness' spot in his heart that didn't get filled."

These desperate parents looking for a solution to their challenging son eventually found Colorado Boys Ranch. "It was kind of sudden," Jack recalls. "We sat down and they said, 'We have to get things straightened out. You're going to the Ranch.' I didn't put up a fight. No, in fact I think a part of me was relieved to be getting out of my situation. It was at the end of June before my sophomore year. I wanted to see what it was like: a ranch, a small town.

"The first people I met were Mr. and Mrs. Zachary," says Jack as he describes his arrival that June day in the late 1970s. The fact that he does not first mention the long drive from Denver or the hot La Junta weather, or even the appearance of the Ranch itself is significant. Jack began his Ranch history with the Zacharys, and even if nothing else had happened to him there, making a relationship with the Zacharys would have been enough.

CBR has always believed that every boy who comes there must find a special someone on the staff. Jim and Juanita Zachary were Jack's "someone." Jack says, "It was just the luck of the draw. Fifth and sixth cottage were both for the older kids. My chance to be with the Zacharys was fifty-fifty." Jim and Juanita made a home for all the boys under their care, and, for Jack, they filled the "closeness" spot he so needed filled.

Jim Zachary refers to Jack as a "model citizen." And, according to Jim, this transformation occurred within the first couple of months after Jack's arrival. Jack comments, "I had parental figures at the Ranch for two years, and I think it is pretty tough to give values like the ones the Zacharys gave to me with only two years to do it."

Jack's adjustment, however, was not without some initial challenges. "I was determined to go out for football. But there is a huge difference between La Junta and Denver heatwise. The team was doing two-a-day practices, and I was sicker than a dog. I quit. School began, and I started to fall in with the wrong crowd."

But then Jack looked around. He figured out that the more he participated in school activities, the more privileges he would receive on the Ranch. But he had also noticed that the kids in school and some of the people in town sometimes judged Boys Ranchers in a negative way. "I figured out that I already had a label as a Ranch Boy, and I didn't like that. I hated people making conclusions about me when they didn't even know me. I didn't want to fall into a mold, so I figured out which crowd I wanted to be with."

Jack became a champion wrestler and an important member of the football team. He made lifelong friends with boys from town. He would enlist with two of them right after graduation. Jack became an integral part of the high school, and consequently, he was a role model for the boys in his cottage at the Ranch. He became the first junior counselor the Ranch ever used. He graduated with his class, joined the United States Army, and built a successful career. He married his army sweetheart and created a loving relationship. He and his wife have successfully parented and nurtured three daughters. Jack is a man who has made a good life. But he would not consider himself a self-made man. He credits Colorado Boys Ranch, and his cottage-parents, in particular, with shaping the teen into the man.

"Almost all my life, I never knew what it was like to be a part of a family," Jack says. "I found out what it meant when I moved into sixth cottage at the Ranch. I found two people, the Zacharys, who really cared about the boys that were in their house, and it showed. Everyone was treated the same: with respect. I learned that you needed to show that same respect back, and things were great.

"I was given certain responsibilities, like chores, and later getting a paying job, and that taught me responsibility," says Jack. "Mr. Zachary was in charge, and we all knew it, but he was not unreasonable. Both the Zacharys led me in the direction that I needed to go, without me really realizing it."

If you compare Jack's situation to the old adage about leading a horse to water, Jack was ready to drink. "The Zacharys were the ones who got me back on track after I quit football," Jack recalls. "When I did something I never thought I could do, it gave me a sense of accomplishment. If one of us was doing a good job at something, we were used as examples. The better we did, the more privileges we got. We all fit together as a family in the cottage. Their house was our house. We talked, watched TV, and just hung out.

"The Zacharys knew, because they had boys from all different backgrounds and races, that each one had to be dealt with in a different way," Jack says. "It also taught all of us guys how to treat each other. Don't get me wrong, the Zacharys could be tough on you when you messed up, but you never felt they didn't care. They opened up their home, and we became friends with all of the grown members of their family. This is where I got my interpretation of what it means to be a real family."

But Jim and Juanita would be the first to say, very emphatically, that they did not operate in a vacuum. The Ranch itself, with its determination to integrate the boys into the town and especially into the high school, was extremely important for a boy like Jack. The Zacharys are also quick to acknowledge how important other staff members have been to their charges. The opportunity boys have to choose from multiple parental figures has always been a strong point at CBR. In Jack's case, it was Mike Cronin, a counselor at the Ranch, who stepped up. Mike and his wife, Peggy, have worked at CBR in various capacities for thirty years and, like the Zacharys, have touched the lives of many boys.

Juanita says, "Jack found out that if he ever got upset with us, he could go down to Mike. We encouraged the boys to go to someone else if they needed to. Jack usually chose Mike, who would let Jack give his speech and then they would discuss it. It was a very good outlet for Jack, as he learned that people are not always going to get along with each other."

Jack remembers, "Mr. Cronin was the guy all of the boys looked up to, kind of like a big brother or the uncle you always wanted to have. He was into sports. He was the guy you wanted to be like and the guy you wanted to like you. Mr. Cronin and Mr. Zachary both filled the need for a father figure very well. Mr. Cronin did rule with an iron fist, but he was always an advocate for me at the Ranch."

Although the people were key to Jack's successful stay at the Ranch, it would be a mistake not to speak about the Ranch itself. Jack enjoyed activities such as learning how to care for horses, participating in the Little Britches Rodeo, and going to Cotapaxi for the cattle roundup, but it was the general structure of the Ranch life that fit so well for him. Not only did it fit for him while he was there, it prepared him for his future career choice in the army. In his words: "I think the Ranch prepped me for the military. I had gotten used to a system, the structure, when I first got there. I don't think I wanted to give that up. I felt safer in the military, and the adjustments weren't all that hard. I mean, it wasn't hard to go to a new place. Heck, I had done that three years ago. So I wasn't worried about it. And there was discipline at the Ranch so I wasn't afraid of it in the army."

During all this growing up, Jack was also getting ready to be a parent. He made up his mind early on that he wanted to do things differently. Not getting annoyed at the interruptions caused by pilgrimages to the pencil sharpener is a fair example of Jack and his wife, Roxanne's, parenting philosophy. Both came from difficult childhoods, and they met in the military. "It was just by luck that we got together and both wanted to raise our kids in the same way. My thing has always been, this is my family," Jack states emphatically.

"If we got in trouble at the Ranch," Jack says, "it was not as if life was over. So, for example, if my girls get in trouble and I get to the point of raising my voice, I will catch myself and come back later. It is an unconscious thing that I got from the Ranch. I think my kids worry more about disappointing me, and that affects them much more than anything else."

Jack and the Zacharys tell a story that illustrates Jack's philosophy. Jack was on an overnight high school trip and got involved in some drinking. As Jack tells it, "One thing led to another, and we had a little beer party going on. One Boys Rancher was walking around the hotel drunk." While Jack didn't initiate the incident, he didn't stop it either. Juanita explains, "I blamed Jack, as he was the oldest. I realized later that it was really another boy, but Jack took all the blame and the loss of face without saying a word." For Jack, "The worst part was not the grounding for a month. It was when Mr. Zachary made me feel about as big as an ant. I always felt worse that I let him down."

The tape recorder is now off and the interview over. Three blond heads are still bent over the spiral-bound notebooks and open textbooks cluttering the table in the next room. The pencils still seem sharp. Roxanne is supervising. Their youngest daughter can't wait to share the news of her upcoming swim meet and the happy fact that her dad will be home to see it. Jack fondly musses her hair. For Jack, family is everything, and that concept was born in a most unconventional place: a ranch cottage filled with boys and two substitute parents out on the eastern plains of Colorado.

—JP

# "Yes"

# Jim and Juanita Zachary

*Juanita Zachary answered the doorbell of her home in Wagoner, Oklahoma, at 6:00 A.M. on a Saturday morning, wondering who it could be at that hour. In the early morning light, she saw three neighbor children she knew well. Becky was standing on the front porch clasping her five-year-old brother by one hand and her three-year-old sister by the other.*

*"Mrs. Zachary," Becky said, "Daddy just shot Mama and then he shot himself. Can we stay with you for a while?"*

*"Yes," Juanita answered without hesitation as she held open the door for Becky and her siblings. "Yes, you can."*

✦ ✦ ✦

Few couples open their doors, or their hearts, to as many children as Jim and Juanita Zachary have. And few couples embrace what it means to form a family with as much passion and success. Although the "yes" that Juanita uttered that morning was only a temporary solution for the three children on her front porch, for the Zacharys it was the beginning of the unconditional acceptance of children in need that has defined this generous couple's entire fifty-three years of married life.

Jim and Juanita Zachary had married young, both just seventeen, during Jim's senior year in high school. Juanita had graduated the previous June, and her family was moving on from the construction job that had brought them to the small Oklahoma town of Wagoner. Determined to stay together, the newlyweds moved next door to Jim's parents, into the former home of his grandparents. It was 1950. Juanita comments, "I was working, and Jim worked after school as well. Really, there weren't too many expenses. After all, we didn't have any rent."

Receiving a university scholarship offer, Jim inquired about bringing his wife with him. The answer "We don't allow married freshman" settled that. Instead, Jim completed his first two years at the local junior college.

Jim and Juanita had both come from large, loving families and did not want to postpone children. Their first child, Chet, was born in 1951. As Juanita says, "I had always dreamed about being a good mother."

A second son, Jimmy, was born nineteen months later. With two children, it was even more of a struggle for Jim to continue his education, especially given that the college where he wanted to complete his bachelor's degree was fifty miles away. But in what was to be characteristic of their life together, Juanita and Jim were undaunted. Jim went to the college and stayed in the dorm that year. When the separation became too difficult for the young family, Jim's solution was to hitchhike back and forth each day.

"He would come back from college every day and be home in time for his shift at the grocery store," Juanita recalled. "I didn't work outside the home. I stayed home with the babies, and they were always 'bandbox clean' for Daddy's return."

Eventually, Jim received his bachelor's degree, and two more children were born to the Zacharys: Judy in 1957, and Kenny in 1958. By that time, Jim had become a high school teacher and a coach. He would eventually become a principal and then superintendent of a rural district.

As a brand-new teacher, Jim was asked to be a class sponsor. "Jim and I went to all the dances as chaperones," Juanita recalls. "So these kids became our kids. He also coached, so that created many relationships. And as our kids grew up, we had their friends with us. We put a pool table in our family room, and it went from there," Juanita says. "We would always have extra kids around. Our oldest son, Chet, never wanted to spend the night at someone else's house, but he sure wanted his friends around. Our youngest, Kenny, was a freshman, and his friends would be over all the time, before school, at noon, and after school. It was like having fifty kids," Juanita says.

Juanita and Jim were sometimes called on to provide more than a pool table and snacks. Juanita remembers, "It was during Kenny's senior year that one of his friends would just appear at our house. He never said much. We didn't actually know what was going on, but we knew he came from a messed-up family. He needed to stay a while. He would talk to Jim some, but mainly he talked to Kenny. He didn't have support from anyone else. He needed food and a good bed to sleep in. He needed a place to get away. He needed a bit of a normal life. The longest he stayed with us at one time was probably three weeks."

Although the Zacharys didn't know it, providing a temporary refuge for this lonely boy, as they had done with Becky and her siblings, was a preview of their future. Ultimately, they were to parent hundreds of kids. It was just doing what came naturally, according to both Jim and Juanita.

With Kenny, the last of their own children, graduating from high school, along with all "fifty" of his friends, Jim and Juanita were facing the emptiest of nests. They really couldn't imagine what their life would be like without kids. Juanita recalls, "They didn't need us anymore. But we couldn't stand the idea of not having children around. What were we going to do?"

Juanita says, "I knew Jim didn't like being a school superintendent. It was too much paperwork and funding problems and not enough time with kids. I had always supported everything Jim had done professionally. So if he had said, 'Let's go jump in a pond and work,' I would have done it."

In an Oklahoma City newspaper, Jim saw an ad that said cottage-parents were needed at Colorado Boys Ranch. He made a phone call. Jim received a letter inviting him and Juanita to come for an interview. The letter was Juanita's first inkling of this new pond, and it looked inviting, just ready for a swim. The Zacharys jumped in feet first, and they soon learned the water was fine. It was almost as if they had created this opportunity by digging the hole and making the rain to fill it.

Juanita recalls, "I remember going to Colorado Boys Ranch for our interview in late April of 1976. It was so green and beautiful, and I thought it would be someplace we would like. It was still a custodial ranch in those days. These boys just needed a place to stay. The Ranch was full. There were kids everywhere. The nice young man that gave us our tour was one of two brothers. He had been there forever and had nowhere else to go. This young man told us that the Ranch had given him a sense of what a real family would be like. He said that cottage-parents would listen to the boys when something was wrong and then help guide them."

The interview, the tour, and the young man's description of the role of cottage-parents gave Jim and Juanita much to talk about. On the drive back to Oklahoma, they asked the inevitable questions: Would they like the work? Would they like the place? Could they arrange to be there when the Ranch needed them at the beginning of the summer, with their daughter Judy's wedding coming up at the end of June?

Just like their reply to the front-porch entreaty from Becky and her two siblings years before, the Zacharys' answers were "Yes, yes, and yes." As Juanita says, "We thought we would like it very well."

Their daughter, Judy, was willing to move her wedding up a month. Juanita quickly made a wedding gown created from five different patterns. With the wedding successfully celebrated, the Zacharys gave most of their furniture to their kids, except for their books and a few special pieces, packed up their car, and headed to Colorado to begin their second career.

✦ ✦ ✦

Within three weeks, the Zacharys, or, as they came to be known, "The Zs," were the full-time cottage-parents for sixth cottage. They had a new home.

Colorado Boys Ranch could not have fashioned a better fit for the needs of the boys in 1976. Jim was a teacher, coach, administrator, and "nuts about kids." Juanita was loving, willing, competent, and accustomed to "fifty kids" at any one time.

In the beginning, Juanita says, "We only had cottage-parent duties." It was summer and school was out of session, so "only" meant making a home for sixteen boys, supervising and planning all of their activities, creating chore rosters, sharing meals in the dining hall, bedtimes, and morning rituals. They were responsible for the boys around the clock, or, as boys say now, "24/7." It was a busy new home for this "retired" couple.

"We set the structure for the cottage that first summer," Juanita says. "It needed someone to come in and say, 'This is what we need and this is how we are going to do it. We will all work together.' That was the beginning. We sat down together and made the schedule and it was put up. The kids knew what they had to do and when. We just had a family of sixteen instead of four. I didn't treat them any differently than I did my own, and they came to know that."

The Zacharys had an apartment connected to the boys' cottage by adjoining living rooms. The door between the living spaces was never shut. In fact, Jim recalls, "The boys would come in with the silliest questions sometimes, but we would just tell them to sit down and we could talk about it."

Juanita and Jim took all their meals with the boys when they were on duty. Juanita recalls, "I was a stickler for manners. We began by setting the table just as it should be set. We were really strict about all of that, and it just became a habit. We gave everyone a spot, and they always sat at the same one, Jim at one table and me at another. The ones who were really doing well were put at the third table. If one began to act up, we put him back at one of our tables." On their "days off" Juanita still cooked for the boys, making endless dozens of cookies or plates of cakes for the boys to enjoy in the evening. "We were just a natural Mom and Dad," she says.

"We wanted the kids to learn comfort and security. While we had all the structure and rules, they had to feel comfortable in that home. Consistency was one of our major themes," Juanita says. "If you're going to punish one boy one day, and then it happens again, they get the same punishment. And, of course," she continues, "there are always those unspoken layers that make up parenting. Some might call it role modeling, others might think of it as 'filling in the blanks.' For many of these boys, it was a brand-new version of family values."

Trust was one of those family values that came naturally to the Zacharys. "We told the boys, 'We have to learn to trust you, and you have to learn to trust us. No one is going to kick you out. We're not going to let you go.' We were all honest with each other."

Juanita says, "We did bed checks at night, not because we thought they wouldn't be there. No, we checked them to make sure they were okay. One time I found a boy who was not feeling well at all. He was afraid to knock on our door. I'm guessing that maybe his mother might have gotten mad in the past at being wakened or maybe he didn't have anyone he could wake up."

Affection was another family value that the Zacharys demonstrated naturally. Jim says, "We were very normal with the kids. And open. We always showed lots of love and laughter and lots of affection. Juanita and I never left each other or came back without a peck on the cheek hello or good-bye. We held hands on

Juanita and Jim Zachary.

and off the Ranch. We showed the boys what it looked like to love each other. I don't believe that many of them had seen a lot of that before they came to the Ranch. I think we were saying that it is all right to show your feelings."

The Zacharys held high stock in humor, a value that many families might not take for granted. Juanita relates, "There was lots of kidding. One day Chuck Wallin, the Ranch administrator, came to our apartment and hid all the pieces of the grandfather clock that Jim had been working on in the bottom of one of our dresser drawers. Jim went crazy and couldn't figure out what was up. I had to pretend I knew nothing of what was going on. The boys thought this was hilarious. Of course, Jim had to get even, and when he finally figured it out, he turned Chuck's office upside down. The boys couldn't believe that adults could do such lighthearted, good-natured practical joking with each other. The boys could see the real and humorous side of adults having fun without hurting each other."

Second careers are often shorter than first, but because Jim and Juanita made an early start in life, their second career, at Colorado Boys Ranch, lasted longer than most. They spent twenty-three years there, filled with twists and turns and opportunities both for the Ranch and for the Zs. It was sometimes difficult, but it was never boring.

Juanita says, "You know, it would be difficult for a husband and wife to be cottage-parents if the husband needed to take over for the wife all the time. It would have been hard to say, 'Well, we need to wait for Jim to do such and such.' Maybe it might have been difficult for Jim, but when I made a decision about something, he would let it stand."

Juanita's ability to handle things on her own became important in 1979. That was a time when, Jim says, "the Ranch, the school district, and I decided I needed to have a degree in special education." It took him three summers to complete the degree at Adams State College in Alamosa, Colorado. "I would leave at 8:00 A.M. on Monday morning and come home Friday night after my last class. Juanita was by herself at the cottage during that time," Jim says. "We didn't hire any extra staff. That made it a bit tougher. She did a great job while I was gone, even by herself at night."

Jim became a special-education teacher at La Junta High School and rode the bus to school every day with the boys. His classes were usually half Ranch boys and half town kids. If there was a problem with one of the boys, the school would call on Jim.

Jim says, "The biggest thing I learned was that you never jumped on a kid in front of anyone. If I could talk quietly, in private, the situation almost always was resolved. We told the teachers we were there to support the kids and to support them. We wanted to know what we could do to make their jobs more pleasant and to make their classrooms run more smoothly."

The district employed Jim for ten years. Eventually, the needs of the Ranch population changed, and Jim Herrel was designated to institute a school on the Ranch premises. Some boys would continue to attend the high school in town. Jim Zachary was appointed principal of the educational program at Colorado Boys Ranch. Jim acknowledges, "I think the Boys Ranch's relationship with the school district was most unusual. I would go to state education meetings and meet with other organizations that had kids in the public schools. And in very few places did they have as great a success as we did in La Junta and at Colorado Boys Ranch."

Jim also took on assistant coaching positions at the town high school. After his combined thirty years of coaching football, Jim was honored in front of a crowd at an All-State game in 1989.

Meanwhile, back at the Ranch, as they say, Juanita was not idle. In 1984, the Ranch was beginning its transition from custodial Ranch to psychiatric residential treatment facility and began to use counselors working in shifts instead of cottage-parents. Juanita took on the job of residential service coordinator and became a unit supervisor with seven counselors providing twenty-four-hour care to sixteen boys. She also went to school and earned her associate degree in psychology from La Junta Junior College. Juanita continued her work at the Ranch by taking on the responsibilities of team leader director.

In 1995, Juanita was named Colorado mother of the year. For a woman who, as a young girl, had "dreamed of being a good mother," receiving recognition at the governor's mansion in Denver for achieving her goal was a most fitting tribute. To participate in the national competition and be feted at the Waldorf Astoria in New York was a well-deserved honor and a dream come true.

Juanita says, "I always had a sense of family. As we grew up, my sisters wanted to be many things, but my goal in life was to be a good wife and mother. I felt that mothering was the most important position in life. I remember how hard my mother worked and the fun she had with us. I had enjoyed my family life so much, and I wanted to do the same thing. I thought it was a real romantic job. Yes, it was a lot of work. For example, we canned all summer long. I peeled and peeled and peeled, until I looked like a peeler. Even so, I always thought mothering was a very, very special job."

In the 1990s, the Ranch was still changing, but the Zacharys continued to say yes to everything that came along. The Zacharys moved into their own home in La Junta and, in addition to their jobs at the Ranch, became foster parents for Boys Ranchers who had no place to go after completing their treatment program at CBR. Helping these boys build on what they had learned at CBR, especially self-confidence and personal discipline, the Zacharys excelled as surrogate parents.

Describing their parenting style, Jim says his wife was the "soft shoulder" and he was the "tail twister." As he says, "The boys have always been able to talk to her easier than to me. She is the one who stayed awake until the boys got home from dates or school functions or other events." Jim, on the other hand, made sure the boys followed the rules, completed their chores, and "learned the two Rs: respect and responsibility."

Jim remembers an occasion when, as the "tail twister," he wished out loud for some kind of punishment for a boy who had played hooky from school. Then it began to snow. Juanita, the "soft shoulder," recalls that same incident, but her memory is of being filled with worry about the boy possibly getting sick from being out in the cold. Both Jim and Juanita were devoted to these boys, but Juanita had a mother's love. She says that as each boy left the Ranch ready to move on with his life, "a piece of my heart left with him."

When changes at the Ranch called for foster parents who were certified as "proctor parents" for those Boys Ranchers who had been referred by the state juvenile justice system, Jim and Juanita not only said yes, but they also worked to get the special certification required. To the Zacharys, all boys, no matter where they came from, were basically good. Said Jim, "We haven't had one boy who I'd call a bad kid. But then, I don't believe there is such a thing as a bad kid."

After forty years of child rearing, the Zacharys began discussing returning to Oklahoma to be closer to their own children and grandchildren. It was the year 2000, and it might have seemed time to move on. But along came Earl.

Earl was a Boys Rancher who had broken his leg badly while playing football. The Ranch felt they could not adequately care for him. One afternoon, Mike Cronin and Chuck Thompson, Colorado Boys Ranch president, appeared on the Zacharys' front porch in La Junta with an appeal. Would the Zacharys foster this boy?

Jim remembers, "We were no longer working for CBR, but they asked us if we could do this, so that his leg would heal."

With another front-porch plea before them, the Zacharys once again said yes.

"We had so much trouble with that leg," Jim says. "It was broken so badly that the doctors had to rebreak and pin it. We stayed with Earl through surgery in Denver and his recovery. So it wasn't foster care or proctor care, but medical care. He was, of course, on crutches, so we would take him back and forth to the high school for classes or to a game. We finally got him on his feet."

"Finally getting him on his feet" is a fitting ending to the story of this couple's life. Jim and Juanita Zachary helped their own four children to stand on their own feet, and then, for more than two decades at CBR, they helped hundreds of young men to do the same. Jim concludes, "The neatest experience of our lives, we think, was being at the Colorado Boys Ranch," to which a large population of boys who will be forever grateful to the Zacharys would add a resounding "Yes!"

—JP

# A Home in Need

## Kevin

*His early childhood was filled with trauma; his later child-hood was normal. Or so he says. Kevin came to live at Colorado Boys Ranch in 1972, when he was in elementary school, and stayed until he graduated from high school. So if normal means growing up on a ranch with sixty to seventy boys, having "cottage-parents" instead of a mom and a dad, building corrals and taking care of cattle and sheep, then Kevin's life was normal—and the only safe, stable family life he had known.*

In the early days of the Boys Ranch, it was somewhat ironically called a home for "orphans with parents." So it was with Kevin. When he was a very young boy, Kevin lived with a mother, a stepfather, and an older sister in a small Colorado mountain town. Two of his sisters were grown and on their own. "We lived on a little farm outside of town, and we were poor," Kevin says bluntly. Kevin speaks from the perspective of a navy veteran of twenty years, a successful husband, and a devoted father of five. With few words, he unflinchingly describes his early childhood.

"My folks were alcoholics, and I hung out at the bar with them," he says. "When I was four years old, I used to sleep with my one older sister still living at home. She was eight. In the middle of the night, my stepfather used to come in the room and kick me out of bed and make me sleep somewhere else." Kevin speaks without emotion, pauses, and adds, "Then one of my older sisters came home, and the next thing I knew we had been taken away."

Kevin spent the next few years in two foster-care placements interspersed with visits to the court. "It seemed like every six months I had to go to court and be asked if I wanted to go back home. I always said, 'No!'"

Kevin's "No!" had a definite exclamation point after it. He says he had no doubts about his decisions. Unhappily, neither of the foster-care placements gave Kevin the home he needed. One foster parent, a preacher's wife, "beat me with a tree limb," Kevin says. The other home, a good placement with a bad location, "was next door to the best friends of my stepfather and mother," he explains, which resulted in malicious harassment.

Kevin needed another home. When his social worker presented a brochure from Colorado Boys Ranch, Kevin, though very young, had, yet again, no trouble making a decision. He knew he wanted to go there. Kevin was "already interested in horses and other animals," he says. And so, that boy of his memory, a "young, skinny little bit of thing," knew immediately that the Ranch was the place for him. Kevin never looked back.

Self-described as "the boy no one worried about," Kevin was a young man who had all the fixings to become a troubled kid. He did not. He worked hard and played hard. And the Ranch, Kevin says with a chuckle, just "stayed out of my way."

Of course, Kevin knows that the Ranch was actually helping him make his way. It opened doors for enough activities to cross any carpooling parent's eyes. Kevin attended public schools in La Junta during all his Boys Ranch years. He was very active in 4-H both at the Ranch and in town, raising his own animals and becoming an animal competition judge. He wrestled on both the Ranch team and for his school teams. He played middle line-backer for his junior high football team. At the Ranch, he built corrals and remodeled barns. He helped birth sheep and worked with the horse program. "They tried to make life as normal as possible for us boys," reflects Kevin. His summers were filled with fishing and camping and "all the other things normal kids do. I never had time to be lonely."

It seems remarkable that a young man with Kevin's painful background could be so successful at so many aspects of his Ranch life. Thinking that his experience was "normal" makes it somehow seem just that simple.

Before picturing a routine image of simple ranch life, how-ever, imagine just for an instant eleven ramrod-straight teenage boys on horseback, lined up two by two with one out in front. They are very smartly outfitted in reproduction cavalry uniforms, bright blue with yellow stripes down the pant leg, topped with Mounties-style hats. You are seeing the 1975 Colorado Boys Ranch Mounted Cavalry, a precision equestrian team.

Normal? Not for life in the inner city, and definitely not for life in an institution. But, yes, normal for Colorado Boys Ranch and its emphasis on unique activities to help boys grow normally into young men.

The Mounted Cavalry, an outgrowth of an existing riding program at the Ranch, used the more-leisurely hours of summer for practice and became an award-winning squad. They went on the road and traveled all the way to Cheyenne, Wyoming, to par-ticipate in the renowned Frontier Days. But winning and travel wasn't everything. Those 6:30 to 8:30 A.M. daily drills and hours of study in horsemanship, with each boy caring for his individual

The Colorado Boys Ranch Mounted Patrol, in formation.

horse, gave the boys invaluable lessons in esprit de corps. Their practice paid off, in recognition and in a sense of accomplishment. At forty-something, Kevin still wears the belt buckle he won competing with the cavalry, and, in his words, is "still a cowboy at heart."

As he matured at the Ranch, Kevin took on jobs such as helping supervise junior boys in his "senior boy" status. He checked off those teenage rites of passage that seem unexpected in an institutional setting: getting a driver's license, having part-time jobs, dating, having friends from town, and graduating from high school. Normal.

Kevin remembers those particular years at the Ranch, the late 1970s and early 80s, as "golden." He also believes, and rightly so, that these were special and unique years for the Ranch itself. Even though every single staffer, acting as chauffeur/coach/tutor/nurturer/nurse—in short, surrogate parent—could have been kept busy just keeping up with each and every kid like Kevin, the Ranch facility itself also matured and evolved. It was a period of considerable expansion. Patched-together remodeled army housing was replaced with brand-new cottages. With the generous help of the citizens of Burlington, a spacious yet homey dining hall was built with a stage for Ranch entertainment and productions. Staff, kids, and volunteers also rebuilt the corrals and animal barns.

With a significant physical expansion came an equally significant philosophical expansion. The Ranch focus began to change. The new boys of a more complicated society, in which the issues of trauma, mental health problems, drug addiction, and gang violence were on the rise, had different needs. New staff came to meet those needs with treatment-based degrees in social work and psychology. The Ranch was developing into a sophisticated treatment facility as well as a home for outcast boys.

While the Boys Ranch evolved naturally to meet the new boys' needs, alumni like Kevin miss the simplicity of the old days. In fact, he remarks rather wistfully, "I feel strongly that there is definitely a need in this world for a place like the Boys Ranch used to be."

Even though Kevin lived at the Ranch during this time of transition, he says that the Ranch more than rose to meet the challenge of his young life. It was, "after all, my home," he says. "I can tell you to this day, that I don't know where I would have been without the Ranch. I had nobody. They were the people who will affect me for the rest of my life. They gave me my start and showed me what life can be about."

Kevin's successful naval career, followed by an equally successful career in a large construction firm, along with his abiding conviction of the importance, and possibility, of normal family functioning, prove the truth in his words.

—JP

CHAPTER
SIXTEEN

# Evolution

# From Orphanage to
# Psychiatric Treatment Facility

*"I remember coming to work one morning and every door
in the administration building had been busted open,"
says Chuck Thompson, recalling an incident that occurred
at CBR in the spring of 1981. When he was hired as
administrator of Colorado Boys Ranch, Chuck was well
aware of the challenges he faced even before he walked
through those doors, busted or not.*

"When I began working at the Ranch, the organization was kind
of at a tipping point," Chuck says. "The needs of the kids were
advancing and more severe than the house parent model could
support. As a result, they were having quite a bit of turnover with
house parents. They were having various episodes where there
would be numbers of kids that were kind of ganging together and
rebelling back against staff."

In the early 1980s, Chuck says, "The Ranch was run much
more on a custodial model. They were focused on daily supervision

Chuck Thompson.

of kids and on their educational needs, but less on a defined treatment plan." Chuck knew, as a master's level social worker from the Denver area, that the Ranch was in danger of losing its credibility. "They were responding in crisis to everything," Chuck says. "In any kind of residential situation, there is a balance point where adults are in control or kids start to take control. And so my job, in essence, was to bring some stability to that and to reexamine the staffing and program model. Hire more trained professionals. We were getting geared up to start dealing with the issues of child abuse, which many of the youth had experienced prior to their arrival at the Ranch."

Many people observing the evolution of Colorado Boys Ranch into CBR YouthConnect over the past five decades, and particularly the last two and a half, will tell you that Chuck Thompson *is* CBR. While Chuck is far too modest to stake that claim, he certainly embodies many enduring qualities of CBR, including resilience and adaptability. Chuck will acknowledge that in the past twenty-five years of working at Colorado Boys Ranch, twenty of those as president, he has overseen significant changes. And he is proud of the organization. But even more, he will stress his pride in the boys who come there and his awe at their capacity to change and grow.

From his viewpoint, which began midway through the Ranch's history, Chuck can look back into the past, up to the present, and even peer into the future to see how changes in society have necessitated adaptations, over time, at CBR. "When you look at what has changed in society over the past forty-eight years, the length of time that CBR has been in existence," Chuck says, "you have to look at changes that occur in two primary domains. One is in the social structure of a society and the other is in the economic structure of a society.

"On the social side," Chuck says, "after the Second World War, we were trying to regroup as a nation. We began to discover that more and more kids were disconnected from their own basic family system and needed specific care outside their homes. People realized there needed to be different alternatives. It was about this point in time that various people and organizations throughout the nation looked at this idea of getting troubled kids away from the cities. The popular thinking," Chuck says, "was 'Let's find places away from the cities where kids can get away from urban pressures, see life from a different perspective, get a breath of fresh air,' if you will. The thought was to give these kids a chance to grow up in happy, healthy ways. That thinking led to the creation of Colorado Boys Ranch.

"Now at that point," he says, "society really wasn't looking at mental health issues. They were looking at social issues and basic nurturing of kids when they could not live at home. Our knowledge base about mental health was a lot less than it is now. We didn't understand the impact, in terms of mental health, of abuse and neglect. We didn't understand, at that point in time, how much body chemistry affects the way people act. And of course there weren't the kinds of medications there are now. So I think what happened is, those kids who were manageable enough stayed within the orphanage structure, and those that weren't ended up in prison systems. CBR began more as an orphanage, but it was an orphanage with a focus on helping kids that were seen to be on a slippery slope. If these boys didn't have adequate supervision and care, they might end up becoming problems for society. I think *criminals* may be too strong of a word, but they might end up as incorrigibles in our society.

"At some point down the line, something happened to the overall family structure," Chuck notes. "More and more kids had to be cared for outside their own homes. Our society began to develop and produce more and more of these dysfunctional kids and families. They were hitting some kind of a critical mass.

"On the economic side," he continues, "society said, 'Uh-oh. This is getting really costly. Now we have to figure out the cheapest ways to take care of these kids who can't live in their families.' Society realized that the state needed to take care of these kids or needed to have a primary role. But government only has so many dollars. When you have more needs than you have dollars, the bottom line is somebody is going to get left out. And so the government hopes volunteers will step up and create non-profit organizations to help those kids that are going to get left out. That is the role the nonprofit organization has been designed to play, to fill the gap that can't be provided by government or is not profitable for a for-profit company." Thus CBR began as, and remains, a private nonprofit nonsectarian organization dedicated to helping troubled youth.

"By the late 1970s," Chuck says, "the concept of orphanages was starting to lose its momentum and was being challenged by advocates throughout the nation. Society said, 'If a child has the behavioral ability to live in a family, they ought to be in a family.' Government formalized the idea of foster care and set up reimbursement systems for foster parents. With the development of foster care, the traditional orphanage system began to be dismantled. That was a very significant thing and a social issue. The other thing that was recognized more strongly by society at this time was the fact that there is such a thing as child abuse. There are kids that really need protection by society against abusive adults. Those two social phenomena began to shift the way we care for these kinds of kids and triggered major change in all of our caregiving throughout the nation.

"There was also a growing social theory," Chuck says, "that kids ought to be in the least restrictive setting possible. This idea of 'least restrictive setting' was included in the 1979 Colorado legislation of Senate Bill 26 that enabled foster care. The theory of least restrictive setting said, 'If they can live in a family, they ought to be in a family; if not, they ought to go up the institutional chain from foster care to group homes to residential child care facilities, all the way up to imprisonment.' *Least restrictive* was also defined as how close to your home community you were going to be. When society defined *least restrictive* as 'the home community,' that placed organizations like Colorado Boys Ranch outside the loop. In other words, we then became, in society's view and by the criteria, a more restrictive setting because we were farther away from the child's home (despite the fact that we have always had, and continue to have, an open, unlocked campus). When Senate Bill 26 was passed, the Boys Ranch realized we were not really ever going to get kids that are less severe. We were only going to get boys who had failed in every other setting possible in their home community."

With the increasing severity of troubled youth coming to CBR, it is no wonder things were at a "tipping point" in the early 1980s, when Chuck arrived on the scene. "Within a year and a half," Chuck says, "my job was to change the staffing model from house parent to shift staff and then to begin to hire more trained and certified professionals. We realized we were going to have to gear up to deal with the most severely troubled boys, so we decided to get the highest credentialing that we could get. We wanted to get accreditation beyond just our state licensing, which was minimal and meager. So a critical decision and juncture within the organization was its decision, in about 1984, to pursue national mental health accreditation. That's when the idea of becoming a Joint Commission on Accredited Healthcare Organizations (JCAHO) accredited facility was born. In 1985, we had our first JCAHO review. I credit my predecessor, Chuck Wallin, for the vision behind that. It really was the right strategy."

In-state referrals to CBR decreased, due to Senate Bill 26, but "We began to get national referrals through our own state department of child welfare," Chuck recalls. "A lady by the name of Bonnie Boyd Wilson would call down from Denver and say, 'Chuck, we got this call from Indiana, and they are looking for a place for a particular boy, and I just want to let you know I gave them your name.' That state then told another state, and by word of mouth we actually built up our population to about half out-of-state referrals without any marketing at all."

"Now," Chuck says, "youth between the ages of ten and twenty-one from all ethnic, cultural, geographic, and socioeconomic backgrounds are admitted to CBR YouthConnect. Our youth are often the victims of severe physical and emotional abuse, compounded by medical and psychiatric problems. Some have drifted into trouble with the law. Others, despite having caring and loving parents, just cannot gain enough control to behave appropriately. By the time youth reach CBRYC, they typically have failed to be helped by several other out-of-home treatment programs, from foster care homes to psychiatric hospitals, and are at risk for continued multiple placements. For many of our youth, CBRYC is a place of last resort.

"Yet, despite their pain and hardships, these boys are remarkably talented and resilient. All but a small percentage of them are able to turn their lives around at CBRYC and avoid delinquency, becoming hopeful and productive citizens."

Chuck goes on to say, "One of the things that I have always been proud of is that the organization itself has a history and has lived out a personality which is really similar to what we are trying to evoke with kids. And that is this idea of being resilient and innovative. Having the will to change and to meet change head on. We try to develop that in kids. And I think that has been a hallmark of the organization. These are some of what I would call the 'branding words' for the organization," Chuck says. "We are resilient; we have the ability to bounce back. We are also an innovative organization because we really are interested in staying current. We have some key leaders in the organization who read voraciously, who really stay on top of the latest theories and information and studies that are coming out. We have participated in research. And we share our knowledge around the world.

"We believe in combining good common sense and the true love of kids with professional theory and practice," Chuck goes on to say. "It's all about motivation. We give kids the opportunity to explore and discover their own interests and talents. That process of discovery ignites the motivation necessary for change.

"When a boy first comes to CBR YouthConnect," Chuck says, "we sit down with him and the meaningful people in his life and we look at testing and observation and history. We plan individualized treatment based on our model of 'the integration of treatments that work: neuroscience, psychotherapy, and an enriched environment.' But, importantly, we include the boy. We say, 'Johnny, this is what we know about you. Based on that, we are going to structure a part of your individualized treatment plan. But the other part will be your choice. What do you want to do? Computers, animals, music, dance?' The boy will begin to explore these things. But often it is the first time he has been asked, 'What do you want to do?' We don't hold him to his first choice. We let him try a variety. Pretty soon he will find something he likes. And then he will pull you through the treatment process.

"Our methodology has advanced in terms of how we implement programming," Chuck points out, "but our basis, or our philosophy, about programming has been pretty consistent throughout the years. We really have stayed connected to the core values that the organization started out with. And those values had to do with the fact that each and every boy is important and unique. The work ethic is important. Giving and doing something for somebody else is important. Understanding the value of a rural setting and the importance of relationships is important. So in terms of the core values, we really have stayed very consistent."

The rural setting of Colorado Boys Ranch has, at times, posed certain logistical difficulties, but, according to Chuck, the value of the rural atmosphere far outweighs the difficulties. "Personally, I think there is something innate in human nature," Chuck says. "Just pick up a little newborn, whether it's a human or an animal, and it evokes in all of us something that is way down deep within our soul and our nature. When you are connected to the other elements of nature, you feel much more at one with the world, more connected, like you belong to the world. We deal with kids who feel disconnected from society, disconnected from belonging anywhere. Although we are an institution, we try to keep experiences in the daily life of each boy that remind them that they are a very precious and individual human being and that they are connected to a wonderful world that is all around them. This emphasis on connecting boys with nature, with therapeutic resources, and with knowledge of themselves and others is what led us to decide to begin using a new name: CBR YouthConnect."

Perhaps even more than he values the rural setting, Chuck values the importance of human relationships at the Ranch. Staff in all areas of the Ranch are incorporated into the treatment team and encouraged to provide feedback on how a boy is doing. Often it is the therapist, but it may be someone in maintenance or in the horsemanship program who establishes that first connection with a particular youth. Frequently, the boy shares his heart and feelings with these staff members and they respond back.

Employees and the boys themselves love to expound on this aspect of the Ranch.

"A good example," Chuck says, "is that we have some people who work for us who get lured by higher pay to go to work at the prison. I had one employee come back and sit in my office and tell me, "Chuck, as soon as we go to work at the prison, the first thing they tell us is, 'Under no circumstances develop a relationship with an inmate, because as soon as you do, you are then vulnerable to manipulation. You've crossed the line, the appropriate line, between caretaker and inmate.' Yet," Chuck reflects, "when you think about it, if the healthy people can't have relationships with the unhealthy people, then who are they going to have relationships with? The other unhealthy ones? Working in the prison system becomes dehumanizing and very mechanical for those employees," Chuck says. "A lot of those employees come back and work at least part time for us, because they say, 'The first thing you have to be able to do if you are going to work at CBR is build a relationship.'

"This focus on relationships takes time. It can't be accomplished in the 90 days usually allowed for inpatient psychiatric hospital stays. At CBR YouthConnect, boys usually stay for an average of 14 months. Our methods have proven to be extraordinarily successful. A recently completed follow-up study of 181 youth three years after leaving the program showed a success rate of 92 percent. Success was determined by how well the boy was doing at home, school, work, and interpersonally. At how well they were handling emotions and being responsible. These results are phenomenal and true.

"To evolve successfully, any organization needs to hang on to what is successful while adapting to a changing and stressful environment," Chuck says. "The length and strength of CBR has allowed the organization to continue serving troubled youth from its own state and from across the country."

Adaptation to a changing economic and social environment has led Colorado Boys Ranch to evolve into CBR YouthConnect, an award-winning psychiatric residential treatment facility with a national reputation for helping troubled youth. Hanging on to its core values has been crucial to the longevity of the Ranch. But without adaptation and evolution, the Boys Ranch would have closed its doors long ago.

—CQL

# CHAPTER SEVENTEEN

# A Brave Heart

# Tom Sutherland

*Tom Sutherland, the second longest-held captive in the Middle East, did not see the sun from June 9, 1985, until November 17, 1991. Six and a half years. During that time, Tom was almost constantly blindfolded, very often chained to the wall, and sometimes beaten and left in solitary confinement. He was wrapped head to foot in duct tape and transported over rough roads in the tire well under the bed of a truck, choking on exhaust fumes. Throughout the ordeal, and through deep depressions, Tom and his fellow hostages held on to hope for survival.*

Nine years after Sutherland's release from the Islamic Jihad, the History Channel produced a documentary about his captivity in Lebanon, focusing on what Tom had accomplished in the years since regaining his freedom. The narrator describes the dark horror of the roach-infested cells where Tom was imprisoned and says, "Today, Sutherland's life is still deeply affected by his hostage experience. Not as a nightmare, but as a mission. Sutherland joined the board of Colorado Boys Ranch in La Junta, Colorado, six years after his release. For Sutherland, this is a calling that increasingly fulfills his life post-captivity."

In the History Channel film, Tom says, "Being involved with that Boys Ranch has given me an insight into just how many young men are abused, some of them brutally abused. And when I look at that and contrast it to my experience, I think maybe I can help here, because I understand what they've gone through. I think they sense that I'm a kindred spirit. That they can talk to me."

The boys do talk to him. Although he has been a naturalized American citizen for many years, Tom's voice is still inflected with his native Scottish burr. "I come from 'Brave Heart' country," Tom says, trilling the letter r and referring to the rugged and beautiful land made familiar by the movie of the same name. "I grew up in a stone farmhouse on the banks of the River Forth near Edinburgh, Scotland."

Sitting at a picnic table at Colorado Boys Ranch with a group of boys, each of whom has his own dark history, Tom discusses the cruelty he was subjected to as a hostage. As he speaks of the abuse he suffered at the hands of his captors, the boys listen intently. One boy tells Tom that he had been beaten too, but not imprisoned like Tom.

"It doesn't feel very nice, does it?" Tom asks. "Who did that to you?"

Almost inaudibly, the boy whispers, "My dad."

Before Tom and the boys saddle up their horses for a ride on the mesa, one boy featured in the History Channel film says of Tom, "I think he should be a mentor for everybody on the Ranch. Most of them have problems that they are fighting with mentally, like aggression and abuse. So I think he's pretty cool for being able to come back like that."

Tom's wife, Jean, agrees. "He never looked back," she says. "He never has flashbacks. He never has nightmares. He can talk about his experience. And I think talking about it and using that experience to benefit others, like those boys, has been his healing."

For Tom, as it is for the boys who come to CBR YouthConnect, healing was necessary physically, mentally, and emotionally. In his account of his hostage experience, *At Your Own Risk*, cowritten by Tom and Jean,

Tom Sutherland.

Tom writes of those dark times when he was blindfolded and chained to the wall. "I couldn't seem even to cope with the simplest mental activities, and began to despair of my mind. ... I fell into extreme depression, and began seriously to believe that I was losing my mind and my sanity. ... At times we were given books and I tried to read them. But, in contrast to my colleagues, when I got to the end of a page, I would stop and ask myself, 'What have I just read? What did it say?' To my horror, I could remember not a single thing of what I had just read *word by word* in the previous five minutes! I truly feared that my mind was disintegrating and that I would never again be right. The end of my intellectual life?"

For Tom, who was the dean of agriculture at the American University of Beirut at the time he was kidnapped, this was a severe blow. He writes, "I was in panic! How I'd come to this point I couldn't say—whether due to the harassment from the guards or from the very fact of being in captivity, I couldn't have said nor did it matter at that time; all I knew for sure was that I was in deep psychological trouble."

Under the stress of captivity, even passing the time by playing a simple game like Twenty Questions with the other hostages was difficult for Tom. Unable to remember that "Casper" was the friendly ghost, Tom felt mortified in front of his fellow cellmates. He writes, "I was being called dumb. I couldn't ever recall having been called that in my entire life, not in earnest and with such genuine feeling, anyway. Had there been anywhere to hide, I certainly would have run for it. But where can one hide in a 14 by 12 foot room with four pairs of eyes bearing on one? The ultimate in humiliation. Could I have come to this in less than three months of captivity?"

Within about a year and a half, Tom says, "I went down to nothing, to a nadir, where I was essentially a blithering idiot." His lowest point came in a particularly humiliating manner. Tom had been in isolation in his cell, waiting hours to be taken to the bathroom. "I was bursting to urinate," Tom says. "Finally, came a rattle at the big door to the guard room. I was at the window of my cell with my blindfold. I didn't speak, but I wanted them to know I was there." After he heard the other hostages being taken to the bathroom, Tom heard only silence. He lifted a corner of his blindfold to see if he had been forgotten. But it was a trick. The guard had been silently waiting, hoping to catch Tom in a forbidden act. The lifted blindfold was enough justification in the guard's mind to give Tom a severe beating.

Tom writes, "He came swooping down on me with a big holler. 'Why you looking?' He went in to his buddies in the guardroom. They took me out of my cell and laid me down on my back and held my feet up and started whacking me on the insoles of my feet with a rubber truncheon. Really, really painful. I started screaming. The guards said, 'No screaming.' But pretty soon they were screaming louder than I was. They were hitting me on my thighs, calves, ribs, shoulders, and by the time they were done I was black and blue from my neck to my feet. Afterwards, they weren't even going to take me to the toilet. I just pleaded with them and eventually they did."

It didn't seem as though things could get worse, but they did. "They blocked off my little barred window with a steel shutter and I was more than ever in the dark. Underground like that it is really dark. I got no outside light, no candle." Tom had to eat in the dark and had no contact whatsoever with his companions. He says, "I was as angry as hops and desperate and I thought, 'I'm not going to put up with this. To Hell with them.' I determined to end it all and commit suicide. I tried three times, but I couldn't go through with it."

Tom was saved by a vision of his wife and daughters. "Before my eyes in my semi stupor: Jean and Ann and Kit and Joan were there, all four as clear as could be. 'God,' I thought desperately. 'God. I can't. I can't do this to them. Not fair!'" The women are endlessly grateful for his courage. "I am here today, and very glad to be here," Tom writes. But at the time, he had to hang on "a day at a time, just get through a day at a time."

The loneliness of captivity was relieved to a great degree when he was returned to the group cell. Tom writes of his relationships with the other hostages and the "power of community." But during years of captivity, Tom's self-confidence had dwindled away. Losing intellectual debates with his cellmate, AP journalist Terry Anderson, had destroyed Tom's self-confidence. Being able to *do* something helped to restore him. Tom was always handy and, when he was able to repair the broken light fixture in their cell, that "did a lot for my self-confidence and mildly improved my standing," Tom writes, referring to the pecking order that was developing among the hostages.

And despite his intellectual conflicts with Terry Anderson, Tom says, "Terry was the biggest restorer of my soul and my faith. Terry would say, 'Come on! Come on! We're not going to let them get us down. Come on! Get up, man!' Frankly, I would say he literally saved my life. We were together for seventy months out of the seventy-seven months that I was there and the eighty months that he was. So he and I were joined at the hip, essentially."

They were, in fact, joined together by chains. And, as much as anything, the two hostages, lying blindfolded on foam pads chained to the wall, suffered from frustration and boredom. In Tom's book, *At Your Own Risk*, and in Terry Anderson's book, *Den of Lions*, both men relate a particular diversion used to maintain their sanity. Terry had a quick and curious mind. He asked Tom, a former professor of agriculture, to teach him.

Tom agreed. Lying blindfolded on the ground, he gave Terry a one-on-one tutorial, from memory, on animal science and other courses. "It turned out to be rather fun and it did pass the time," Tom writes. "Armed with all this new knowledge of agriculture, Terry had an idea. There were plenty of kids that were going wrong where he came from and he had this idea of saving these kids from going completely astray. He was going to build a school that was part of a farm. He would have the kids working on the farm and that was to be their salvation. Giving them something to do."

Tom had been an agriculture professor at Colorado State University but was not familiar with Colorado Boys Ranch before going to Lebanon. Thus, when Terry asked Tom to help him devise a plan for a farm facility for troubled boys, they thought they were working from scratch. Tom recalls the many questions that Terry had for him as he planned his farm. "He would ask, 'What do you feed a cow and how much? How do you get milk out of a cow? What's a milking parlor?' All these things that were second nature to me," Tom says.

"Then Terry realized he was going to have to have pretty special teachers to handle boys who were on the edge of getting in trouble with the law. And Terry wasn't sure how he was going to get the money to do this. Having just been a dean and having had to get money for various projects," Tom writes, "I told him about seeking grants from individuals and foundations.

"It all took weeks and months at a time and kept our minds very occupied—all the while talking from behind blindfolds with no pencil or paper," Tom writes. "In subsequent cells, we had paper and talked of revising the project and of honing the budget. I was giving him all these ideas and he was writing them up for his proposal. Endless hours of discussion and planning. But time we had."

Terry was so attached to this plan to help troubled boys that he "wrote it all out, every detail, in the smallest handwriting I have ever seen," Tom writes. "He wrapped the pages, perhaps eight to ten of them, in plastic and hid them in the one place where the guards, given their extreme prudishness, never ventured—in his crotch." But eventually the guards did discover the notes and took them away. "We never saw paper or pen again until the day of my departure," writes Tom.

With freedom, Tom was able to celebrate with friends and family back in Fort Collins, Colorado, but he was not content to simply retire to a life of ease. In the sixteen years since his release, he has shared his experience and knowledge wherever, and in whatever way, he feels it can do the most good. Tom has lectured at countless venues about his experiences as a hostage in the Middle East. And despite, or perhaps because of, having been beaten and abused by young men during that time, Tom has devoted himself to the education and treatment of troubled youth, especially helping troubled boys at CBR YouthConnect.

"After my release," Tom says, "I learned about Colorado Boys Ranch while on a skiing trip with my friend Owen Smith, a CBR board member. I was prejudiced in favor of CBR since it was in a rural setting. I think it has a lot of calming influence to be out in the country. When I was a dean at the American University in Beirut, my agriculture students never saw many plants. Kids growing up in Beirut, even wealthy kids, all they saw were a few plants on their balconies. It wasn't safe to go out into the countryside. When I got those students out to the AUB farm in the

Bekaa, they felt it was the biggest, most wonderful happening in their whole time at the university. It was a revelation for them.

"Owen drove me down to the Boys Ranch and we spent a day there with Chuck Thompson, CBR president, and I thought, 'This is a good place, and Chuck Thompson is a good man,'" says Tom. "I thought he was such an articulate spokesman for the boys and such a sympathetic guy. He really had the interest of these boys right at heart. I was interviewed, and they decided to invite me to be on the board.

"Owen and the other board members cared so much about the Ranch," Tom says. "Somehow it gets a passion in people, and that's what's passed on to other people. What I enjoy most about working on the board and with Chuck is feeling that it is a mission that is worthwhile doing. Chuck Thompson is a saint. The people on the CBR board are really diverse: doctors, lawyers, professors, businessmen, and realtors. They really get in there and pitch like crazy. It is the hardest-working board I've ever been on. And you feel like you can get things done.

"At the Boys Ranch," Tom says, "they give something that those boys have never had before, and that is give them love. I think that's a big part of it.

"I've talked to Chuck about it," Tom says. "They ask those kids, 'What would you like to do when you come to the Boys Ranch here?' It's almost the first time they've heard that question, "What would *you* like to do?" *Telling* them what to do doesn't work with kids.

"After I learned about CBR," Tom says, "I called Terry Anderson from Colorado and said, 'Hey, Anderson, remember that farm you were going to create in New York?' And he said, 'Yeah.' And I said, 'I found it. We've got it right out here and I'm joining the board.'"

Terry came out to Colorado to visit CBR with Tom and several other board members. He got a thorough tour of the campus from

Chuck Thompson and learned about the extensive professional staff: psychiatrist, psychologists, social workers, teachers, nurses, educators, and vocational specialists who work with the boys. "I want to tell you," says Tom, "You never saw guys so engrossed in what a man had to say as we were. When Chuck was done talking, Terry said, 'Boy, you and I were sure naïve. This whole operation is so much more complicated than I ever even dreamed it was.'"

On October 9, 1999, Terry Anderson and Tom Sutherland spoke on behalf of CBR at the University of Denver. Roger O'Neil of *NBC Nightly News* acted as master of ceremonies. Nearly 300 people listened as Sutherland and Anderson described their long ordeal as hostages in the Middle East. Terry commented on how valuable it would be if the stories of the troubled boys at CBR, who have overcome their own psychological captivities, could be told in their own words and shared with the world. That was the immediate catalyst for *The Hero Within*.

It is the spring of 2005. Tom and Jean Sutherland sample the Scotch eggs at the Stonehouse Grill in Fort Collins, Colorado. The cozy eatery, recently opened by their daughter and son-in-law, is named after the stone farmhouse in Scotland where Tom was raised. They laugh in delight with their daughter Kit as she unpacks a box of kilts to be used as garb for the waitstaff. The atmosphere during the busy lunch hour at the Stonehouse Grill is one of relaxed and cheerful family togetherness. Tom and Jean's meal is frequently interrupted by the greetings of friends and neighbors, but they don't seem to mind. In fact, they relish it. There were so many years when they and their daughters, Ann, Joan, and Kit, could only dream of such a gathering.

A photo of Tom's boyhood farm home is displayed on the restaurant wall, along with another of Tom in his youth, a handsome young man kicking a soccer ball through a goal. Tom tells a story about soccer that is emblematic of his tenacity as a youth and as a hostage.

"Growing up in Scotland," Tom says, "I was always nuts about soccer, and when I went to school, I was eager to be in it. On the playground, we set up two goals, and the two best guys would choose the teams, one each, until all were chosen. One of the hotshot players doing the choosing was named Alfie McNab. Well, I was the last one chosen, and I went to the other guy. I remember Alfie laughing and saying, 'You got stuck with Sutherland!'"

Tom says, "I thought to myself, 'You ridiculed me! You son of a gun. I'll show you!'" Tom honed his skills, and in 1949, as a senior at Falkirk High School, scored fifty-five goals in a season, a school record that still stands. He went on to be chosen to play outside left for the Scottish Youth International Soccer Team against England, Wales, Ireland, France, and Holland, and was signed by the Glasgow Rangers.

Sutherland scores a goal during a soccer match in Scotland.

Tom's triumph over his ordeal as a hostage shows the same kind of tenacity he had as a young soccer player. The strength of the Sutherland family as they waited for Tom's return displayed a similar resolve. Their dedication, each for the other, was tested during those years of Tom's captivity in Lebanon and found to be as sturdy as any house of stone. Tom and Jean's commitment to peaceful solutions to the difficult problems of the world, already strong when they arrived at the American University of Beirut in 1983, has only grown since those days.

Tom is now chairman emeritus of Colorado Boys Ranch Foundation/CBR YouthConnect board, doing work very similar to that which he and Terry dreamed up while in captivity. Amazingly, Tom holds no bitterness for his captors. "A lot of people think I should feel angry and bitter that these young guys treated me so badly," says Tom. "But I honestly felt sorry for them, because they had never had a chance in life at all. Any of them. I never felt like I should be angry at them." Sympathy and empathy seem to come naturally to Tom. His sympathy and empathy for the troubled boys of the world, like those who come to CBR YouthConnect, is what makes Tom work so hard on their behalf.

—CQL

# CHAPTER EIGHTEEN

# The Contents
# of a Mother's Heart

## Claire

*"The ordinary man is involved in action. The hero acts,"
according to the playwright Henry Miller. It is doubtful
that Claire has ever thought of herself as a hero. More
likely she sees herself as simply John's mom, a parent who
had to act. She shares her story in hopes of helping other
parents of troubled youth. In her words, "Part of the reason
I give you all this information is that I trust you not to use
it to describe us as a family, but to put in perspective the
complexity of these kids. I have given you the contents of
my heart."*

In one rural community, a divorce wreaked havoc on the lives of
everyone in the family. It is possible for kids to bounce back from
a divorce, especially when a very loving and competent stepfather, like the one that John had, comes on the scene. But for
John, mental illness associated with a brain injury complicated
his reactions to the devastating family upheaval. He began to act

in uncontrolled and uncontrollable ways. As for Claire, she began a journey that took her to unfathomable places. It required great courage. Had she been a fortune-teller, she might well have folded up the tent along the way.

But packing it in was never an option for Claire. Although nothing is easy when you are dealing with a special-needs child, she was committed to her son from the beginning. "When John was in second grade, we realized that he had far greater problems than we could provide for, and he was placed in special education," Claire says. "It was clear to me that a parent needed to stay very, very involved. As there are limited resources within a school district, I soon found out that the squeaky wheel gets the grease."

This early realization of the need for advocacy has shaped Claire's life and work for more than two decades. Although she continues to work in mental health advocacy, including lobbying with state governments, from the first her passion was her son. "It was my job to advocate for his welfare. It also became clear to me that this was not a common and accepted practice," Claire says. "The bottom line is that an involved, articulate parent who knows the rules is not a welcome sight at the conference table."

The ramifications of John's mental illness and his mother's fervor to obtain help for him have come at great cost. She removed him from their home for his own sake. She watched incompetent and sometimes uncaring health care workers unsuccessfully try to treat him. She placed herself and her parenting methods under constant scrutiny. She saw the family finances shredded and attempts at privacy insensitively doomed. She watched her loving son become almost unlovable. She struggled to keep him a member of the family while constantly grieving for lost opportunity. And she sobbed herself to sleep on more nights than she cares to remember.

"One day we realized we just didn't have any more rabbits in our hat," says Claire as she begins to describe the process of getting help for John in her rural area. Although due in part to her efforts, day care and group homes now exist in her small community, eighteen years ago they did not. Eventually John would make it to Colorado Boys Ranch, but not before many difficult stops along the way.

Placing John away from home for the first time may have been the hardest stop on the road. "He was ten," Claire recalls. "We took him to a locked facility, and they wouldn't let us see him for a week. It was the hardest thing I have ever had to do, to watch my son sobbing behind the glass of the locked door." Although she tried to drive away, Claire says, her voice breaking, "I couldn't even drive. I sobbed in the parking lot for an hour and a half."

When John returned home, things got worse. He was only in sixth grade when he tried to take his life. Claire describes the agony of the moment when she discovered her child no longer wanted to live. "John had come home from a residential psychiatric stay, cut school, and taken a handful of pills. Thank God I didn't have many pills in that bottle.

"Later that night," she says, "when I was holding him on his bed and he was crying, he said, 'I know you and Dad love me and I know you want me to be okay, but I just can't hold it together. You can't understand. I feel as if I am going to fly apart and I will never find all of myself again. I know you don't want me to go back into treatment, but you don't understand, it helps hold me together.'"

Claire pauses. "It was shattering. Just shattering."

Shattering because she had to admit truthfully to her son, "I don't know how to help you. I have to get help for you. I can't lose you."

For most parents, the stakes are not nearly so high, but for Claire, every decision she made had about it the feeling of life or death. As hard as it was for Claire to place John in yet another residential facility, she knew that he needed more help than she could give. "The point came when all those traditional things that we assume will work with troubled kids didn't work. And sometimes, even though residential care is very unpopular, these kids need it. They need the parameters, the structure, and the control that can be given in an institutional setting."

Despite the need to place him outside his home, Claire remained determined that she and John's stepdad would be part of the treatment team. She knew that once a child is institutionalized, it is often assumed that the family is no longer involved. Claire was adamant that John and everyone involved with his care know that he had a family and was a part of that family.

"John had so many poor service providers who were determined to take control of him away from us," Claire says. "We fought from day one to be his lifetime care managers and would say to professionals, 'We will help you. We want you to help our son, but you do not have final authority over him. He will stay a part of this family.'"

It was a constant and dispiriting challenge. On one occasion, the family drove for seven hours to a meeting that had been on the calendar for over a month only to be told that the social worker was "too busy" to see them. They waited. When the social worker finally arrived in what appeared to be disheveled and dirty gardening clothes, he said, "I don't have time for this."

Claire said, "You're fired."

He said, "You can't do that."

"Watch me," Claire replied. "You will get out of my son's life because you do not care about him."

As tough as that and other experiences were, Claire is not bitter. She believes it is essential for her to forgive so that she can go on. Her voice softens as she asks, "Can I forgive the service providers who looked down on our family? Who hurt us more than they helped us? They were limited by the system and by their own limitations and humanness. But I never met a person who wanted to do a bad job or set out to hurt us. It is easy to forgive. They were just human."

Forgiving herself continues to be more problematic. "Forgive myself?" she asks. "That's the hardest of all. There has never been a day where I haven't revisited John's separation from the family while in treatment," Claire says softly as her voice breaks. "Only God knows how deep the pain is. I worry about what I could have done differently or better to help him sooner, quicker, and more at home. I know I didn't have the skills I needed, and I am sorry for that. It is a part of me and the journey that I will always work on."

As advice for any parent facing difficulty with a child, Claire says, "You know, our kids do not come with instruction books. I am just a parent; I am not a therapist. But," she says, "don't mistake me. I know we are not a normal family." Claire hesitates as she tries to explain. "Normal is a setting on the refrigerator," she says. "We all have our dysfunctions. But love was never lacking. I used to tell John that I wasn't perfect. He didn't get to order me from Sears, and I didn't get to order him. We did the best we could. Obviously God gave us to each other for a reason. And so we make the best of it."

"Making the best of it" is so easy to say, but so tough to live. Claire recalls those difficult days: "I looked around at all my neighbors with their 'perfect kids.' At work, I would be at coffee break and someone would be talking about his or her son being captain of the football team. And there I was, not saying anything. I mean, what do you share? 'I just left my son in residential treatment?' Or 'He's in the children's psychiatric hospital?' It is the most incredibly painful and isolating experience."

When a child suffers from mental illness, normal parental pride is distorted by pain. "Your family is struggling," Claire says. "You are struggling with shame. People think you are bad parents.

How could anyone know how very painful it was? How could anyone know we were struggling just to keep our family together?

"For me, for families like us, it was agonizing to let our child go into an institution," Claire says. "We ran into the assumption from other people that we didn't care. My in-laws thought that we couldn't be bothered, and nothing was further from the truth."

If it was hard for her to face neighbors, coworkers, and family members, the stress of dealing with mental health professionals was, surprisingly, even more difficult. If ever there was a time when parents of a mentally ill child would want to make a good impression, it is around the conference table. After all, this is when they are trying to get proper care for their child. Claire has advice for the mental health professional scrutinizing such families:

"When talking about families or looking at records about families who are so desperate that they have either lost their children or placed them voluntarily in residential treatment, be aware. By the time those kids get to a center, you bet the professional sees a dysfunctional family seated across the table. They are so beaten down by that time, so desperate. There is nothing left. And what you are seeing when a family finally gets there is not the true, whole picture. You see a wounded animal, a desperate person."

Even getting to the conference table was an ordeal. The prospect of having the family's life and personal finances put under a microscope was appalling. As it became more and more challenging to afford John's care, Claire and her husband were forced to look to the government for help.

Once private medical insurance had been tapped, there were few choices. "And so that is when we first had to be involved with social services," Claire says. "This is very problematic for most parents, and it is when some give up custodial rights to the state. There are ways to get help and continue to keep custody, but it isn't easy."

She describes the process of finding funding for John as dehumanizing. "You give up a great deal. Your finances are in shambles. When we finally accessed the help we needed, we had no privacy left, and certainly no dignity. The government looks at everything, not only your financials, but also your complete social history. They look at everything about your kids and your family. Here you are, fighting to keep your family together, and you have people looking at you and being very judgmental. But having to submit to their scrutiny is what we needed to do to get money for treatment."

Claire had to do more than just submit to intrusive social workers and wait for them to make critical decisions about paying for John's treatment. Claire had to give up the dream of a normal son. In talking about this unique pain, her voice tightens. She is in tears.

"It was so very difficult. You know these are the kids that need the most love and yet they often make it almost impossible to love them. Kids with emotional and behavior problems defy you to love them. They throw it in your face. I can't tell you how many times he has told me he hated me. They push you away, say awful things, and tell you that you and everyone else are the source of their problems. They suck the marrow out of your bones and leave you emotionally and physically spent."

But despite her pain, Claire could see behind the façade of her angry child. "At the same time, they want you to love them," Claire says. "They do not internalize responsibility or remorse for their actions; they are angry and intense. What would I do then? I would just hold him and say, 'Tough, 'cause I love you so much and there is nothing you can do to make me let go or quit loving you. So live with it.'"

Grieving is still a part of Claire's life. "John and I have cried about all the lost years. It hurts so much, the time we lost and will never get back. I cried myself to sleep wondering if we had sold him down the river for our peace of mind."

While no one would accuse Claire of selling John down the river, no one would have begrudged her some peace of mind. Unhappily for the family, although many modalities were tried, nothing seemed to work. True, John was a complicated case, with both physiologic and psychological components at work. And, although he was bright, he was an expert at self-sabotage. "Anytime he began to get successful at something—school, friendships—then he would sabotage it."

Coming to Colorado Boys Ranch was a last resort. "It was a true effort to get his life on track," Claire remembers. "If they continue to screw up, they will end up incarcerated. And that is unthinkable. And then we have thrown away a life."

Claire considers Colorado Boys Ranch, and in particular one CBR therapist, a great gift. "He understood that the young men who came to the Ranch were not throwaways. They were not society's trash. He believed that they are individuals who, for a variety of reasons, failed to make it in the real world. They need help, patience, and someone who believes they have worth."

She continues, "If we think these kids are hard to deal with, we can't forget what it is like to be a kid living in that mind and body. He can't walk away from it. He is desperate. And that is where John's therapist intervened. He knew this kid was not a free-falling pod from outer space. His sincere dedication to John saved him."

That therapist's dedication also gave Claire some peace of mind. She no longer had to fight to be kept in the treatment loop. She no longer had to fear losing her son to a closed-in institution or to ineffective therapy.

"This man understood how deeply we loved John and that we would never let him down or let him go. He knew I had to be a part of the treatment planning. He believed me when I said we were an integral part of John's life even though we were many miles away. He believed in me, trusted me. He worked with me as a partner so that we were on the same page of music, orchestrating our actions and messages to support healing and success."

And for maybe the first time since John's problems began, Claire felt understood. "The therapist's gentle acceptance of my fears and heartbreak," Claire says, "gave permission for me to be honest enough to cry and share without my feeling that he would think I was a bad parent."

Another important factor for John and his desperate mother when placing their trust in Colorado Boys Ranch was that it was in a rural setting. This was critical to Claire, as John was a "runner." In fact, running away was one of John's earliest problem behaviors, and Claire thought a large city would be risky for John. "I worried about him bolting and ending up on the streets. His running didn't disappear at the Ranch, but his therapist and I just laughed. I mean, where can you run to out there? He would run, come back, and want his dinner."

Of course, it wasn't only John's CBR therapist or the Colorado Boys Ranch setting that gave John the tools to finally be successful. Claire elaborates: "The CBR programs, like working with animals and various classes, taught self-sufficiency skills, anger management, and assuming responsibility for your actions. When traditional settings failed us, CBR offered an alternative to failure and gave John a chance at a successful life."

This story, like life, has an ending in progress. John has taken the gifts CBR had to offer and has created tools for himself to move forward in life. He cowed his demons. He is leading a full and meaningful adult life, which includes work and marriage and a young son.

✦ ✦ ✦

A flood of traumatic events may sweep apart a family in peril. But the heroic parent holds on mightily, pulling the family safely to shore. The heroic parent acts. Claire, John, and the rest of the family continue to work hard to make up for lost time, always acknowledging the unbreakable bonds of love that join this family. "John always knew from the bottom of his heart that he was loved deeply," says Claire. "We never backed away. We never let go."

—JP

# CHAPTER NINETEEN

# Orphan Annie

# The New Leash on Life Program

*Though there are no Broadway lights for this not-so-little "Orphan Annie," she is a star at Colorado Boys Ranch. Annie, a Great Pyrenees, is everything the American Kennel Club's Web site says about her breed. She is "gentle, confident, affectionate, unsurpassingly beautiful and elegant, possessing a keen intelligence and a kindly and regal expression." But when this abandoned dog first found her way to CBR, she was not looking very regal.*

Could CBR YouthConnect have found a better auntie dog for its boys than Annie? It's doubtful, if one considers that Great Pyrenees are "patient, tolerant, attentive, fearless," and, perhaps most importantly for Annie's adopted nephews, "loyal." However, the Annie of today is not the same Orphan Annie that first showed up on the stoop of Colorado Boys Ranch one June day in 1996.

Using animal-assisted programming to help the boys was not new to the Ranch, but in 1994, when Charleen Cordo was hired to run the program, it was ready to grow. After arriving on the job, nearly the first thing she said to herself was, "This place needs a dog." Although in past years Boys Ranchers had been allowed to have dogs as pets while at the Ranch, there had not been a dog at CBR for some time. They were using sheep, horses, and other farm animals as well as a menagerie of rabbits and other small animals in therapy. But as Charleen's husband remarked, "There is nothing like a boy and a dog."

Keeping that idea in the back of her mind, Charleen began her work by suggesting that CBR begin a trial program to determine if having the boys work with unwanted dogs from the local animal shelter would have a beneficial effect on their ability to cope with their own similar issues of neglect and abuse. Charleen got the go ahead and became the coordinator. The new program was named "New Leash on Life."

The New Leash on Life program pairs troubled boys on the Ranch with dogs from the local animal shelter. In ten-week sessions, the boys bond with their dogs and train them in obedience. At the end of the sessions, the dogs are adopted into the community with "Canine Good Citizen" certificates. Charleen says, "What we found was that these troubled boys could empathize with the dogs who were fearful, unsocialized, and unruly. With time and patience, the dogs become loving, obedient, calm, and able to function in society."

While developing the New Leash on Life program at CBR, Charleen continued to believe that the Ranch needed a dog of its own, one that would remain on the Ranch and not be adopted out. Charleen wanted to find a large-breed dog, one "who could take care of itself." Deciding that a Great Pyrenees was the best choice, she set out to find one. Charleen called a local Great Pyrenees breeder and described the kind of dog she wanted: older and trained. No luck.

Two days later, as Charleen was walking into work, a great grimy white ball of fur appeared behind her. "I couldn't believe my eyes," Charleen says. "Here was this dirty, skinny 'Great Pyr' who I couldn't get near. She was wild, fearful, and in pretty bad shape. With the help of a Boys Rancher, I put down food and water and then finally got a leash around her neck. Of course, I wanted to keep her right then, but we fostered her out for two weeks while we advertised just everywhere." Lucky for the Ranch, no one did claim her, so the abandoned, abused dog, newly named Orphan Annie, had a new home.

New activities for Annie almost always involve a relationship with a boy. Charleen and the other staffers neglected to tell Thomas, a CBR boy who took on the care of Annie, that entering her in a dog show was probably not in the cards. Maybe they should have explained that, generally, this breed is not very trainable in the normal dog-show kind of way. Great Pyrenees' fierce independence makes them the perfect guardians for herds of sheep, but not the most obedient show dog material. So maybe it was Thomas's youth, at thirteen years of age, and his positive CBR experience in training two other dogs that made him want to rise to the challenge of schooling this skittish dog. Or maybe Thomas simply saw no barriers to the places where Annie could venture, for as Charleen says, "Annie would let Thomas do anything with her." And so, surprisingly, a trip to a dog show with Annie and Thomas was planned.

Part of getting a dog ready for a show is the beautification component. For shorter-haired breeds, grooming is a smaller part of the process. But that was not the case for coat-blessed Annie. Charleen says, "It took Thomas a good half hour every day to get her groomed. He was even more painstaking when he had to spend a full three hours to get her show-ring ready." The grooming included combing, brushing, bathing, blow-drying, and a final full-body combing to separate each and every hair. Thomas did such a beautiful job that once he and Annie were at the fair, the judges were sure the CBR staff had done Annie's meticulous grooming. Not so. Charleen says Thomas "worked diligently to get out every mat" in that beautiful, but very abundant, white coat.

After several months of hard work, both with the brush and practicing the many obedience and show requirements, it was Thomas and Annie's chance to show their stuff at the Colorado State Fair in Pueblo. Competition day did not begin well.

"Here we were," says Charleen, "already running a bit late, and the Boys Ranch car broke down on the way to the competition. We had to wait for another car. We had thought we would have an hour or so for Thomas to get changed into dress clothes, get Annie used to this new environment, and run through her routines. But just as Thomas walked into the arena, they called his name."

Without a chance to warm up, Thomas and Annie were on. "He had barely been able to get his pants changed and shirt tucked in," Charleen remarks. Thomas, a skinny, tiny-boned, barely five-foot-tall African-American boy, made quite the impression as he

Orphan Annie.

entered the ring with this huge, fluffy, perfectly behaved and groomed white dog that came up past his waist. The class had thirty-six dogs, and Annie was, as might be predicted, the only Great Pyrenees. Thomas and Annie had already won Grand Champion Honors at the Arkansas Valley Fair in Rocky Ford. On this day, at the Colorado State Fair in Pueblo, they won sixth-place ribbons in both showmanship and obedience. For a day with less-than-auspicious beginnings, it was a triumph.

Given Annie's condition upon her arrival at CBR, it is a testimony to the power of boys and dogs and to the healing care they can provide one another that, just months after her arrival, Orphan Annie and Thomas managed to take home 4-H honors at both the local and state levels. Going from victim to victor is a success story for CBR youth trainer Thomas, the animal-assisted therapy program, and, of course, Annie herself.

Annie's adventure with Thomas was only a beginning. She continues to play a critical role in the New Leash on Life program. For many boys at CBR YouthConnect, having their own New Leash on Life dog is a sought-after privilege, and the first step begins with Annie. Due to her unique temperament, Annie will not approach a boy who comes to her with anger or hostility. "If a kid is having trouble, even if we know nothing about him, we know it the second he walks in the door. If Annie feels unsafe, she will not go to the boy; she will stand between me and the boy or she will go and hide under the desk," says Charleen. Annie and her instincts have been pivotal in a number of boys' lives, according to Charleen. "Without getting through to Annie, there is no way for a boy to get his own dog to train."

Getting through to boys and dogs is what the New Leash on Life program is all about. "When we first get the dogs from the shelter, it is like the beginning of an unknown journey," she says. "All of these dogs have problems and respond with what people classify as inappropriate behavior. Since most of these dogs have already been the victims of abuse, including yelling, hitting, kicking, having their feet stepped on, being hit with rolled news-papers, tethered and ignored, etc., we use no aversive treatment whatsoever. Not only does this reassure the dogs, it is an impor-tant lesson for our boys, many of whom have experienced brutal treatment or neglect."

Charleen believes that "all of these dogs, even the ones who try to jump up and nip at you, are driven by the need for atten-tion and affection." Her approach is positive. She teaches the boys to react only to appropriate behaviors on the part of the dog and to use only "soft, kind words and touch combined with lots of treats and praise." She has found that such training works. "By the second week," Charleen says, "most dogs stop using their inappropriate behaviors to get the attention they so crave.

"Gradually," Charleen says, "trust develops and the dogs begin to relax and present happy, playful behaviors such as fetching, tricks, and just calmly snuggling in their boy's lap. This may be one of the few places where a boy feels he can express affection, and his dog will express affection in return. I've noticed that an uncanny bond develops between boy and dog. The boys become capable of making incredible strides in rehabilitating not only themselves, but also the dogs with whom they work."

Witness Dwight. Monklike, with his hooded sweatshirt pulled deep over his face, he came every day into Annie's realm. "He was so depressed. He would not say a word to anyone. With his large size and almost menacing appearance, Dwight came in, lay his head down on the table, and went to sleep," says Charleen. "He had no interest in anything at all."

During this time, Annie needed regular medication and vita-mins, and Charleen needed a "hook" for Dwight. Since Annie would not approach Dwight in any way, not even when Charleen asked Dwight to give Annie a treat, Charleen suggested, "Why don't you help me remember to give Annie her meds and vitamins?"

This small step led to Dwight learning how to pet Annie, give her treats, and, eventually, have a successful experience with his own dog in the New Leash on Life program. On graduation day, Charleen and another staffer watched in amazement as Dwight, smiling and gracious, greeted the adoptive family for his dog. One said to the other, "Do you remember the first day Dwight came to us?" No doubt Charleen also remembered the first day a wild, white ball of fur bounced out of the weeds.

Annie's story does play out a bit like a Broadway musical. Amidst a chorus of other dogs that come and go on the Ranch, not-so-little Orphan Annie still shines brightly in her starring role. She continues to play an important part in the many "boy-meets-dog stories" that unfold on a daily basis at CBR YouthConnect.

—JP

# CHAPTER TWENTY

# Flash

# A Dog and His Boy

*Is it really better to have loved and lost than never to have loved at all? If you had asked fifteen-year-old Jimmy that question in the spring of 2001 after his first loss while at CBR, he'd have likely answered, "No way, it hurts too much." Volunteering for another possible loss when your young life has already been filled with it is not easy. Yet it was just what Jimmy did—and then did again.*

Sometimes CBR YouthConnect staff must want a crystal ball. They must wish they could predict with certainty what might happen to these emotionally fragile boys with any given therapy. But if such a therapy predictor existed, would anyone have had the courage to pair Jimmy with Flash?

Charleen Cordo is a brave soul. She selects dogs from the local animal shelter and guides the pairings of dogs and boys in the New Leash on Life program, knowing full well that ultimately the boys and dogs must part. She saw a match in Flash and Jimmy. "Flash," a shepherd mix, "was scared of everything and

Flash.

everyone," says Charleen. "Jimmy," a slight, dark-haired boy, "was troubled, full of anger, and very shy and quiet," she continues. "I sensed Flash and he would be a good match."

Charleen has had years of experience with boys and dogs to guide her judgment. In the eleven years since she founded New Leash on Life, it has become a nationally acclaimed program that has been featured in numerous publications and on television, including "Animal Planet" and *NBC Nightly News*. More than 125 dogs enrolled in this unique program have found new homes and new lives as companion animals. The dogs, who probably would have been destroyed, do indeed get a new "leash" on life. In return, these dogs help troubled boys heal. Boys graduate from New Leash on Life with invaluable lessons in giving, loving, trusting, and, ultimately, letting go.

These were exactly the lessons Jimmy needed to learn. Both Jimmy and Flash came from backgrounds that made connecting with others tentative at best.

Boys in the New Leash on Life program begin training their dogs by trying to get the dog to take a treat. For most dog owners, it is difficult to imagine a dog not turning itself inside out for a special tidbit. "Not Flash," says Charleen. "We could not get him to take a treat of any kind, and Jimmy was getting enormously frustrated. I really had to encourage Jimmy to stick with Flash until finally, finally Flash took a piece of cheese."

It was still slow going, but after about three weeks of hard work for both dog and boy, there came a moment of truth. A wild rabbit appeared when Flash was off the leash. As Flash took off, Jimmy thought surely he would never see the dog again. But within a few moments, Flash was back, and a huge sense of relief and satisfaction washed over Jimmy. He knew they had arrived. As Jimmy wrote in a poem:

> Every weekday we ran and played.
> By my side, he always stayed.
> On the weekends, I'd sneak a visit.
> The love he showed
> Made me feel quite exquisite.

When the training period nears completion and the dogs are ready for adoption, it can be a complicated time for the boys. They feel sadness at losing their dogs, but they also feel pride for effecting such positive change in these once-abandoned creatures.

> He learned to sit, to come and stay.
> He was the perfect dog
> In every way …
>
> He wasn't the best looking dog.
> But does that matter?
> Looks aren't the only thing
> Possible to flatter.

Looks can count, as it turned out, for Jimmy's beautifully trained, lovable dog could not get a nod from a traditional adopter. However, Marsha Shoemaker, special-education teacher at Plum Bear Ranch, a working ranch located 100 miles

southeast of La Junta and one of several ranches donated to
CBR over the years, saw Flash through Jimmy's eyes. "Flash
was gorgeous, a beautiful dog," she says, "and we wanted him
for Plum Bear Ranch, which was used as an extension of CBR
at the time." Marsha, an already enthusiastic animal lover,
began to share a new relationship with Flash and Jimmy. "Flash
was king, and I mean king, with all the CBR boys wanting to
visit him!"

One boy in particular. Jimmy worked hard in his therapy
program at CBR and finally earned enough behavior points to
visit the Plum Bear facility after Flash's adoption. Marsha anticipated Flash being so excited to see the CBR van that he would not
initially realize Jimmy was in this particular group of boys. Flash
had a different set of instincts. Jimmy was sitting in the back of
the van when the door slid open. Flash lived up to his name and
leaped into the van, over the seats and luggage, and covered
Jimmy's face with huge, wet kisses.

> I was so happy
> To finally reunite
> It was like love at second sight ...
>
> He showed me around
> His yard and his house ...
>
> When I left
> I felt kinda sad
> But, hey, he was happy
> So I didn't feel all that bad.

Flash lived at Plum Bear Ranch for six canine-heaven
weeks. One evening, as Marsha was walking from the garage to
the workshop, she heard the coyote cries. "Flash was right by
my side, as usual," she says. "He followed me to the house door

and I patted his head and said, 'Good boy,' and that was the last time I saw him. Five minutes later, I called, 'Flash! Puppy!' and there was no answer."

Marsha believes that Flash thought he had found new friends in those predator cousins. She found his lifeless body not twenty feet outside the window of the bedroom where he slept each night at the foot of her bed. "All I could think of was how I had let Jimmy down. He had trusted me with Flash. I loved the dog, too, and now he was gone."

Called into the office back at the main campus of CBR, Jimmy immediately knew something was wrong. "I told you this would happen," he blurted through his tears. For Jimmy, who felt as if he always lost everything he loved, Flash's death had become a self-fulfilling prophecy.

> The news that I always dreaded
> It came unexpectedly.
> Flash heard some dogs
> In the distance.
> He walked in that direction
> Without any resistance.
> He was killed by coyotes—
> Bitten right in the neck.
> His last few seconds
> Were one big wreck

On the grounds of Plum Bear Ranch, the current group of visiting boys and staff had buried Flash in a homemade casket with "Flash, Our Friend" burned onto a wooden cross. And, as is often true at CBR, the next hours and days became times to figure out life and reactions to loss. Everyone grieved, especially Jimmy. Ultimately, instead of an ending, Flash's death became, like many tough times at the Ranch, another beginning.

Jimmy needed to grieve, and his therapeutic community encouraged it. No one rushed him. He visited Plum Bear Ranch and Marsha. Together they visited Flash's grave and, as mourners will do, reminisced and were sad together. They spoke of all the things they wished they had done and all the things they did do. Marsha told Jimmy that something good had to come from this. He made a memorial in his room with Flash's collar, a wooden sign, and several photos. Jimmy spent time alone in his room. He was sure he could never love another dog. He wrote "Flash" on his arm in ink. And he wrote a poem.

> They took Flash's life away.
> I will pray for him every day
> There is not a moment
> I don't think about him.
> In my dreams and in my thoughts,
> Flash, I love and miss you,
> Lots and lots.

In many places the story might end there. It didn't. Jimmy's therapists hoped he could be persuaded to take another New Leash on Life dog. Jimmy, however, was adamant that no dog could ever compare to Flash. But Charleen was beginning another class with four other experienced youth trainers, and she thought Jimmy would be perfect to complete the group. He reluctantly agreed, but was a day late in joining the class. He was left with the only remaining dog, a sad and sorry-looking Shitzu puppy, Mattie.

"This program teaches the boys how to become attached," Charleen says. "They need to become attached. When Jimmy lost Flash, I think he went through every stage of grieving a person could go through. He threw stones at the coyotes. He wanted to kill them. And then he began to heal. I was hoping he could get attached to something else," Charleen shares. "When Jimmy said, 'Yeah, I guess I will give it a try,' I knew we could do this."

But doing is sometimes much more difficult than anticipated. "When Jimmy took on Mattie," says Charleen, "I never imagined the dog would need so much medical care. We screen the dogs to avoid what happened to Mattie. But there we were, believe it or not, with Mattie needing to have her eye removed because of a tumor! I couldn't believe Jimmy would be faced with yet another difficult situation."

But Jimmy rose to the occasion and was extremely meticulous with Mattie's care and grooming. "There was even one time when CBR rules were stretched and Jimmy was allowed to care for her overnight in his room," says Charleen. "Mattie needed round-the-clock nursing, and Jimmy had to set his alarm and get up every hour to put cold compresses on Mattie's eye. The staff was pretty sure then that Jimmy had attached. When his therapists saw that he had made an acrostic in ink on his arm with 'Flash' written in one direction and 'Mattie' in the other, we were sure."

```
            F
            L
    M   A   T   T   I   E
            S
            H
```

"Nine times out of ten, you can't replace that first dog of your life—it is the best dog," Charleen muses. Certainly, no dog would ever replace Flash in Jimmy's heart, nor would their hard-won friendship ever be forgotten or lost. But in terms of life's lessons, what Jimmy did for Flash and for Mattie, who was happily adopted, could be compared to graduating with honors.

—JP

# Lucking Out

## Luke

*Dear reader,*
*When I came to the CBR, I was mad at the world. No one*
*would listen to me or what I had to say. Instead, everyone*
*else made the decision on where I would be placed. This*
*time I lucked out.*

When Luke pulled a chair up to his kitchen table and began his
letter with "Dear reader," he had already taken quite a journey. It
was 2001 and Luke was twenty-four years old. His journey began
when he experienced a profound loss that was to color his entire
young life. In Luke's words, "It all started when my mom and dad
got divorced. I was just four, and I didn't understand it at all. As
I got older, my dad would try to come and pick me up, but at that
time he was drinking, and my mom wouldn't let me go with him.
I knew that my dad had planned all kinds of neat things, like
camping, and when we couldn't go, I became very angry."

Young, confused, and upset, Luke lied to the authorities
about his father's new wife, claiming she had struck him, and set

into motion circumstances that altered his and his family's lives forever. His lie did not accomplish what his four-year-old mind had hoped it would do: allow him to see his father. In fact, it did just the opposite. Meanwhile, Luke's anger took over his life. He began to act out, starting with little things like carving on a dresser but quickly escalating into terrible school performance, out-of-control behavior, and running away from home.

From age seven to age sixteen, Luke spent more time in an assortment of institutions than in his own home. He provoked numerous battles and responded to almost any goading with his fists or by running away. As Luke said, "Fighting was my middle name."

Luke faced the world with his personal life-defining mantra: "If I didn't want to do it, I wouldn't do it." Lack of resourcefulness was never a problem. Luke admits to becoming "very good at never being good at all." Although bright, it became impossible for him to keep up with schoolwork. He was consumed by anger. He attempted suicide several times.

At one point, Luke was sent to a residential treatment center in a large metropolitan area. It was his home for three years. "I hated the place," says Luke vehemently. "I was just miserable." For example, Luke recalls being required to stand at attention outside his door to request toilet paper, a humiliating exercise that he wryly notes "really required advanced planning!"

Luke became resigned to the fact that, for him, there were no easy outs. "Pretty much, if you show them, you know, how to fight, then you become the guy to beat." At times, he fought for the underdog, but often the fight was about a basketball or anything else that touched the now well-defined chip on his shoulder. Living his doctrine of "only doing what he wanted to do" was easy, according to Luke. But, he says, "I was a pretty smart kid, and I knew I would have to act in a certain way to get out of there." He took his time, as fighting and acting out continued to give him the sense of self that was hard to give up. Though Luke might feel remorse after a fight was over, or even astonishment that he had fought over something unimportant, while he was in the fray, "it just felt good."

Still, underneath all the anger, the conscience of the adult Luke was emerging. It is what "got him through" some of the tough days. There is one young woman from the metropolitan treatment center who may well remember young Luke's kindness.

Sherri was gawky and trying to find her spot amidst a group of adolescent girls. Bragging, falsely, that handsome young Luke was her boyfriend was a way for Sherri to grab a bit of attention. Overhearing both Sherri's untrue boast and the derision that greeted her, Luke sauntered casually into the crowd. He describes it as a "swarm of vultures" about to eat Sherri alive. To cover her embarrassment, Luke said, "Yeah, didn't you know? We have been going out for about two weeks now." Later, Luke helped Sherri gracefully resolve the deception. He arranged for her to "dump him" in a very public display with his pseudoprotestations clearly overheard by the swarm.

Even though Luke did sometimes drop the "tough guy" persona and follow his conscience, for the most part he simply didn't know how to behave. In Luke's words, "A big problem is that when you have been at a place like that center, when you get out, you really don't know how to act, even if you think you do." Due to the many disruptions in his life caused by his problem behavior and subsequent treatment time, Luke was extremely far behind in school. Entering seventh grade is difficult for many young adolescents, and being overwhelmed academically magnified Luke's adjustment difficulty even more. His reaction? Fighting.

"For about the eighth time, they sent me to the principal's office with a kid I had beat up pretty bad—I can't even remember why. But I do remember the principal getting right in my face and yelling and yelling at me about being a 'problem child.' I decked him." Hitting the principal resulted in Luke being expelled from the district. After a brief stay in yet another psychiatric facility—with yet another stay-ending fight—there were few options left.

In 1993, Luke's desperate family and his dedicated social worker had run out of options to help Luke at home. At nearly thirteen, Luke had the opportunity to go to CBR. Once the decision had been made, his caseworker thought it would be better if someone familiar drove him to what, with luck, would be his last placement. So the caseworker and Luke, under a deceptively bright blue sky on a bitter cold winter day, passed under the Colorado Boys Ranch's gate and drove up the driveway to the end of a very long journey.

Luke, a well-seasoned veteran of institutions, expected no surprises. But CBR was no ordinary institution, and it would surprise Luke. As Luke says, "I got lucky."

If you believe that luck is a capricious and unsolicited event, then perhaps luck does not adequately describe Luke's experience. But if you believe that luck is the place where opportunity meets preparation, then Luke was indeed lucky. His past placements—for good or ill—the persevering love of his mother and stepfather, his intelligence, and his own physical and emotional development all contributed to a readiness. CBR, too, was ready. It was ready with opportunities to help Luke conquer his demons and his roadblocks to success.

Opportunities come in a variety of forms. For Luke, a first opportunity came through CBR's celebration of the holidays. The Christmas season was fast approaching when Luke arrived. Being new to the Ranch made this holiday especially difficult for Luke. He missed his family very much. But it turned out to be one of those moments of opportunity. As Luke recalls in his letter:

> I was facing the worst Christmas I would ever see—
> being away from loved ones and getting nothing. But I

was wrong. Some generous people found a way to get all of us something. I was given a catalogue and a price limit and was told to pick out whatever I wanted. Although I don't believe in Santa Claus, some very generous people made it happen, and it reminded me that although I don't know their names or what they look like, that some people still care.

Expecting nothing, Luke was surprised by CBR customs. "They gave us a catalogue and told us we could spend $85, and unless the item was out of stock, we would get what we wanted. I remember thinking, 'Yeah, right.'" It seemed too good to be true.

"Christmas morning arrived, and the unit staff woke each of us up. They had hidden everything and then wrapped the presents. So for our fifteen guys, there was quite a pile under our tree. It wasn't the same as opening presents with your family, but here we were, still opening presents that someone had bought and wrapped for us. For me, the lasting impact was not what I got that day, but looking at the other guys. For once, everyone was smiling.

"In a manner of speaking, it changed my life. I was able to see how it was to receive something from a stranger, and it only built my curiosity and generosity."

Luke filed that memory away. He remarked, "After I left CBR, I kept going back to that morning and wondering why people who didn't even know us would give us something. I wondered what there was to this 'giving thing.'" It took several years for Luke to find the answer.

It began one day in his late teens. Luke realized he had enough money in his pocket to buy a new stereo, and he gave the old one to a "music-loving cousin" who didn't have one. His surprise at the cousin's gratitude and the new relationship they then discovered awakened something in Luke.

Years later, after he was married, Luke found out he was being transferred out of state for a new job. He had a truck that was in excellent condition, his pride and joy. In fact, he had done a good deal of the work on it himself. It was a shined-to-perfection, black four-wheel-drive number just perfect for Colorado. He discovered it was going to be too expensive for him to move it across country. Noticing that a single dad and his son in the apartment below did not have a vehicle, Luke decided to offer them his.

"I'm moving and wonder if you have need of a truck?" he said to his neighbor.

"How much do you want for it?" asked his neighbor cautiously.

"You can just have it, if you take good care of it," Luke replied.

As the door closed, Luke could hear the boy ask his father about the truck. "Oh, it's probably just some piece of junk," said the neighbor. Later, as Luke and the neighbor stood out in the parking lot, Luke said, "Here's the truck and title."

"So which one is it?" the neighbor asked.

"It's the black one over there," said Luke.

"What!" the neighbor and son shrieked together.

The neighbor jumped in the truck, revved up the engine, and, according to Luke, was nothing but smiles. "I felt very good about myself," Luke says. "I remembered those Christmas smiles at the Ranch and I think I got it.

"I wanted to see what it would feel like to give something away to someone who needed it. I found out! I gave my truck to a family that did not own a vehicle. The disbelief in their eyes was more than I could have paid to see—it felt awesome. But all I wanted to do was give the feeling that I had to somebody that I didn't know. Make them feel like I felt when I thought there wasn't any more good in this world."

Another opportunity at CBR led to Luke finding something he thought he'd lost forever. And he found it after believing that he was completely responsible for losing it in the first place. It was, in Luke's words, a lucky opportunity, and without doubt a turning point.

"I met a man named Martin Masar (CBR YouthConnect director of the Office of Admissions and Clinical Affairs), and instead of telling me what I should be, he listened to who I already was—no one had done that before.

"I told him that I really missed my father, who I hadn't seen in seven years," Luke says. Luke did more than confess to wanting to be with his dad, he confessed to the guilty secret he had carried since he was four years old. At the time, Luke had been forbidden to see his father due to his father's alcoholism. "My dad had remarried," Luke says, "and I didn't like my stepmother. In my four-year-old head, I had this crazy notion that if I said my stepmom had done something bad to me, then they would blame her and I could be with my dad. So I told my mother that my stepmom had broken my nose."

Actually, Luke says his nose had been broken in a wrestling match with his brother, but the lie's damage was done. A restraining order was put into effect. His dad and stepmom moved out of state. "I felt incredibly bad about this lie. I didn't know how to undo it. In fact, I had kept it a secret for all these years."

Finally confessing, years later, to Martin at the Boys Ranch, Luke expected a shocked remark along the lines of "How could you have done such a thing?" Instead, Martin responded gently and in a matter-of-fact way, saying, "Yes, I can see how a four-year-old might think like that."

Relieved by Martin's response, Luke was emboldened to ask if there was any way he could talk to his dad. Martin promised to look into it. Luke remembers thinking, "Sure, everyone tells me stuff like that—what they will do for you—but no one ever does."

Martin Masar.

This time, someone did. Martin Masar is a soft-spoken yet extremely articulate man, and he is as good as his word. He takes these boys' lives as seriously as any true professional should. And he lets the boys know from the start that he will never give up on them. This helps the boys to never give up on themselves. Of course, there were steps that needed to be taken to remedy Luke's situation. First, Martin would determine that no restraining order currently existed. Next, he would establish parental fitness. And then, he would do many phone interviews and make many conference calls.

Finally, Luke was told to come to Martin's office. When the door opened, instead of Martin, Luke's dad walked out.

"You've grown!" his dad choked.

"You've shrunk!" Luke giggled.

And they talked and talked and talked. After eight years of being apart, there was a great deal to share. Luke reflects, "The minute I saw Dad, my thinking changed. I wanted to live with him. All of a sudden, my actions at CBR meant something. Before, nothing seemed to matter much. I didn't care and some-times ruined my own chances just because I thought I was bored. Now, I cared. I was discharged into my dad's custody about seven months later, on my sixteenth birthday." Luke had found what he had lost. He could move on. Luke writes:

> Martin saw my need to be reunited. He brought my dad
> back into my life, although it wasn't easy. My dad and
> I to this day can't thank him enough. In my eyes,
> Martin had created the impossible. I moved in with my

father upon my discharge and found everything I have
waited for and more.

Reluctant to take credit, Martin says, "Everything at
Colorado Boys Ranch is accomplished on a relationship level. I
believe that there is always somebody here for somebody there.
And that is the beauty of this program. It's not always the therapist. It could be the housekeeper, or the voc. ed. guy. Whatever
relationship becomes important to a boy, it is our job as therapists
to strengthen it and build upon that. To utilize the relationship."

Luke says as much when he writes:

> During my stay at Colorado Boys Ranch, my interest
> tended towards the corral program. I was able to ride in
> parades and rodeos, and thanks to an old cowboy
> named Jim [Kerr, director of Horsemanship], I was good
> at it. For once, somebody acknowledged me at being
> good at something, as did my ceramics teacher Mary
> Ann [Hale], and I thank them too.

For Luke, preparation did meet opportunity at CBR. No
rabbit's foot was necessary. And, as Luke says in his letter, he continues to be grateful for his "luck." Luke's letter, begun years after
his stay at Colorado Boys Ranch, concludes with this message to
troubled boys and their sponsors:

> To CBR residents: There is a world out here, and no
> matter how negative your peers can be, you should
> listen to people like Martin, Jim, Mary Ann, and Rudy,
> the shift manager on my unit. They are not there to
> make your life miserable. They are there to listen and to
> try to help. Don't cut them off short. I didn't, and now
> I have a home with nice possessions, a good job, and a

beautiful wife. Your future is not just tomorrow, but the rest of your life. So don't cut yourself off short either. If you hold all your feelings inside, it's kind of like tying the hands of those who do want to help.

To the sponsors, this may sound sort of dumb, but, with your donations, you gave the people who helped me room to work. A gift is just a material possession, but the meaning behind it is something that can't be taken away. I won't lie. It wasn't until after I was discharged that I began to appreciate it.

In closing, to the Boys Ranchers, I want to say, please do not tie the hands of those who care about you as an individual. I'm not able to remember all the names, but I remember your faces and what you did.

Sincerely yours,

Luke

—JP

# CHAPTER TWENTY-TWO

# Don't Leave Me

## Martin Masar

*"I was sitting in a staff meeting listening to the terrible history of abuse that one boy had endured," recalls Martin Masar, a therapist and the director of the Office of Admissions and Clinical Affairs at CBR YouthConnect. "Hearing what that boy had been through, I started to get sick to my stomach," Martin says. "I was sitting there on the floor, and I thought, 'Oh my gosh, Martin, you're too close. Your system is saying you can't take it anymore."*

Many of the boys who arrive at CBR YouthConnect have histories of abuse. Martin knows the common themes. "The fact that one boy's mother tried to drown him at the age of two is not unique," he says. "It had happened before to other boys. The fact that a boy's parents are in prison is not uncommon. We had a boy whose mom had been using him as a prostitute for her female clients. Some of these parents have perpetrated unspeakable forms of abuse on their own children."

As a mental health professional, Martin also knows he should not be surprised by his own visceral reaction. "There is language out in the mental health arena about vicarious trauma," Martin says. "Emergency-room personnel, police, and child-protective service workers are prone to it. There is a mental health dynamic where a worker is exposed to a significant amount of depressing cases and it begins to effect you in non-healthy ways.

"Some handle it in a negative way, with drink and violence," says Martin. "Others get numb. They get indifferent and callous. They lose perspective. Awareness is half the battle. I knew I had some work I had to do," Martin says. "I had to keep my perspective. I had to keep a healthy boundary between my personal and professional life. When I left the Ranch at the end of the day, I needed to leave my work behind."

But for Martin, who admits he has a "passion that not one single child should be hurt again," leaving thoughts and feelings behind at the end of the day is easier said than done. For him, as well as the other professionals at CBR YouthConnect, forming relationships is the key to helping these boys.

Martin, who has a master's degree in social work and is a licensed clinical social worker, recently presented a paper at an international symposium of mental health workers in Dubrovnik, Croatia. His paper, which describes the CBR YouthConnect treatment model, is titled "The Integration of Treatments that Work" and was published in Issue 11 of the 2004–05 *IUC Journal of Social Work*. It begins with a story.

Martin writes, "Joseph was sixteen years old when he was admitted to CBR YouthConnect. Reading his history, I discovered that Joseph had been in forty placements before coming to our facility. During his early childhood, Joseph was repeatedly beaten for his behavior and then locked in a dark closet for hours. His earliest memories are of stark isolation, terror, and fear. In Joseph's mind, the world was a terrible place, and he had come to expect the worst. Imprinted in his mind became a solution: use aggression and strength to control others, thereby controlling the fear he had of the world.

He was a stout young man who learned to survive by using his strength and aggression to his advantage. Soon after he was admitted to our program, in a show of power and defiance Joseph forcibly removed an entire toilet from the bathroom floor. Over the next several months, Joseph became increasingly aggressive with staff and peers.

"In our treatment sessions," Martin writes, "Joseph continuously demonstrated his physical power through the use of strong words and threats. He would say things like, 'Don't even go there, if you know what's good for you' and 'I'll do whatever it takes to get out of here. I could easily beat you and then they will take me out of here.' He had this look, and you knew he meant business.

"One night, as I worked late, the residential staff called my office asking if I would speak with Joseph. He was very angry and threatening to hurt anyone who got in his way. I had Joseph brought to my office. After numerous attempts to assist him with his current problems, I asked him bluntly, 'Tell me, what makes you angry?' Joseph stood up in what seemed like an irate explosion, turned around, and, grabbing his shirt, lifted it above his head. There on his back were the scars of many beatings. Embedded forever were the deep scars of his childhood, of his rage, of his hatred."

Despite Joseph's anger, Martin did not give up, and Joseph successfully completed eighteen months of treatment at CBR YouthConnect. The importance of the relationship they formed was proven three years later when Martin heard from Joseph in a letter that said, "I'm living with my uncle and doing really good. I'm graduating from mechanics school. I'm doing good, I'm doing real good. I'm glad you're still there. Thanks, Joseph."

Another boy's story comes to mind as Martin describes the balancing act he must maintain between professional and personal duties. "I was at home with my wife and kids when I received a phone call at about 9:00 P.M. Paul, a boy at the Ranch, had been hurt participating in a touch football game. After an especially rough down, he had sustained a black eye. I went straight to the campus to be with him. As I drove out to the Ranch, I thought about Paul's history.

"I knew Paul as a rambunctious twelve-year-old youth referred to CBR by his adoptive parents. Before his adoption, Paul had been the victim of severe physical abuse, neglect, and eventual abandonment. As an infant, he suffered extreme physical trauma. His earliest memories were not of love and affection from his parents, but of loneliness, hurt, and pain.

"Paul's adoptive parents had tried their best to provide him with love, affection, safety, and security. They wanted to give him those things that most children thrive on and need. They would have changed the world for him. But for Paul, the world remained an angry place, full of those things he had learned long ago from his biological parents: neglect, distrust, hurt, anger, and abuse.

"Throughout his early life, Paul traveled in and out of therapies and placements. Nothing seemed to work. Despite the solutions focused on his behavior, he merely intensified his anger, violence, and rage. When he entered CBR, he entered into a different treatment philosophy and a value system founded on relationships.

"For Paul, this meant the tearing away of his established belief system, a process that he would reject with force, aggression, destruction, and running away. But over the course of two years at CBR, Paul had demonstrated, ever so slowly, the ability to accept newfound beliefs and attitudes about his world and the people around him. Yet for Paul, there remained a doubt, an uncertainty, that these people caring for him were indeed committed to him. This important step was seen as essential [in order] for Paul to understand his world as a much better place.

"When I arrived at the nursing station at CBR the evening of Paul's eye injury, Paul said, 'Martin don't leave me. Please go with me to the hospital.' And of course, I did. Paul's favorite blanket and pillow came along.

"Paul was seen at the local emergency room in La Junta, but was immediately referred to a hospital sixty miles away. An eye surgeon would see him there. When we got to that hospital, the number of patients shocked us. Broken legs, broken arms, fights, heart problems, and a myriad of other problems were waiting to be triaged. Paul's eye was examined. He was X-rayed and tested and CAT-scanned. We soon learned that surgery was needed. However, there would be a three-hour wait. It was now midnight.

"For the next three hours, Paul and I remained in the emergency room and watched as people came and went. Knowing that surgery was forthcoming, Paul's impatience grew. He was hungry, tired, and thirsty, saying, 'I just want to go back to the Ranch.' He was full of questions: 'Can't you take me home? Why does a black eye need surgery? Why does everything take so long? What will happen to me? Will you be here? Will you stay with me?'

"I discussed everything the physician had told us, and I consoled him. I realized that it was not the surgery that Paul feared most. It was being left alone.

"At 3:00 A.M., the nurses came to take Paul to the operating room. They told him to take off his pants, socks, and underwear. 'My underwear too?' Paul asked, alarmed. 'Martin do something! I'll be naked!'

"I reassured Paul that his privacy and dignity would be maintained. Behind a curtain, Paul put on a hospital gown and got under a blanket. As the nurses wheeled him out of the room and down the hall, Paul tearfully called out, 'Martin, take my hand.' Running to the side of the moving gurney, I grabbed his hand and walked along beside him.

"We entered the surgical area with doctors and nurses hovering about. Our surgeon came over and began discussing the procedure. It wasn't until I was asked to sign the consent form that I discovered that Paul was still tightly clenching my hand. 'Will you be here?' he asked. I assured him, in the most gentle of ways, that I would.

"During the procedure, I called Paul's adoptive mother who lived in another state. I had maintained phone contact with her all evening and throughout the night. She, too, had not slept. Although Paul was not my own child, we talked over the phone at 3:00 A.M. as two tired, concerned, and exhausted parents. She turned the conversation around, asking, 'And how are you holding up?' As parent to parent, we shared the fears, concerns, and worries of having children go through these difficult times in their lives.

"For the next two hours, I remained in the surgical waiting room and paced, as any anxious and concerned parent would do. It was time to think how lucky I have been to have the privilege of working at CBR and to have my life enriched by the young men and their families that come through our doors.

"The surgeon finally came out and said that the procedure had gone well. Paul's eye would be fine. He would be back playing football soon. I waited until the nurses wheeled Paul down the hall and back to his room. As we entered the elevator, I gently reached for his hand and in a soft voice told him, 'I am right here.' Paul squeezed my hand and whispered, 'I'm okay. You can go home.'

"Other staff from the Ranch had arrived to relieve me. They would continue to watch over Paul for the remainder of his stay. It was finally time to let go.

"I left the hospital and stopped at a convenience store to fill my coffee cup. As I headed back to La Junta, the morning sun was rising above the horizon. I smiled and enjoyed the hour drive home. I thought about my long years at Colorado Boys Ranch and the many young men who also called out, 'Don't leave me.'

I hear from them often. They call back, years later, to share their stories as working men, husbands, and fathers."

To perform the balancing act required in his role as therapist, Martin knows he needs to keep things in perspective. One way he does that is by paying attention, not only to the long histories of abuse these troubled boys have endured, but also to their small moments of happiness. He smiles when he hears how another professional at CBR helped create one of those moments. Lorraine Reynolds, a nurse and program director, says, "Many of these boys have only sad memories of past Christmases. We have one boy who has never had a Christmas tree, and he's sixteen years old. So we woke him at 11:30 P.M. to go outside and play in the year's first snow. He loved it," she says. "We were making memories."

Martin has happy memories of his own of joyful winter moments on the Ranch. He shares them with other mental health workers in a professional newsletter: "As the icy north winds blow across the frozen plains of southeastern Colorado," Martin writes, "I watch as three young men build the finest of snowmen. The snowman's rounded belly and cheeks stand firmly against the winter wind, a testimony to the hands and hearts that carefully create its form. The boys fashion their creation in moments of laughter, strength, nurturance, vision, and endurance. Upon its completion, the snow-covered youths brush the icy particles from their coats and hats and watch the snowman as if in a moment it will come to life and dance merrily down the street. These magic moments in time, when the world seems to stand still, bring a feeling of serenity to the campus of the Colorado Boys Ranch.

"Looking at the splendid snowman and the snow-covered boys, I think about all children and the energy it takes to bring form and shape to their lives. Long before children enter this world, and continuing through the years, nurturance and love are the foundations that allow them to take their first timid steps into life. They feel a sense of safety and belonging in knowing that, if they should fall, a compassionate adult will be there to protect them.

"As they grow and move further away from their trusted support, children gain strength. Their legs, arms, and bodies learn how to work in harmony and build the endurance needed to go the distance. Along the way, they will encounter pain, frustration, anger, and resistance. Their endurance allows them to persevere, but somehow laughter just seems to make the life journey so much more fun.

"Children learn that nothing is really perfect and that most obstacles can be overcome with a little smile and patience. With knowledge comes the ability to question, argue, and confront their world. They have experienced the past, lived the present, and will become the visionaries of the future. Like the snowman fashioned from the formless blanket of snow, their vision of the future begins to take shape, meaning, and purpose.

"Eventually the boys who build the snow creation move with weary arms and chilled hands to the shelter of their cottage. I know what awaits them. Nurturance in its warmest form. Something that each of us could use after a long day braving the icy north winds. A frothy, comforting cup of hot chocolate."

Despite the horrific stories of trauma that Martin hears on a daily basis, he can keep on doing this work because "I really believe in what we do at CBR YouthConnect. The mental health care and the education are very important. But most important are the relationships, the human connectedness. And just as important as the time a boy spends in a CBR office with a clinical therapist," Martin says, "is the time he spends outside with other boys getting muddy and dirty. The freedom he can feel riding a horse on the mesa, playing football, flying a kite, making a snowman."

—CQL

# Uprooted

# Mike

*Because of serious emotional problems, Mike was trans-
planted to at least ten different institutions while still a
child. Like the mandrake plants in a Harry Potter novel
that scream when they are repotted, Mike was furious
about being uprooted so many times. His continual relo-
cations did not allow Mike to establish roots or develop
relationships. He was an angry, unsettled young man. But
then Mike met a gentle cowboy and found a place where
he could grow.*

The lanky young man ambles into the restaurant amid cries of
"Mike! Good to see you!" and "How are you doing, Mike?" The
locale is not Boston, and it is certainly not Cheers, but at the
Cracker Barrel Restaurant in southern Colorado, it seems everybody knows his name. Dark haired and in his late twenties, Mike
wears jeans and a T-shirt with the words *World's Greatest Dad*
emblazoned on the front. "A Father's Day gift from my wife and
kids," he explains with a crooked grin, folding his long legs into a

booth by the window. Mike winces from the pain of a recent and serious back injury, but then smiles as he talks about his family.

"My oldest boy will be six years old on August 2," Mike says as he gives the menu a cursory glance. He looks up. "The middle one is thirty-one months. And the youngest is a girl. She's nineteen months old." The matronly waitress beams down at Mike like a doting aunt, more interested in hearing how he and his family have been than what he wants to eat or drink. "I'll have my usual," he confirms, closing the menu and handing it back to her. Before the noon hour has passed, teenage cashiers, middle-aged waitresses, and the restaurant manager have all gone out of their way to greet Mike by name and ask how he is. And just like the crew on *Cheers*, they all seem truly glad he came. But few of these friends know Mike's whole life story, how far he has actually come, or how especially proud Mike is to be wearing a World's Greatest Dad T-shirt.

"I never knew my real dad," he says quietly. Mike's words echo a refrain heard frequently from men who once lived at CBR. "My stepdad was a drunk," he says. "Beat my mom."

Like most of the boys who have passed through the gates of CBR YouthConnect, Mike's early life was impoverished in a variety of ways. "There were seven of us kids living in a two-bedroom trailer," he says. "We were poor. We were raised old fashioned, the hillbilly-type deal. People called us hillbillies, rednecks."

But Mike liked the simple, old-fashioned way of life. "You see the old Westerns?" Mike asks. "What I wouldn't give to live in those times," he says. "Being around horses and working with them is the closest thing you can find to living back then."

As a young boy, Mike got acquainted with a pure-white horse that belonged to his great-grandmother, "Grandma Two Shoes." "That was her nickname," Mike explains, "because if she went to the grocery store she'd wear her tennis shoes but take a pair of slippers. She'd get into the car, sit down, take off her tennis shoes, and put her slippers on. Then, when she got to the store, she'd take her slippers off and put her tennis shoes back on. Everywhere she went she carried two pair of shoes."

Mike also enjoyed the physical labor that was part of his rural upbringing. "One of my uncles had an old sawmill. We'd go out in the woods and cut lumber. We had a vegetable garden the size of this building," he says, waving his hand to indicate the dimensions of the dining room at the Cracker Barrel. "Pulled weeds by hand."

But what little Mike had was snatched from him at a young age. "When I was ten years old, my mom died of cancer. Cancers," he says, correcting himself. "She had a whole list of them. She was only thirty-five. My mom had been in the hospital for two years before she died. So for those two years while she was in the hospital, my stepdad was the one raising me," Mike explains. "I was being raised by a drunk."

"He didn't bother me much," Mike says, sloughing off old hurts. "He didn't beat me. The only person he gave a hard time was my older sister because she knew everything he was up to. Heck, he had two kids born two days apart by two different women. So you know he was cheating. He's worthless to me."

It may have been for the best when Mike's stepfather pulled himself out of the young boy's life. "Right after Mom died," he says, "my stepdad took his own four kids, the younger four after me, and left me and my two older sisters in the trailer. By ourselves. And we lived in that place for about a week with nobody, just us three kids. And we were kids. We were just kids."

Mike and his sisters didn't know what to do. "We called Grandma because she just lived two miles away," he says. "She'd come check on us, and she'd say, 'Oh, he'll probably come back. He's just on a binge.' But he never come back. He had moved across town. Nobody could contact him. They'd go over and knock on his door, but he wouldn't answer. So they moved us three kids to my grandma's house."

From then on, Mike was the one who was uprooted, time and time again. Grandma's house was the first stop, but it was not the solution for Mike. "They say I was a problem child. Probably was," he admits. "My grandma was elderly. She couldn't take care of me. So they put me in a military school."

Mike did not object. "The military school was strict," he says as he digs into the plate of huevos rancheros the waitress has set before him. "But they weren't as strict as you hear in a lot of stories. They had the rules, and that was the rules. They weren't all that bad. I did good there for a while, about two years. But I got into some trouble, so they kicked me out."

A series of out-of-home placements ending in rebellions and rejections became a pattern in Mike's life. "They sent me back to Grandma's house," he says, but he was not welcomed with open arms. "When we pulled up in the driveway," Mike recalls, "my grandma had social services and welfare already there. They took me to an alternative house until they could find a group home to put me in. Then they sent me to another place. I got kicked out of there for beating a guy up. I lost my temper. Then they sent me to a hospital, a psychiatric facility. They said I was crazy. I don't know.

"They've diagnosed me with multiple things," Mike says. "Compulsive explosive disorder. Something like that. I wasn't the kind of kid to stand down and let things happen. Because I grew up in such a way as I did, you had to fight for everything you got. So you learned how to fight.

"As a kid, yes, I was mad. I won't deny it. I was pretty mad," Mike says. "This is what someone told me, they said, 'You were a perfect little angel until your mom died. Then you were a devil.'"

Mike can now look back on his childhood with greater understanding. "Even as a grown adult, when you lose someone, it's hard," Mike says. "It's hard on anybody." He has become philo-sophic about his mother's death. "I think you're on the earth for

a mission," he says. "You've got a set objective. When God feels
you've met that objective, he takes you. How he takes you is different. My mom, she must have done what she had to do on the
face of the earth. That's how I look at it. I always hear that saying
'The good die young.' My mom must have been damn good."

Mike has traveled a long road to arrive at his philosophical
conclusions. "After my mom died and my stepdad left us, I was
sent to ten places altogether," Mike says. "There was the military
school and the group home and the psychiatric hospital. That
hospital was only short term, only ninety days. It wasn't very
long. And then I was sent to another hospital in Chicago. Then
they sent me to a school in Maine for twenty-three months."

Mike has good memories of that placement. "The school in
Maine was neat, back in the middle of the woods. Snow up to your
hips in the wintertime. It was cool. I never was good in school.
Never cared for school. I'd rather work. I learned how to cook. I
was there about two years. Then they put me in a foster home."

This time the transplantation did not take well. "I stayed in
the foster home for maybe a school year and part of the summer,"
Mike says. "My foster mother liked me, but I don't think her husband ever really wanted me there. She was having a lot of medical
problems with a pregnancy. One night she went to the hospital
because she had placenta previa, where it detaches. So I went to a
friend's house and got drunk. You know how kids are. Teenage kids.

"My foster parents had said that they didn't want me
smoking cigarettes," Mike recalls. "I told them, 'I won't quit, but
I'll have enough respect for you that I won't smoke around you.
I won't smoke in your house. Out of respect.' Well, the night my
foster mother went to the hospital and I was drunk over at my
friend's house, my foster dad come over and slapped the cigarette
right out of my face. So I said, 'All right,' and I went out and
wrecked his truck. They kicked me out of there," Mike laughs rue-
fully. "Go figure.

"Teenagers," Mike says again, shaking his head, perhaps anticipating the day when he himself will be the father of three such wonders.

"After that, I was sent to the Colorado Boys Ranch," Mike says. "Before I even got to the Boys Ranch, I had been, what you call, 'institutionalized.' I already knew the games. At that point, I had the feeling, 'Why care? Nobody else cares.' At these other places, I had the feeling, 'It's a job.' That's what it was to them, a job. They didn't get close to people. So many kids come and go. Why should they?

"At Colorado Boys Ranch, I went to work with Jim Kerr, in the horsemanship program," Mike says. "And that's what changed me. That's the honest-to-God's truth.

"Jim took me under his wing," Mike says, "and kind of led me the right way, you know what I'm saying? He's kind of like the dad that I never had. He took a father-figure role. Still to this day, I talk to him. I run out and visit him. It's cool. And you know what? He didn't have to. He didn't have to care. He could have just went there, did his job, and went home. There was days he'd get to work at six thirty or seven o'clock in the morning, and I remember still seeing him there at nine or ten o'clock at night. Talking to kids. Talking to me. I'm sure he didn't get paid for all that. I'm sure he didn't. Jim, he's *gen-u-ine*," Mike says, elongating and emphasizing the word. "He cares. And it's true."

For a young man who likes old Westerns, it's not surprising that Mike was impressed first by Jim's appearance. "He looked like John Wayne or Clint Eastwood. He was rough, you know, a lot of hard years working outside."

But very soon, Mike was more impressed by Jim's actions. "When I got to Colorado Boys Ranch, Jim was really involved with two kids, teaching them how to ride," Mike says. "I got involved with them two kids, and that's what got me to loop into the horse-manship program. Then those two dropped out of horsemanship, but I kept going. Jim seen I showed an interest in it and I really cared about it. After that, Jim and me became friends.

"It wasn't like a relationship between staff and patient," Mike explains. "It wasn't like that. It was more like a friend. I had my troubles there and things like that. And he'd stay after hours and talk or whatever I needed. It wasn't about the money, I'll tell you that. It's about his heart and his character. To be honest with you, if the world had a couple more of him, it would be all right.

"At first," admits Mike, "I had an attitude. I'd snap when somebody would look at me wrong. I had a lot of anger because I was institutionalized all my life. The staff at some of those places would come in with a power trip because, you know, some people do that. I didn't put up with it. But Jim wasn't a power-happy person. He was one of the more powerful people at the Ranch, but he didn't flaunt it. Not at all."

Mike makes clear that Jim was not a pushover. "I'm sure there were times when Jim would put his foot down and say, 'Wait. That's going over the line.' He'd use his authority, but that's what it's for," Mike says. "He didn't abuse it."

Jim Kerr of the CBR Horse Program.

Mike can recall from years of experience at a variety of institutions people who did abuse power. "It's egotistical," Mike says of them. "It's sick. Makes those people look like fools, if you ask me. They think they're Billy Bad Asses. They're messing with a little kid who's sick. Not sick in their stomach, but sick in their mind. I would tell some of those guys, 'If you want a power trip, join wrestling in college and see how much power you really have. Mess with somebody your own size. See how much of a Billy Bad Ass you really are. Because there's always someone bigger out there.'"

At CBR, Mike saw Jim use natural strength in a positive way. "You take Jim, for instance," Mike says. "He's tall and slender, like me. He's not built like a tank, but he's one of the stronger people I know. He used to wrestle in high school in Las Animas. He was one of the first people to ever win a state championship from Las Animas, back when they didn't even have school divisions. Jim's family had all that land out there, and they did it all by hand. That makes a person strong."

But when it came to working with horses and boys, Mike saw a different kind of power in Jim. "He was more finesse," Mike recalls. "He finessed the horses. He's been doing it forever. It's just talent. He knows what to do. He wasn't really rough."

In Jim's sheltering shadow, Mike learned gentleness and empathy for horses and for people. "A horse can genuinely feel emotion," Mike says. "It's my belief. I may be wrong. But they can feel emotion. You can tell. They can feel when a person is down or happy or whatever. I believe they can, because I've seen it. When a person is mad or angry, the horse is going to be mad or angry too, and it will hesitate. But it's different when a horse is loved. And when a kid is sad, I've seen horses come up and put their head on a kid's shoulder.

"There was a horse I really cared about at Colorado Boys Ranch," Mike recalls. "Her name was Lacy. She was an aged mare, probably about a twelve- or thirteen-year-old quarter horse, that I showed in halter and rode in western pleasure. She was a good horse. When I was putting her on a hot walker, she could tell if I was frustrated. Maybe Jim had been on me because this was my 4-H project and I had to do it. And maybe I didn't want to do it that day. Well, I had to. And he's on me to get it done. I'd get frustrated. The horse knew when I was mad or sad or happy. She responded to me."

Along with an understanding of emotions, Mike gained an appreciation for honesty while he worked in the corral at Colorado Boys Ranch. Mike admired the fact that Jim was a straight shooter, like his Old West movie heroes. "Jim is business," Mike says. "He'll tell you straight out if you did something wrong. He wouldn't beat around the bush. He don't do none of that. You kind of respect a person more for that too.

"You get him in a pickup," Mike says, "him and me together, and with our relationship, if he had something to say, he'd say it. He could tell me straightforward. That's the relationship him and me had. He didn't put nobody down."

Some of Jim's lessons have helped Mike as an adult in the work world. "Jim helped me learn to control my temper," Mike says. "Jim told me one day while we were working in the corral, 'I can tell you what to do because I'm the boss. And you can get pissed off at me and cuss and call names. But you don't do it to me. You walk around that barn and you kick a rock and cuss me all you want. Because after, you still got to do what the boss says.'

"I learned that from him," Mike says. "That makes a person go a lot further, because you learn respect for authority. You may not believe what the boss is saying is right. You may know better ways. But there's going to be a jerk wherever you go, and you're going to want to cuss him up one side and down the other. But you can't. You go around the corner and say, 'That no-good son of a bitch,' and kick a rock, and then, when it's over and done with, you do what you have to do. And it's done."

The lessons he learned from Jim have stayed with Mike for years. "If you ever get down to Colorado Boys Ranch," Mike says, "look on the wall in the tack room. Jim's always got a motto on there. More like little philosophies. The one that was on there the longest while I was there, if I remember it right, said, 'Where does good judgment come from? It comes from experience. And where does experience come from? It comes from bad judgment.' I used to know it word for word. It's been about ten years ago. It breaks it down to 'Yeah, you screwed up, but you learned from it.'"

Jim was not the only fount of wisdom at Colorado Boys Ranch, or even in the horsemanship program. Mike also learned lessons from other staff, and he continues to go back to the well. "When I'm down there, I'll still make it a point to swing in there, and Jim may not be there, but Debbie's there or Monty or Vern or Sean or Lorraine. I'll stop by and say hi. You go in the tack room, and there's always a statement there on the wall. There's always something different."

Another staff member that Mike credits with helping him get his roots established is Linda Thompson, a reading teacher at CBR. "I wasn't much into education," Mike says. "I can read, but it takes a little longer. There are a lot of people like me out there. When I got to the Ranch the only class I would go to was the horsemanship program. But they told me you can't just do that. So I entered into some GED classes, and if I took them, then I could work with the horses. They hooked me up with Mrs. Thompson. She was getting me better at reading. So I would go to her class, and I got my GED. Linda Thompson is great."

As part of a vocational job placement program, Mike worked as a veterinary assistant at Colorado Beef. Jim Kerr then helped him get a job at Bara Farms. "I also worked for a company called River's Edge, training Morgan horses," Mike says. "I was a groomsman. We went to horse shows all over the country: Santa

Monica, California; Louisville, Kentucky; and Denver. All over. These people I worked for were top notch. They'd take fourteen horses to the world championship and come back with thirteen world champions. When you work with people who are doing that, you're working for the best. It's a lot of hard work. A lot of hours. But anytime you're dealing with livestock, it's hard work. Nothing's easy about it."

Mike eventually took up a new career. "I've always been mechanically inclined. When I quit working with horses, I ran a small engine-repair shop. I was doing what I liked and making a living. Lucky. But with the drought and the economy, people aren't fixing their lawn mowers, and things are kind of slow right now. I've got three kids and have to pay the bills.

"Last spring I went to work for a concrete company and broke my back," Mike says. "I was carrying a concrete form for basement walls," he explains. "It's a four-by-eight-foot sheet of wood, inch and a half thick, soaked with oil. It weighs about 150 to 200 pounds. The wind was pretty heavy, and it took that form, just like a sail, and picked me up and threw me down in the hole. I've got several spinal fractures and four torn discs. The bad thing is, doctors told me I'd never be able to do work like I always have. I'm used to working twelve to fifteen hour days, six or seven days a week, but it doesn't matter, because you've got to do what you've got to do to make a living. And now they're telling me I'll never be able to do that."

His situation would be enough to discourage and upset most people. At twenty-eight, Mike is still a young man, but no longer an angry one. Experience and fatherhood have mellowed him beyond his years. "Now that I'm older," Mike says, "I get angry, I get frustrated, but I don't sweat it. If you talk to people who knew me then and know me now, they would say, 'Different man.' They'd tell you now I'm one of the most laid-back people you'll ever meet. My kids have changed me. I'm an adult now, and it's time to face reality. I can't blow up like that anymore. So I find ways to deal with it. I don't know who it was that told me, but it stuck with me, 'Don't sweat the small stuff. And it's all small stuff.'

"Did I learn my parenting style from Jim?" Mike asks, leaning back as the waitress takes his empty plate. "I'm sure I did," Mike says, drawing out the words. "I'm sure I did. I learned that what I do now will affect me the rest of my life. What's more important, taking care of my kids or running out and partying with the rest of the guys? I don't party. Jim taught me a lot of that. The Boys Ranch taught me a lot of that."

Mike unfolds his six-foot, one-inch frame, eases himself out of the booth, and walks stiffly out of the Cracker Barrel Restaurant. He waves good-bye to his friends and promises to come back soon with the wife and kids. As he steps out onto the wooden porch of the restaurant, he pauses, not quite ready to let the story end. He is thinking about birth. "I had already had my son," Mike says, "when I went back to Colorado Boys Ranch to work graveyards. I worked the night shift during foaling season. Horses are real personal. They'd rather wait until night. I was the one who delivered most of the colts. It was neat.

"I was present at the birth of all three of my kids," Mike says. "All three of them, I was there. If anybody's going to have a kid, be there when it's delivered. It will change your life. That's the honest-to-God's truth. You'll never look at a woman the same way. Women are tough. Jeez. My wife never took any pain pills, and my kids were all big. Nine pounds, two ounces; ten pounds, two ounces; and the smallest was seven pounds, twelve ounces."

Mike grins. This young man, once a fatherless, rootless little boy, has finally found his ground and set down roots to last. He has developed the heart and character it takes to be a father. According to the T-shirt his wife and children gave him, Mike is not just an average dad, but the world's greatest.

—CQL

# Boy Whisperers

# The Horsemanship Program

*After the release of the hit movie* The Horse Whisperer, *the notion that some people have an almost magical ability to communicate with horses became commonplace. Perhaps that same kind of magical process is at work at CBR YouthConnect in the horsemanship program. The needs of both boys and horses are addressed with calm and reassurance. Training boys. Training horses. Working some magic with these very challenging kids. Boy whisperers at work, one might say.*

A variety of animals large and small are available for boys to interact with in therapy programs at CBR YouthConnect. Perhaps the most impressive animals are the horses. Why horses? You can ask Jim Kerr, director of the horsemanship program at CBR since the mid-1980s. With his slim body, shirt neatly tucked into jeans, and his ever-present western hat, he is the consummate cowboy, at ease with both boys and horses. "When you're learning about horses, you're learning about life," Jim says. "Look at a bunch of mares who have been messed with or who haven't been handled well. If they know you're not going to hurt them, you can do anything. They learn to trust."

When it comes to learning to trust, a quiet approach works best. "You cannot train a horse with shouts and expect it to obey a whisper," said Dagobert Runes, an American philosopher, in the mid-twentieth century. It is probably no stretch to say that prior to their arrival at the Ranch, most boys who come to CBR had experienced a lot more shouting than whispering in their lives.

Given their size, whispering to horses seems almost paradoxical. Horses are large. In fact, at an average weight of about 1,000 pounds, they are the largest domestic animal with which we humans make relationships. Given the size of the problems that boys bring to CBR YouthConnect, whispering to them might seem paradoxical as well.

But the size of a boy's problem doesn't seem to bother the horse or the staff. Debbie Henderson, a fifteen-year CBR staff member and the only woman currently in the horsemanship program, says, "Horses are nonjudgmental. They don't care if you act tough. But they only respond well to gentleness. Horses are intuitive and sensitive."

One might say the same for the staff of the horsemanship program. "I wonder what the chemicals are that travel between a man and a horse?" wonders Wes Sterner, now retired but previously on the CBR horsemanship staff for fourteen years. Wes is convinced that everything in human life relates to horses. "Maybe it is because a horse is a universal animal," he says. "Every action that a horse does, society does as well. Birthing. Nurturing. Loving. Horse people recognize this. So we can, with different experiences, relate almost every sentence we say to a boy to something he has in common with the horse. The boys do not object to this, because the horse is a mighty animal and a beautiful animal that has all the basic instincts of a human being."

The horsemanship program at CBR is not about one boy, one horse, or even one staff member. It is about an idea, an idea that began as a recreational riding program. Wouldn't it have been a pity to waste the inviting mesa out in back of the Boys Ranch, which just begs to be explored by horse and boy? Eventually, the idea of a riding program grew into something more. It evolved into the passionate belief in the therapeutic value of animals and, in this case, horses, in the care and recovery of troubled boys. It is the horsemanship program where, the CBR staff says, "Every day we witness minor miracles."

Horse folk seem to instinctively recognize the value horses can provide to troubled boys. Wes says, "What Jim was doing with the kids and the horses got around, and pretty soon he was getting donations for CBR: Magness Arabians, donations from the Kansas Quarter Horse Racing Association, and many other private donations as well. CBR eventually had really outstanding stock."

Having such a herd led naturally to the creation of a horse-breeding program, which, not surprisingly, led to some whispering by the boys about that part of life. Contrary to what one might assume from graffiti boasts on the back of bathroom doors back home, this was an area where few of the boys had had much positive experience.

"The boys would brag about their conquests," Wes says, "but they can't tell a male horse from a female horse. We would show the kids the entire process and, when necessary, would have a therapist around to explain things maybe better than we could. We would make sure they learned everything the right way." Observing breeding horses could be a very powerful experience for the boys. But Jim crafted the program as a blessing to be appreciated, a tool for teaching, and as a model for living.

"First of all," Jim explains in *That's My Baby*, a documentary film about CBR's therapeutic horsemanship program shown on television's *Animal Planet*, "the mare's pregnancy is fun for all the boys and staff at the Ranch. We use the breeding program to help the boys. They get to witness a mother like Mightshebe, really laid back and nurturing. I personally teach a foaling class at the Ranch with the true intent to go over mating and conception through pregnancy and birth. I breed horses at the Ranch so that the boys can see the true way of it. It can be a thing of beauty."

"It is real, and the result is a miracle," Wes adds. "A seed and an egg. Bang. There's a baby. This *is* a miracle."

Although all the boys in the horsemanship program take an interest in the pregnant mare, it is usually one boy who is in charge. He will pamper the mare with special foods, often do research in the library to learn about her pregnancy, paint her birthing stall, attend her labor, and maybe even make a home-made pink or blue sign for the barn to announce the birth.

During all of this exciting fuss, quiet lessons are learned. As Jim says, "A foaling program allows the kids to see firsthand what nurturing looks like." And as one young man put it in the *Animal Planet* film, "It makes me feel good to know that I was there when he was first born and while he was growing up and becoming an adult male horse."

Jim adds, "I think the boys come to respect the mother more and understand what their own mothers went through. We turn all that back to the boy's life and behavior of the boys and their moms and dads."

If the horsemanship program is the main meal of the day, then the foaling program is the dessert—more exciting than the meat and potatoes, and oh so sweet. However, as any parent knows, while pregnancy and birth are miraculous and powerful, it is in the everydayness of child rearing that consistent learning takes place. It is not much different at the Ranch. Whether a boy is satisfied with learning something about horses and their care by grooming, mucking out stalls, and hefting bales of hay or if he wants to become more involved with riding and showing, both the boy and the horse seem to do a lot of whispering back and forth.

More often than not, these troubled young men come to CBR YouthConnect with problems in human-to-human communication. They are frequently angry and may lash out or are so quiet as to not say anything at all. That all changes when they get involved with the horses. "The kids feel they can talk to the horses," Wes says. "More than once we have seen a kid out in the corral talking to a horse. I've even seen a kid out there in the pasture with his horse's head in his lap. And I don't interfere with that. They really communicate. If someone walked up, the boy would just stop talking. So I would just set back and let the horse be the teacher."

Some of the horse-to-boy lessons are a bit more dramatic than others. As Wes tells it, "We assigned a weanling to this slender little twelve-year-old boy with a pretty hot temper. He was trying his best to get this horse under control while trying to halterbreak him. He wasn't having much luck. Finally, the boy was being dragged on his belly a little ways and there was an outburst from him. Then the boy stopped and said, 'Now, I know why my mom was so mad at me all the time.'"

Sometimes it is the boy who whispers to the horse, learning, for perhaps the very first time, what it might feel like to nurture. Wes recalls, "I remember a white horse. We had trouble with her. She didn't like people, and we even had trouble saddling her. One day, I don't know how it happened, she had a piece of barbed wire tangled in her mane. We'd have had to rope her or something. She was standing about 100 yards or so up a hill, and I was talking to a group of kids. I turned around, and one of the kids was gone. And there was the boy, about twenty feet from the horse. I thought, 'Oh, gosh, kid, you're going to get hurt.' But I didn't want to yell and scare either of them. So I just eased my way nearer in case something happened. The boy ended up standing there for a couple of minutes and then just walked right up to the horse. He untangled the wire from the mane and walked back. 'Son,' I said, 'didn't you know that horse was kinda ornery?' 'Yep,' he answered, 'I just wanted to get that wire out of her mane.'"

In the corral, it seems almost too easy to find a lesson everywhere you look. Want to teach about difference? The staff tells of the white mare that gave birth to a black foal. Natural and normal in the horse world, this event surprised the boys. According to their concrete ways of thinking and their own experience, black and white don't always mix. So they were even more surprised to witness the universal acceptance of the mare and her foal by the rest of the herd. To the boys, this was a lesson.

Want to teach academics? For one boy who had dyslexia, his horse literally was the teacher. Dry Hollow Robin, a wise old horse, showed his boy the right direction to go to make a figure eight, which they needed to do in order to perform in a barrel racing event. Jim recalls another boy who learned to read using books such as *Black Beauty* and who mastered basic math by counting stacked hay bales and change at the feed store. "He would have to get down on the ground and write with a stick sometimes, but when he was at the Boys Ranch, he could come up with the answers quicker than I could."

Want to teach ethical behavior, for example, putting others first? Wes relates, "We had this one boy who could blow up really, really bad. When any of the boys has a blowup, we have to figure a way that we can take care of it." Wes cogitated about this particular boy, and then came up with a solution for the next time this boy blew up. "I have a pair of really ratty knees," Wes says. "So I was out in the corral and walked three steps and stumbled. I went to my knees on purpose. This kid must have had a soft spot in there somewhere, because, as mean as he was getting ready to be, he came over to me. I asked him if he could help me. I put my arm across his shoulders, and I hobbled with him as he helped me down to the unit. That is how we got him back. There was good in that kid, and I gave him reason for it to come out."

While it might be easy to find lessons in the corral, the horsemanship program at CBR YouthConnect is neither simple nor magic. It is, however, a place of small miracles. It is a place where magnificent animals come together with boys who have important lessons to learn. It is a place where a dedicated, intuitive staff understands just how powerful the art of persuasion can be, even when you are speaking in a voice that is barely above a whisper.

—JP

# CHAPTER TWENTY-FIVE

# Growing Boys

# The Horticulture Program

*In the early days, when CBR YouthConnect was still known as Colorado Boys Ranch, agriculture was regarded as a natural tool to be used in raising the boys. The necessity of filling up those empty stomachs with wholesome food was obvious. But helping things grow can keep body and soul together in more ways than one. CBR saw the potential that agricultural pursuits have to fill up other empty spaces within these troubled boys as well.*

You can't have a ranch without plants and planting, and you can't raise a boy without watching him change and grow. From the beginning, boys at Colorado Boys Ranch marked their growth with the seasons. As the "CBR Rancher" newsletter reported in its early days, "This is a place where the work of a regular ranch is an important part of daily life."

On most summer mornings, boys at CBR knew it was time for relaxation after the two-hour morning work detail was over at 10:30 A.M. Successive cuttings of hay just laid in for the livestock measured the progress of the summer. With personal pride, the boys saw the freezers fill with their own handpicked "finger-lickin' good" sweet corn for the winter months. They knew summer was near its end when they made their annual trip to the Colorado State Fair in Pueblo. The boys recognized autumn's arrival by helping harvest fifty tons of Colorado Boys Ranch onions, ready to be sold in five-pound bags on its behalf. And, when the summer turkey-raising project was completed in November, everyone knew it was time to set the holiday tables at the Ranch and in the community.

The boys could also measure their own personal growth by their accomplishments in the fields or in the corrals. Some boys knew their skills were developing when they were chosen to be a part of the haying team. Other boys became part of the 4-H wrangler ranch management program, learned about being a full-time rancher, and saw themselves seriously preparing for their own futures.

With the shifting needs of boys in the 1980s, CBR evolved from a ranch that raised boys to a psychiatric facility that treated boys with serious mental health problems. Although vegetables were still grown and livestock continued to graze, these enterprises became the background for a stronger focus on treatment.

Along with an increasing number of professional staff, including psychiatrists, psychologists, social workers, and educators, the 1980s was also the season at CBR when the more engaging and dramatic aspect of agriculture, the raising of livestock, became more therapeutically structured. The horsemanship program and the animal-assisted therapy programs were developed. Plant therapy took place on a small scale, but for the most part, as these other programs took shape, the quieter horticultural sibling sat dormant, waiting for another cycle to come around.

And come around it did, with interesting results for the boys and the Ranch.

In 1996, CBR hired a new chaplain, Reverend Rodger Harris, who also happened to have a degree in agronomy and twenty-five years of experience working for a seed company. Thus the horticulture program began in a way some might call coincidence, but Rodger Harris calls providence.

As is suitable for tilling, planting, watering, and weeding, the horticulture program at CBR started quietly. Initially, it was a summer program with a small but successful flower garden. Rev. Rodg, as the boys call him, saw a patch of land and thought it should be planted. As for the boys' interest, he says, "I just brought gardening catalogues from home and left them on my desk." The boys saw them and wanted to help.

Any avid gardener can describe the therapeutic nature of scratching around in the dirt pulling weeds, nurturing seedlings, and crossing your fingers that there won't be hail this season. But there are now formal organizations such as the American Horticultural Therapy Association with research databases and a journal to attest to the therapeutic power of plants.

CBR instinctively appreciated the need for some of the boys to discover their strengths and talents in the garden. As the days grew cooler, CBR staff recognized the value of the summer garden project by making it an ongoing program, creating the first official CBR horticultural program, which is part therapy and part vocational education. Textbooks were gathered, curriculum created, and classes set up to give the boys, with staff help, yet more options to create their own personalized treatment program. And Rev. Rodg was there to cultivate his seedlings and his boys.

The quiet horticulture program reaches boys in different and subtle ways. Some experience growth by learning the lessons of patience and hard work in the garden, both necessary skills at CBR and in life. And, as happens in other programs at CBR, such as music or art, boys are inspired by the relationships they encounter as well as the knowledge they gain as they move through the program.

For boys who choose to participate in the horticulture program, a relationship with the instructor, Rev. Rodg, is the way they learn about patience and hard work. Patience is a virtue that Rev. Rodg has learned the hard way. A childhood bout with polio left him with a withered and nearly useless right arm, which he holds close to his body. But having only one good arm hasn't slowed the reverend down. The boys watch the reverend as he enthusiastically goes about his manual and spiritual labor. When this quiet yet tuned-in farmer-minister talks to the boys, they listen. He sometimes tells the boys about the uselessness of throwing what he calls a pity party. The boys know when they look at Rev. Rodg's shriveled arm that he could throw a few pity parties for himself if he wanted to. But they see he has no time for entertaining negative notions.

While the boys are "learning that all living things need attention and nurturing to thrive, a concept unfamiliar to many of them," Rev. Rodg says, they are growing as well. But, as the reverend suggests, gardening is not a quick accomplishment. Patience and hard work come first.

Rev. Rodg has seen the horticulture program work its slow miracles. He recalls one boy in particular. "Gary just sat there," Rev. Rodg says. "He was so shut down and so hurt. I would suggest something for him to do, and often he would just look up … barely. Ironically, he said to me, 'I can't do it as well as you. I have to use two hands.'"

Rev. Rodg didn't say anything. He just looked at his own arms, so unlike the two strong arms of the young boy. Gary looked too, until the logic of his statement, or lack thereof, became apparent to them both.

"I went ahead and asked him to mix the soil for the flats we were going to plant melon seeds in next," says Rev. Rodg. "Gary

Reverand Roger Harris, Horticulture Program director.

spent nearly thirty minutes with his hands in the dirt sifting and mixing. It was clear that it was therapeutic. As he progressed, I could push him further. Sometimes he resisted, but often he would come along. He has done well, and Gary still calls back today to tell me how he's doing," Rev. Rodg says with pride.

Pride grows better than any other crop at CBR YouthConnect. As the boys brush freshly pulled radishes on their pant legs and pop them into their mouths or share their homegrown tomatoes and peppers with staff and other boys in the living skills program or see their carefully planted Easter lilies brightening the grounds of CBR in springtime, the boys grow and blossom themselves.

Institutions have cycles and seasons and a need for growth as well. CBR has measured the seasons of individual and institutional growth every year for nearly five decades. The need for regular donations in order for CBR to remain a healthy nonprofit organization is ever apparent. Although reimbursements from the boys' home states cover a majority of their expenses at CBR YouthConnect, those special programs that make CBR so successful, such as horsemanship, horticulture, music, art, and vocational training, would not exist without private charitable donations.

The boys at CBR have always depended on the kindness of strangers. Early fund-raising efforts for CBR began when the staff rolled up their sleeves to package and sell Colorado Boys Ranch onions. They purchased a school bus with Gold Stamps, a different version of Green Stamps, given by hundreds of individual donors. A "Buck a Month" club brought in donations one dollar at a time.

Times changed. And the way that the seasons and growth at CBR are measured changed as well. CBR's financial health was tested as the more-complicated needs of the new boys and programs became evident. Gold Stamps and the Buck a Month Club could not do it all.

Grants from a variety of charitable foundations supplemented the gifts of generous individual donors. Although CBR was prepared to build a greenhouse one donated dollar at a time, it was truly a gift when they received a check from the Wallace Genetic Foundation that enabled the horticulture program to operate year-round. It was an especially exciting day for the horticulture program when the boys, volunteers, and staff began construction of the greenhouse. The Wallace grant signaled a new season in the horticulture program at CBR.

Now, all year long, in the searing summer months under unbelievably blue Colorado skies and in the harsh bitter cold winters of southeastern Colorado, boys can garden. For those experiencing the entire gardening year, they will do it all: study plant biology, prepare garden beds in the spring, plant seedlings, water and unenthusiastically weed, joyously harvest, put the garden to bed, prepare potting soil and pots, plant new seeds, transplant the seedlings, and watch it begin again.

A local seed company also noticed the growth of the horti-culture program at CBR and wanted to help. Fifty-year-old Hollar Seed Company from Rocky Ford, Colorado, is a noted national seed producer in the squash/pepper/watermelon family. After three years of research, Hollar Seed produced a new seed for an ornamental and edible mini-chili pepper called the Prairie Fire. Hollar has given CBR permission to do anything they want with the seeds, including marketing and distribution. So, with two dif-ferent donations working in concert, a perfect donation marriage, the boys grow the Hollar seeds in the Wallace greenhouse, pro-ducing the most perfectly delightful ornamental and edible plants.

Joan Murray of the Wallace Foundation describes her mother's love for gardening in these words: "My mother's belief is that all people can be changed for the better if they only work in the garden and care for the soil. She feels that few things bring such happiness as planting seeds, watching them grow, and then enjoying whatever sprouts—even wayward tomato plants that thrive in the middle of her compost pile." To that, Rev. Rodg and the boys at CBR YouthConnect would say, "Amen."

—JP

CHAPTER
TWENTY-SIX

# Local Hero

# James Lopez

*James Lopez was a gang member from Denver's north side. He had been in prison for a gang-related assault and had been involved in other criminal activity. In 1991, fourteen-year-old James arrived at Colorado Boys Ranch, and he is still there. But James is no longer one of the resident troubled youth. He is a college graduate, employed as the librarian for CBR YouthConnect. James vividly recalls the encounter that eventually led him to CBR. It was a cold Christmas Eve, a night that changed his life.*

"We were leaving a party on Denver's west side," says James. "It was Christmas Eve. There were five guys and three girls. We were walking past the King Soopers parking lot. Four guys came around the corner and started talking smack to us. One of my friends, Chris, had a lot of mouth, and he started up with them."

As Chris launched his verbal barrage, James kept silent. Despite his small stature, fourteen-year-old James never needed to say much. Although just a few inches over five feet in height, he possessed strength and speed, as well as quiet charm. A handsome teenager with dark hair, large brown eyes, and a quick smile, James was well liked by his friends from the north side. But the gang confronting him and his buddies were from a rival gang on the west side. James and his friends were on foreign turf.

"One of the guys from the west side gang pulled out a gun and was pointing it at us," James recalls. "Most of the kids took off. The four of us, Chris, Tommy, Ken, and I, stayed and started circling the guy with the gun. Chris kept running his mouth. The west side guy just kept turning and pointing the gun in different directions at us. He pointed the gun at Chris."

James recalls thinking, "I'm going to do something or else I'm going to get shot." He reached into his pocket. "I had a knife," James says. "I ran and stabbed the guy three times in his side. Three times. He had clicked; he had pulled the trigger, but nothing came out. He went to the ground."

James and his friends took off running. He was worried about what would become of the young man he had stabbed, but he didn't know what to do. He just kept running. Hours passed. In the early hours of Christmas morning, James and his friends walked across the Colfax Avenue bridge toward their north Denver neighborhood. Five police cars pulled up behind them. "We could have kept running, but we didn't think," James says. "We just kept walking, and the police came up on us. They handcuffed us and took us in."

James had been in other scrapes with the law. The assault with the knife landed him in jail. To James' relief, the gun-wielding west side gang member survived his stab wounds, but James was charged with first-degree assault for the stabbing. At the Gilliam Youth Services Center, a detention center in the Five Points area of downtown Denver, James waited behind brick walls, high fences, and locked doors for his court date. His grandmother's home happened to be just across the street from the detention center, but James could not see it from his cell. There were no windows to the outside.

James's mother, Georgia, had prayed that her son would not turn out to be like his father. The only thing James knew about his dad was that he was in prison. At the court hearing, the judge asked Georgia what she thought the court should do. "Keep him in. Lock him up. Straighten him out," she pleaded. James lowered his head when he heard his mother speak those words. But he knew that she wanted to help. The judge gave fourteen-year-old James a two-year prison sentence. James was about to find out for himself what long-term incarceration was like.

Like the other young inmates at Gilliam , James had to wear turquoise-colored scrubs. All the inmates wore the brightly colored shirts and pants except for the boys on suicide watch, who wore white scrubs. Those most severely depressed needed closer observation, and white scrubs made them stand out.

At the detention center, James sometimes played basketball or cards with other juvenile prisoners, but mostly he kept to himself. He sometimes had a bad attitude when his mother came to visit. He complained of missing his homies. Georgia would have none of it. "See, James," she'd say, "you're here because of your friends."

"No, it's because I want to be here," he said with the defiant logic of a fourteen-year-old. But he listened when his mother said, "James, pray. Just make sure you pray." And after she was gone, he did.

Although James was classified as a high-risk juvenile offender, an assessment process determined that he qualified for a different kind of rehabilitation. After six months behind bars, James was offered the opportunity to go to Colorado Boys Ranch. He took it.

Sitting in the backseat of a detective's car for the three-hour drive to La Junta, James had no idea what to expect. He looked down at the handcuffs and leg shackles on his wrists and ankles, a sober expression on his boyish face. The restraints were nothing new. He had worn shackles to and from the courthouse when he faced the judge four or five times in the past six months. He looked up. In the rearview mirror, James could see Denver recede into the distance, and he realized he was leaving everything he knew behind.

✦ ✦ ✦

James, the only son of a hardworking single mother, had grown up in the shadow of Denver's Mile High Stadium. Georgia, the tenth of twelve siblings, was the only one in her family to finish high school. She had a good job with the federal government. Even though the neighborhood was rough, Georgia was proud of the home she was able to provide for James and his little sister.

Georgia tried to keep bad influences out of her home by attaching iron bars to the doors and windows of her tidy bungalow. To match her sunny disposition, she painted the stucco exterior and the bars on the windows a pastel yellow. But her concern for her children's safety was the exception on the block. A few doors down from their home, a dilapidated three-story apartment building was in need of a lot more than paint. Small children played outside in the gravel yard without supervision. Above them, tattered dirty curtains hung askew from open windows. No parent had thought to install bars or even screens to prevent a fall.

James and his sister were more fortunate than the kids at the apartment building. In the front room of their home, a television and a computer flanked a newly upholstered couch. A photograph on a shelf showed James as a baby in the arms of an aunt at his baptism. Flowers and religious paintings covered the walls. An engraving of *The Last Supper* hung in the dining room next to a cabinet filled with pink china.

Georgia doted on her two children. For Halloween, she dressed eight-year-old James as a jar of jellybeans, a costume she constructed with different-colored balloons and clear plastic wrapped around James's little body. As he got older, she enrolled her son in youth athletic leagues and cheered him at his games. "Get the lead out!" Georgia would yell, and James would run faster. She taught James how to use a baseball glove and how to twist and turn for wild balls. For James, Georgia was both Mom and Dad.

But the young boy still had his neighborhood to contend with. Fistfights, broken bottles used as weapons, knives, and guns weren't unusual on Denver's north side. James had to learn survival skills at an early age. He had his first fight in second grade.

At age twelve, James was "jumped into" a neighborhood gang, the North Side Mafia (NSM). The initiation required James and six boys to fight nine older guys at the local elementary school playground. They had to prove themselves.

James already knew some members of the North Side Mafia. He was especially close to two older gang members, Andy and Rudy, and often hung out with them after playing football or basketball in the park. Five or six years older than James, Andy and Rudy were like a pair of elder brothers, which he never had, or like the father he never knew.

At the "jumping in," James and the six younger boys kicked, punched, and wrestled with the veteran gang members until the younger boys were all lying in the dirt. When the playground brawl was over, the smaller boys struggled to their feet and smiled. They were in.

Despite its Sicilian-sounding name, the North Side Mafia was a mostly Hispanic group, but James notes wryly, "We didn't discriminate." Later, James and his friends branched out from the NSM and formed their own gang, which they called the Local Boys Posse, the LBP, or simply the Local Boys.

It was good to have friends in the neighborhood. Going it alone could be dangerous. Once, while walking home from school by himself, James had been beaten up by five guys. They attacked him in an alley, where they had been hiding, and beat James with a bat until his face was swollen and his back was bruised. That was the worst attack he endured, but James recalls being assaulted a couple of other times, "just being by myself."

When James turned thirteen, he stopped participating in organized sports. The son Georgia had hovered over was put on probation by the court for gang fighting and was given a court-ordered curfew. James ignored the curfew. Georgia became frustrated with the probation officer, who looked the other way. She lectured her son. She tried to use the locks and bars on the doors and windows of her home to keep James safely inside, not just to keep danger out.

But James was determined to escape. His friends were too important. He was small, but Georgia was even tinier. Nevertheless, she was a formidable opponent. Despite the size difference, she would take his keys, wrestle him to the floor, and sit on him in a vain attempt to keep him from going out on the streets with the gang. "Mom, let me go," he would protest, but he never threatened to push her or fight with her physically. He would just wait until she was asleep in her room and then slip out the front door. He was breaking curfew the night he was arrested for stabbing the west side gang member.

As James was driven in shackles south out of Denver to Colorado Boys Ranch that summer morning of 1991, he made a decision. "I don't want to live like this for the rest of my life," he thought. "My dad is in jail. He's in and out. I don't want to live like that."

Looking down at his hands joined together by handcuffs, his thoughts were as solemn as his mother's prayers. James made a vow. "I am going to change. I am going to do something other than lead a life of crime and gangs." But he realized it was one thing to make that resolution mentally, another to perform it. He wondered whether Colorado Boys Ranch would be the place where he could prove himself.

Three hours later, the detective opened the car door. James got out and shuffled into his cottage at Colorado Boys Ranch. The cottage supervisor, Mrs. Zachary, was there to greet him. She asked the police officer to remove the handcuffs and shackles. So accustomed to being behind bars, it was days before James realized there were no iron bars, no tall fences or locked doors, let alone handcuffs or shackles, keeping him at the Ranch. Colorado Boys Ranch was not a prison and not a part of the penal system. He could leave if he wanted to. He could run away.

He didn't. James had arrived at CBR on June 21, 1991. Mrs. Zachary remembers that day well, even ten years later. "It was my birthday," she recalls. "James was wary and proud, but he wasn't belligerent. I could tell right away that he was determined to stay out of trouble. He was determined to keep a grip on himself."

With time, Mrs. Z, as James came to call her, continued to witness his determination. "James did not want to get involved in anything wrong," she recalls. "There were just a couple of minor incidents when James tried to defend his roommate from some verbal abuse by other boys."

James was beginning to learn that fighting was not a good solution. "If a bunch of boys started getting riled up, James would come back to his cottage and go to his room. The CBR staff didn't make him do that. It was James's choice, and the staff supported it," Mrs. Z recalls. "My staff and I said, 'This is great. Let him alone. Let him settle it down himself.'"

Mrs. Z knew that James needed his time out. "I really respected my staff because they could see which child needed to be left alone and which child you needed to go with to make sure he was okay." Mrs. Z didn't push James to talk. "You have to let the boy make the first move," she would tell her staff. "You don't push. You can't push. Let them know you're there. If they think you're going to push, they're never going to open up to you."

As their relationship developed, a bond of mutual respect grew between James and Mrs. Z. He says that, from the first day, she treated him like a young man, not like a criminal. He realized she was firm but fair. She was there for him.

James attended high school in La Junta that fall, where he played varsity baseball, football, basketball, and ran track. Mrs. Z loved sports and attended James's events, often bringing the other boys from their cottage to watch him play. Other CBR staff often came to the high school games as well, even when it wasn't their night to work. Like Mrs. Z, most employees at CBR were "full-time and then some."

Not long after James arrived at Colorado Boys Ranch, he saw his first cow. He'd never seen one before, except on television. He also rode a horse for the first time. "That was different," James recalls with a smile. "I did a lot of things at the Ranch that I had never done before. Doing these things opened my eyes to the fact that there's more to the world than the realms of the neighborhood I had lived in." When Georgia came to visit, she could see that the rural environment was good for her son.

"All James knew before was the city," Georgia remembers. "This was all foreign to him. Everything he was learning at Colorado Boys Ranch was new. And that was good, because it set a new challenge on him. I think the individual attention and counseling he got really helped him as well."

James's grades were good. He felt he had made a fresh start. "Since nobody knew me in La Junta, I didn't have to worry about anybody trying to 'sweat me'—you know, cause a fight or get in trouble," James remembers.

On one occasion while living at the Ranch, James was with friends at a La Junta drive-in restaurant when a car full of teenagers pulled up. Accustomed to the impending violent confrontation this would have signaled in his old Denver neighborhood, James prepared to flee. But all that happened was somebody's car got egged. James had to laugh. He made it through his freshman year and half of his sophomore year, showing such improvement that the state decided he could go back to Denver. James didn't want to leave.

When the probation officer called Georgia to report how great James was doing and tell her that he could return to his Denver home earlier than planned, Georgia said, "What? You're sending him home? How can you do that?"

"You act like you don't want your son," the probation officer said.

"No! It's not that I don't want him," Georgia cried. "It's just that I want him to have his education. It's so important for him to have that. It's the middle of the school year. If he comes back here, he'll get caught up with his friends and he won't finish this grade. We're going to have trouble."

Mrs. Z and her husband, the education director at CBR, understood James and Georgia's feelings, even if the probation officer couldn't. They supported the close bond he shared with his mother, but they agreed he might get into trouble if he returned to Denver. "We don't want that. James wants to do better. What can we do?" Mrs. Z asked her husband.

Since James was no longer eligible to stay at CBR, the Zacharys decided to buy a home in La Junta and open it up to boys like James. James was able to live with them and finish out the year. Everyone involved was pleased. Georgia was grateful to the Zacharys for the care they gave James.

"They were able to show James that two people living together can love one another without bickering," Georgia recalls. "That was good. I didn't give him that," she says as a tear rolls down her cheek. "They showed him love."

The Ramirez family, another La Junta couple, later cared for James. James continued to excel. He was the first CBR boy to be elected homecoming king at La Junta High School. His mom and sister came down from Denver to see him ride in the homecoming parade. His senior year, he won a trophy for rushing a thousand yards. He earned a football scholarship to college along with another scholarship from CBR. On graduation night, the high school superintendent stepped aside and allowed Mr. Z to personally hand James his diploma. Looking on proudly, Mrs. Z and James's mother held on to each other and cried. To top it all, James was named Mr. La Junta High School for 1995.

Years later, James's little sister still keeps her revered brother's homecoming crown hanging on her bedroom wall. Next to it, wrapped in plastic, is a scepter James received in college, where he was also elected homecoming king. In the bottom of the china cabinet of their dining room, Georgia keeps albums full of newspaper clippings describing athletic feats that James accomplished and scholarships he was awarded. She pasted a headline to his high school football picture. It says "James Lopez Plays the Hero Again."

"That one I made up," she laughs. But tucked in her albums next to poems and Mother's Day cards from James, there are real headlines and newspaper clippings that recognize James for his volunteer work with the Probation Department.

More than a decade after he first arrived, James is back at CBR. No longer a boy, he is now a young man in his late twenties. With a bachelor's of arts degree in sociology, James is a valued employee. "Mr. Utility," as Chuck Thompson, the president of CBR YouthConnect, likes to call him, James has filled in wherever he is needed. He has worked as a substitute teacher on campus and as an administrative assistant. He is now the school librarian. He mentors a recent CBR alumnus at Otero Junior College in La Junta. He attends the nondenominational chapel on the CBR YouthConnect grounds every Wednesday night and fills in when the pastor is away. In his free time, James is head football coach at Swink High School and assistant basketball coach at La Junta High School, where he has coached several boys from CBR. And every year, on June 21, he still calls Mrs. Z to wish her a happy birthday.

Many of the gang members from the North Side Mafia and the Local Boys Posse don't believe the success James has achieved. "Maybe they can't relate or they never thought I was capable of it," James notes. Most of their stories have sad endings.

"Last year, my old friend Andy was shot and killed as he tried to make a drug deal," James says. "Andy was still living the

James is the head football coach at Swink High School.

fast life, making $1,000 a day dealing drugs. Now he is dead. We had been good buddies for fifteen years. I lost a lot of tears at his funeral."

Rudy, the other friend who was like a brother to James, has survived. "My old friend Rudy is doing okay," James says. "He's done some time in prison, but he's straightened out. He is working and taking care of his family. I'm proud of him."

James is the librarian at the CBR campus library.

Most of the old friends have not done as well. "Another friend of mine is still in prison, doing twenty-five years to life for manslaughter," James says. "He was sentenced the same year I came to the Boys Ranch. He was sixteen when he went in," James notes. "All of my other friends, if they didn't die, I lost them to prison."

In the education building at CBR YouthConnect, there is an office where boys in crisis can go to talk to a counselor. The walls are plastered with a collage of news articles and photos of heroes. Some, like John Elway, who performed his Mile High exploits just blocks from James's Denver neighborhood, are nationally known. Others are local heroes. James is one of these. His picture is prominently featured in an article published in Denver's *Rocky Mountain News* in 1994. The headline reads "From Homeboy to Homecoming King." The article tells how James made it from the gangs of Denver to the fields of glory at La Junta High School. It describes how he went from being a member of the Local Boys Posse to becoming a local hero.

Sometimes a troubled new boy at CBR YouthConnect who is sitting in the crisis office upset and unwilling to talk with anyone will look around and see that article on the wall and realize it's about James. The boy may later come up to James, perhaps at the library, and ask him about his life. James is still the quiet type. He doesn't brag about his accomplishments or push his story on the boys. But if they ask, he'll tell them.

—CQL

# Epilogue

# Imprisoning Mentally Ill Youth: the Harsh Reality

The lack of appropriate programs for troubled youth, which Colorado's county judges noted and addressed in 1959 and which led to the creation of Colorado Boys Ranch/CBR YouthConnect, is now being documented on a nationwide level. In July 2004, a congressional committee reported "Thousands of mentally ill youths are unnecessarily put in juvenile detention centers to await mental health treatment every year.

"This is a serious national problem. Major improvements in community mental health services are urgently needed," according to that report, the United States House of Representatives Committee on Government Reform's *Incarceration of Youth Who Are Waiting for Community Mental Health Services in the United States.*

The report states, "The U.S. Surgeon General has found that debilitating mental disorders affect one in five U.S. youth, but access to effective treatment is often limited. This report documents a serious consequence of the health system's failure to ensure effective mental health care: the inappropriate incarceration of youth who are waiting for community mental health services to become available. Without access to treatment, some youth with serious mental disorders are placed in detention without any criminal charges pending against them."

Society seems unaware that this alarming situation is occurring around the country. But it is true.

In addition, youth who have mental illness and have been charged with crimes but are able to be released must remain incarcerated for extended periods because no inpatient bed, residential placement, or outpatient appointment is available, according to the report.

The 2004 study, presented at a hearing of the Senate Committee on Governmental Affairs, contained responses from more than 500 juvenile detention administrators in forty-nine states representing three-fourths of all juvenile detention facilities. The statistics found that "Over a six-month period, nearly 15,000 incarcerated youth waited for community mental health services. Juvenile detention facilities spend an estimated $100 million each year to house these youths, not including any of the additional expense in service associated with holding youth in urgent need of mental health services. Children as young as seven years of age are incarcerated because they do not have access to care."

The statistics are sobering, but even more startling are the quotes from some of the administrators. A detention center administrator from Oklahoma wrote, "To put it simply, we are the dumping grounds for the juvenile system. Understand this and understand it well: when the system is unable to get youth placed in a treatment facility or a mental health facility, they will be placed in a detention facility. If a youth needs to be detained in a mental health facility it will not happen; they will be placed in a detention center."

Another administrator from Louisiana commented, "The availability of mental health services in this area is slim to none. ... We appear to be warehousing youths with mental illnesses due to lack of mental health services."

The report was prepared at the request of Senator Susan Collins (R-ME) and Representative Henry A. Waxman (D-CA).

Senator Collins was quoted as saying, "This misuse of detention centers as holding areas for mental health treatment is unfair to youth, undermines their health, and is costly to society."

On July 7, 2004, an Associated Press report on the hearing quoted Representative Waxman as saying, "Thousands of youth who are in need of community mental health services are stuck in jail until these services become available. This is deplorable."

*The New York Times* published an article on July 8, 2004, on the congressional report, including testimony from witnesses. The witnesses at the Senate committee included experts in psychiatry and juvenile justice and had this to say: "Dr. Ken Martinez of the New Mexico Department of Children, Youth and Families said the data showed 'the criminalization of mental illness' as 'juvenile detention centers have become de facto psychiatric hospitals for mentally ill youth.'"

Judge Ernestine S. Gray of New Orleans Juvenile Court testified that 70 to 85 percent of the youngsters who appeared before the court had mental health or drug problems. "All too often," Judge Gray said, "children charged with delinquent behavior are identified early on as needing mental health services. But because the services are not available, the children are sent back home until there is another violation. After several brushes with the law, the children are incarcerated so they might have a chance at getting mental health services."

How can it be that more than forty years after Colorado's county judges had the foresight to conceive of a place like Colorado Boys Ranch, a congressional committee can report such a dearth of mental health care facilities and programs for youth in America?

In his testimony before the Governmental Affairs Committee, Representative Henry Waxman stated, "The problem is real and affects millions of families, yet without corporate lobbyists in the hallways or the prospect of sizeable campaign contributions, the needs of children with mental illness have received little attention."

Clearly, the message needs to get out. These troubled children can be helped. Change can occur. Almost half a decade after judges in Colorado sought and found citizen support for troubled youth, it is clear that troubled youth continue to need champions, adults across the country who will care for them and believe in their potential.

One such champion, a judge in Colorado, came to the fore on children's behalf as recently as June 2006. "At-Risk Kids' Cuts Blasted," a *Rocky Mountain News* article, reported that "In a scathing, seven-page order handed down recently, District Judge Chris Melonakis used the term 'child dumping' to describe what was presented to him in court as a plan to downgrade the care of 120 children who now live in centers where they receive professional care." Medicaid cuts in residential care were cited as the reason a county social services director had planned "to move children with mental and behavioral problems out of residential treatment to balance his budget."

That cut in funding is being bandaged to some extent in Colorado with legislation designating an official category of care, psychiatric residential treatment facilities. These types of Medicaid-reimbursable facilities, such as CBR YouthConnect, require a stringent accreditation process, for example regular in-depth review by the Joint Commission on the Accreditation of Hospitals. Residential care facilities without this type of accreditation are losing funding all over the country.

Existing psychiatric residential treatment facilities across the country worry that even stringent accreditation and a history of success will not save them from Medicaid cuts that may come in the near future. Funding mental health care for troubled youth is like navigating a complex maze through county and federal coffers. Very little is covered by private insurance. There is never enough money and, thus, never enough accredited facilities, which explains, in part, the number of mentally ill youth unjustly put behind bars.

If government is a reflection of society and society is made up of basically caring human beings, then, once again the question arises: why is the care for troubled youth in this country insufficient? If it is caused in part by a lack of awareness that these boys can change, then the stories of Colorado Boys Ranch/CBR YouthConnect can help counter that misapprehension. Even the toughest of the troubled boys, those boys who have been through multiple out-of-home placements without success, boys whom some people would call "the worst of the worst," do well in this supportive environment.

Yet parents, grandparents, and extended families continue to struggle, desperately seeking access and funding for programs like CBR YouthConnect to help their children heal.

After years of work on this book, I returned recently to the campus of CBR YouthConnect, wondering how to get this urgent message across.

After attending a board meeting on campus, I walked over to the education building. I met three young teenage boys struggling with their English assignment. Nancy Bennett, a teacher who has worked at CBR for almost twenty years, was there to help. She showed me a poem tacked up on the wall written by a boy at the Ranch. His poem was not just an English assignment. It was a plea.

> Who will cry for the little boy in love and
> away from his amor
> Who will cry for the little boy misunderstood
> and confused
> Who will cry for the little boy lost and looking for the way
> Who will cry for the little boy who is helpless
> and lonesome

Who will cry for the little boy inside the man

Who will cry for the little boy sad and homesick

Who will cry for the little boy who has loved and

feels he can't feel the same way again

Who will cry for the little boy who felt he can never

make the right decision

Who will cry for the little boy who always seems

to make mistakes

Who will cry for the boy inside of me

—Josh

As I walked back to my car, I thought to myself, "Who indeed?"

—CQL

# Afterword

# Hope and Healing

Imagine. Just imagine a world in which healthy and emotionally secure children and youth play, interact, share thoughts and ideas, enjoy their diversity, and find peaceful ways to solve their differences.

Imagine the national and global impact for our next generation, if they are able to live on this planet in harmony with others. These are thoughts well worth imagining. They stimulate hope and confidence in the future for all humankind.

To move our society in this direction, we must understand and respond to the damaging effects of trauma and injury to our children and youth.

In clinical terms, the *Diagnostic and Statistical Manual of Mental Disorders* (DSM IV) defines a traumatic event as one in which "the person experienced, witnessed, or was confronted with an event or events that involved actual or threatened death or serious injury, or a threat to the integrity of self or others." The trauma may have many sources, including neglect, physical abuse, psychological abuse, sexual abuse, witnessing of domestic abuse and other violence, community violence, school violence, traumatic loss, medical trauma, natural disasters, war, terrorism, refugee trauma, and others (National Child Traumatic Stress Network, 2005).

Traumatic events often set off lifelong consequences, such as distress and impairment at home, in school, at work, and in

271

---

**Childhood abuse or neglect
increases the likelihood of
arrest as a juvenile by
59 percent and as a young
adult by 28 percent.
The likelihood of arrest for
a violent crime also increased
by 30 percent.**

(National Institute of Justice
Research, 2001)

---

other areas of functioning. Children re-experience thoughts and emotions related to the trauma. Research is demonstrating the effects of trauma on brain development and neurochemical pathways.

The connection between trauma, mental illness, and delinquency is also well documented. In 2004, the National Association of State Mental Health Program Directors and the National Technical Assistance Center for State Mental Health Planning published a report that included the following information:

- A history of trauma that is pervasive among youth (especially minority youth) in the juvenile justice system. In one study of juvenile detainees, 93.2 percent of males and 84 percent of females reported a traumatic experience. Males were more likely to report witnessing violence, while females were most likely to report being victimized by violence.
- Each year, between 3.5 and 10 million children witness the abuse of their mother. Up to half of these children are also abused themselves.
- Between 20 and 50 percent of abused children will have some degree of permanent disability as a result of abuse.
- Childhood violence is a significant causal factor in 10 to 25 percent of all development disabilities.
- Sexual abuse predisposes children to drug and alcohol addiction, unprotected sex, increased sexual partners, prostitution, and HIV/AIDS.

- Childhood abuse is correlated with increased truancy, running away, and homelessness.
- Boys who experience or witness violence are substantially more likely to commit violence than those who do not. Reenactment of victimization is a major cause of societal violence.

Why do we allow, even encourage and support, our society's drift toward violence and trauma and promote its consumption by our children and youth? Sit back and observe the focus of news media and the preoccupation of entertainment media with violent and traumatic themes. Where is the counterbalance to this bombardment on our children's minds? Match these media trends with the rise in domestic violence and the exponential growth in prisons and juvenile detention facilities.

**Before a child turns eighteen, he or she will have witnessed more than 200,000 acts of violence on TV, including 16,000 murders.**

(Huston, et al., 1992)

**More than 85 percent of the most popular video games are violent.**

(Provenzo, 1991)

Where do troubled and traumatized youth come from? Sometimes troubled youth come from caring and well-meaning families, yet those children suffer neurological problems from complications during birth, high fevers, or accidental head injuries. One boy who came to CBR had a difficult birth and began "head banging" at seven months of age. By age four, he had uncontrollable tantrums, poor vision, and coordination. By age eleven he was suicidal. His problems were accidental.

Many, many other troubled children come to CBR YouthConnect as victims of family chaos and dysfunction, experiencing severe neglect, abuse, and often damage from their mothers' drug use during pregnancy. One boy was suffocated as a baby. His mother couldn't tolerate his crying as an infant, so she put him in a dresser drawer, closed it, and then waited until he lost his breath and stopped crying. She did this again and again. His problems were induced.

In both scenarios, troubled youth really know how to push people away and how to create chaos around them. As a result, they often experience multiple out-of-home placements in foster homes, treatment centers, psychiatric hospitals, detention centers, you name it.

Unfortunately, their impulsive mental health behaviors often predispose troubled children to placement in juvenile detention centers instead of treatment settings. When mentally ill youth are mislabeled and placed in detention centers and prisons, very little that is positive occurs. In this environment, they are further traumatized and damaged.

These youth need environments where they can be taught to build relationships and take responsibility. They need environments where staff have patience, self-control, and the ability to listen and know when a child is ready to share his or her pain and confusion. They need the opportunity to explore and discover their interests and develop their own unique talents and abilities. When this happens, there is a dramatic shift in self-perception that sparks hope. Their hope then leads to success.

As a mental health professional, I am in a position to observe how youth with trauma-related mental illnesses are mislabeled and misplaced in detention and correctional settings. However, I have also experienced how in therapeutic settings, these problems can be overcome and replaced with hope and success. I have witnessed healthy and therapeutic environments where safety and security are predictable and young minds grow and develop. I have seen and experienced the magical transformation from trauma to health through integration of psychotherapy and neuroscience within an enriched learning environment.

Do not let the doubters in our society influence your thinking.

**They say, "It's too late—teenagers can't change."** Absolutely not true! Traumatized youth can and want to change. They desperately want to be happy and healthy, and with support they can sort out their feelings and change their behaviors. Their brains are still growing; neurological pathways are still being developed.

**Others say, "It's too complicated—these boys are a lost cause."** Yes, it is complicated. But with enough time and resources, it is proven that the pieces of the trauma puzzle can be put back together through integrated treatment and education.

**Still others say, "It's too costly—just ignore the problem."** In truth, the more the effects of trauma and its correlation to troubled behavior are ignored, the faster our prison-spending crisis will grow.

Facts on the prison population explosion are hard to ignore.

- According to the "2000 Sourcebook of Criminal Justice Statistics," the total state and federal prison population in 1970 was about 190,000, or a rate of 96 per 100,000 in the population. By the year 2000, that figure had grown to 1,321,137, or a rate of 478 per 100,000.
- The latest report by the U.S. Department of Justice puts the 2005 prison population at nearly 1.5 million, and, if local jails are included, it brings the number to nearly 2.2 million. (U.S. Department of Justice Programs, Bureau of Justice Statistics Bulletin: "Prisoners and Jail Inmates at Midyear 2005")

- Nearly six in ten juveniles return to court by the time they turn eighteen. (National Center for Juvenile Justice: "Juvenile Offenders and Victims 2006 National Report")
- Nationwide between 1990 and 1999, the jail inmate population for prisoners under age eighteen increased by more than 300 percent. ("Juvenile Offenders and Victims 2006 National Report")
- In Colorado, since 1982 the overall prison population has increased 528 percent while the population of the state has grown only 59 percent during that time. (Colorado Criminal Justice Reform Coalition)

**Each high-risk teen prevented from adopting a life of crime (including future adult offenses) could save the country between $1.7 million and $2.3 million per youth.**

(Cohen, 1998)

The financial costs of imprisonment are staggering. According to the Bureau of Justice Statistics, correctional authorities spent $38.2 billion to maintain the nation's state correctional facilities in 2001, including $29.5 billion specifically for adult correctional facilities. When adjusted for inflation, this was an increase of $5.5 billion in five years. The increase in cost of corrections outpaced the rise in cost of health, education, or natural resources.

Which is really cheaper: prison or treatment? The Bureau of Justice Statistics reports that the average annual operating cost per state inmate in 2001 was $22,650, or $62.05 per day. When compared to the cost of a child's stay in a psychiatric residential treatment center at hundreds of dollars a day, it might sound cheaper to just lock kids up. But, the revolving prison door caused by high recidivism costs society much more over the long run than does effective treatment for youth. More importantly,

society cannot afford to lose the tremendous value and contribu-
tion of these youth as productive citizens.

Recently a Building Bridges Summit was initiated by the
Federal Center for Mental Health Services. The summit and
follow-up plans are evidence of critical new partnerships and
demonstrate a strong commitment to transforming children's
mental health care in America. The following shared principles
were among many adopted at the summit:

- Achieve and maintain clinical excellence by providing the
  highest possible quality of care that is trauma informed,
  uses the latest research evidence, and employs continuous
  quality-improvement practices that use relevant data and
  feedback to improve services
- Ensure that children, youth, and families feel safe and nurtured and have a sense of belonging and that children and
  youth have a developmentally appropriate role in their care
  and in creating rules, regulations, and policies that govern
  their living environments
- Demonstrate in word and deed the utmost respect for children, youth, and families and for one another, and create
  environments that value cultural differences, self-examina-
  tion, listening, and learning from each other

It is now time for a call to action for all of us. I encourage
you to consider and to act in the following ways:

- Be a role model. Demonstrate by your own actions that you
  value children and youth and that you understand the neg-
  atives of trauma.
- Join with others. Be supportive of family, school, and community efforts to support children and youth.
- Look for the trauma beneath mental illness and delinquent

behavior. Take time to examine what is causing the problems of children and youth around you.

- Nurture youth to develop their own inner strengths. Ask them to think things through and take responsibility for their own actions, with your help.

Imagine. Just imagine a world in which healthy and emotionally secure children and youth play, interact, share thoughts and ideas, enjoy their diversity, and find peaceful ways to solve their differences.

Imagine the power of the hero within.

—Chuck Thompson, president,
Colorado Boys Ranch/CBR YouthConnect

# Acknowledgments

We wish to acknowledge the founders of Colorado Boys Ranch, whose love and caring have reached across generations to give hope to thousands of troubled boys. Without them and countless other volunteers, not only would there be no Ranch, but there would be no heroes within.

We heartily thank all the dedicated, talented, and caring staff of Colorado Boys Ranch, past and present. In particular, we acknowledge the assistance of Chuck Thompson, Martin Masar, Pat Hobin, Judy Heerschap, Paula Mahoney, Dee Quick, Darlene Blair, Linda Thompson, Gerri Henson, Debbie Klieman, and Edy Hughes, all of whom were instrumental in the production of the book.

To the alumni, who are the real heroes, we are grateful for your honesty and humbled by your courage as you relived your pasts for our interviews. To those we interviewed whose stories are not contained in these pages, you remain in our hearts and memories.

Our great thanks goes to Jean Sutherland; without her tremendous support, encouragement, insight, and inspiration, this book would never have become a reality. Jean and her husband, Tom, are heroes of the first order.

Our good friend Cate Boddington acted not only as copy editor during the writing process, but was our first reader and first responder, offering insightful editorial opinions and advice.

We wish to thank Fulcrum Publishing, especially Bob Baron, who had faith in this project. And what better or more apt name for an editor could you wish for than Faith Marcovecchio?

Many thanks to them and all at Fulcrum, especially designer Patty Maher for turning this work of love into a work of art.

For his willingness not only to tell his story but also to donate the use of his painting *A Path to Follow* for the cover of this book, we are extremely grateful to former Colorado Boys Rancher Eldon Warren. Thanks to Jean Sutherland for gifting the painting to CBR YouthConnect, where it will be an inspiration to troubled boys for years to come.

Individually, Judith wishes to thank "my steadfast and encouraging family: husband, Tom, and daughters, Katie and Rebecca. Who else would read everything I write from the first draft with never a complaint? And I want to thank Cindy, my writing partner, muse, and the best possible book project manager/editor/friend a writer could ever hope to have. I'm grateful for the day when I picked up the phone and heard these words: 'How would you like to write a book?'"

Cindy wishes to thank "my coauthor, Judith, who has been truly wonderful to work with. Her talent, dedication, and friendship made the writing of this book a joy. I also want to thank Deborah and David Douglas, excellent writers and excellent friends. I am lucky to have the support and encouragement of my family: husband, Bill Landsberg, daughters, Sarah and Rachel, and son, Sam—the lights of my life. My late husband, David Quicksall, gave me not only the insight and love I have for the Ranch, but when I first divulged my desire to become a writer, he also gave me a fancy set of extra-sharp pencils. And, although a computer was used to compose this book, it was important that at the time of my second marriage my husband, Bill, gave me not only encouragement and praise, but also a very fine journal full of blank pages that he urged me to fill."

—Cindy Quicksall Landsberg and Judith Pettibone

# Appendix

## Resources
## on Juvenile Delinquency
## and Mental Health

For more information about juvenile delinquency and mental health, the following sources are helpful:

1. "Incarceration of Youth Who Are Waiting for Community Mental Health Services in the United States." Report of the United States House of Representatives Committee on Government Reform, Minority Staff, Special Investigations Division (July 2004). Available at www.juveniledefender.org/pdfs/incarcerationof%20youthwithmentalhealthneeds.pdf.

   "This report documents a serious consequence of the health system's failure to ensure effective mental health care: the inappropriate incarceration of youth who are waiting for community mental health services to become available. More than 500 juvenile detention centers in forty-nine states, representing three-quarters of all juvenile detention centers, responded. This report, the first national study of its kind, presents the results of the survey. The report finds that the use of juvenile detention facilities to house youths waiting for community health services is widespread and a serious national problem."

2. The Office of Juvenile Justice and Delinquency Prevention, http://ojjdp.ncjrs.org.

   The Office of Juvenile Justice and Delinquency Prevention (OJJDP) is charged by Congress to support local and state efforts to prevent delinquency and improve the juvenile justice system. Congress enacted landmark legislation with the Juvenile Justice and Delinquency Prevention (JJDP) Act (Pub. L. No. 93–415, 42 U.S.C. § 5601 et seq.) in 1974 and reauthorized the act on November 2, 2002.

In addition to the JJDP Act, other pieces of legislation are relevant to OJJDP and its policies and priorities; several are listed below. Search online for these and others on GPO Access, which contains the text of public and private laws enacted from the 104th Congress to the present.

- The Adoption Promotion Act of 2003 (Pub. L. No. 108–145)
- Child Abuse Prevention and Treatment Act (Title I, Pub. L. No. 108–036)
- Methamphetamine Anti-Proliferation Act (Title XXXVI, Pub. L. No. 106–310)
- No Child Left Behind Act of 2001 (Pub. L. No. 107–110)
- PROTECT Act of 2003 (Prosecutorial Remedies and Other Tools to End the Exploitation of Children) (Pub. L. No. 108–021)
- Protection of Children from Sexual Predators Act of 1998 (Pub. L. No. 105–314)
- Runaway, Homeless, and Missing Children Protection Act (Pub. L. No. 108–096)
- Strengthening Abuse and Neglect Courts Act of 2000 (Pub. L. No. 106–314)

OJJDP produces numerous publications and products each year. Recent publications include:

- Teplin, L. A., K. M. Abram, G. M. McClelland, A. A. Mericle, M. K. Dulcan, J. J. Washburn. "Psychiatric Disorders of Youth in Detention." Bulletin NCJ 210331 (April 2006). Available at www.ncjrs.gov/pdffiles1/ojjdp/210331.pdf.

    "This report examines the prevalence of alcohol,

drugs, and mental disorders among youth at the Cook County (Illinois) Juvenile Temporary Detention Center by gender, race/ethnicity, and age. Drawing on research conducted by the Northwestern Juvenile Project, this bulletin finds that even when conduct order is excluded, nearly two-thirds of males and three-quarters of females studied met diagnostic criteria for one or more psychiatric disorders. This suggests that on an average day, as many as 72,000 detained youth have at least one psychiatric disorder. The bulletin presents information that can help the juvenile justice system detect youth psychiatric disorders and respond with an integrated system of services."

- Snyder, Howard N. and Melissa Stickmund. "Juvenile Offenders and Victims: 2006 National Report." Washington D.C.: U.S. Department of Justice, Office of Justice Program, Office of Juvenile Justice and Delinquency Prevention. Available at http://ojjdp. ncjrs.org/ojstatbb/nr2006/downloads/NR2006.pdf.

    "This report was prepared by the National Center for Juvenile Justice, the research division of the National Council of Juvenile and Family Court Judges. It gives reliable data and relevant research to provide a comprehensive and insightful view of juvenile crime across the nation. The report offers Congress, state legislators, and other state and local policymakers, professors and teachers, juvenile justice professionals, and concerned citizens empirically based answers to frequently asked questions about the nature of juvenile crime and victimization and about the justice system's response. Among other information contained in this report, the following statistics are noted: In 2003, Child Protective Services received and estimated 2.9 million referrals alleging child abuse or neglect against 5.5 million children. This equals 39 of every 1,000 children under eighteen years of age. Twenty-six percent were substantiated."

- Snyder, Howard N. "Juveniles Arrested 2002." OJJDP Juvenile Justice Bulletin (September 2004). Available at www.ncjrs.gov/pdffiles1/ojjdp/204608.pdf.

  "This report states that in 2002, law enforcement agencies in the United States made and estimated 2.3 million arrests of persons under eighteen years of age, according to the Federal Bureau of Investigation."

- Loeber, Rolf, David P. Farrington, and David Petechuk. "Child Delinquency: Early Intervention and Prevention." Child Delinquency Bulletin Series (May 2003). Available at www.ncjrs.gov/html/ojjdp/186162/contents.html.

  "Compared with juveniles whose delinquent behavior begins later in adolescence, child delinquents (offenders younger than age thirteen) face a greater risk of becoming serious, violent, and chronic juvenile offenders. OJJDP formed the Study Group on Very Young Offenders to examine the prevalence and frequency of offending by children younger than thirteen. This study group identified particular risk and protective factors that are crucial to developing effective early intervention and protection programs for very young offenders."

3. The Northwestern Juvenile Project. Linda A. Teplin, PhD, principal investigator. Available atwww.psycho-legal.northwestern.edu/about/.

   "Many studies have investigated general-population youth to see who becomes delinquent. Far fewer studies examine health needs and outcomes among youth in the juvenile justice system. This is the first large-scale longitudinal study of mental health needs, services, and outcomes among delinquent youth. We are studying only delinquent youth because they are at such high risk for psychiatric disorders, HIV/AIDS risk behaviors, life-threatening problem behaviors, and death. Our data will help plan needed intervention strategies for delinquent youth.

"Goals include determining how alcohol, drug, and mental disorders develop over time among delinquent youth, investigating persistence and change in psychiatric disorders and associated functional impairments. We will also investigate whether delinquent youth receive needed services after their cases reach disposition. We will assess if and when juveniles who need services (including services for substance abuse/dependence) receive them. This study will provide needed data on a very high-risk population. These data will help direct the types of prevention programs that best fit the needs of delinquent youth."

4. The National Center for Juvenile Justice, http://ncjj.serve http.com/NCJJWebsite/whoarewe/whoweare.htm.

"The National Center for Juvenile Justice is a private, nonprofit organization. It is the research division of the National Council of Juvenile and Family Court Judges, with substantial support from public and private sources doing independent and original research on topics related to the field of juvenile justice." Publications include:

- Hurst, Hunter. "Juvenile Justice and Mental Health Trying to See Eye to Eye." Reprint from *Juvenile and Family Justice Today* (Winter, 2002). Available at http://ncjj.servehttp.com/NCJJWebsite/pdf/mental healthhod.pdf.
- National Center for Juvenile Justice. "Mentally Ill Juvenile Offenders: Responding to a Critical Need for Services, Assessment, and Collaboration." Compiled by Imogene Montgomery. 2000. Available at http://ncjj.servehttp.com/NCJJWebsite/pdf/insummental health.pdf.

5. "President's New Freedom Commission on Mental Health Achieving the Promise: Transforming Mental Health Care in America." July 22, 2003. Available at www.mentalhealth commission.gov/reports/FinalReport/toc.html.

"Executive Summary of the President's New Freedom Commission Report." Available at www.mentalhealthcommission. gov/reports/FinalReport/FullReport.htm.

"The mission of the president's New Freedom Commission is to 1.) Conduct a comprehensive study of the United States' mental health service delivery system, including both the public and private sector providers; 2.) Advise the president on methods of improving the system. The goal is to recommend improvements to enable adults with serious mental illnesses and children with emotional disturbances to live, work, learn, and participate fully in their communities."

6. "Mental Health: A Report of the Surgeon General." Available at www.surgeongeneral.gov/library/mentalhealth/home.html.

"This report makes evident that the neuroscience of mental health—a term that encompasses studies extending from molecular events to psychological, behavioral, and societal phenomena—has emerged as one of the most exciting arenas of scientific activity and human inquiry. We recognize that the brain is the integrator of thought, emotion, behavior, and health."

The summary of Chapter 3: "Children and Mental Health" from the surgeon general's report makes the following statements:

- Approximately one in five children and adolescents experiences the signs and symptoms of a DSM-IV disorder during the course of a year, but only about 5 percent of all children experience what professionals term "extreme functional impairment."
- Mental disorders and mental health problems appear in families of all social classes and of all backgrounds. Yet there are children who are at greatest risk by virtue of a broad array of factors. These include physical problems; intellectual disabilities (retardation); low birth weight;

family history of mental and addictive disorders; multi-generational poverty; and caregiver separation or abuse and neglect.

- Preventive interventions have been shown to be effective in reducing the impact of risk factors for mental disorders and improving social and emotional development by providing, for example, educational programs for young children, parent-education programs, and nurse home visits.
- Primary care and the schools are major settings for the potential recognition of mental disorders in children and adolescents, yet trained staff are limited, as are options for referral to specialty care.

7. "Report of the Surgeon General's Conference on Child Mental Health: A National Action Agenda." U.S. Department of Health and Human Services. 2000. This report represents an extraordinary level of collaboration among three major federal departments: the Department of Health and Human Services, the Department of Education, and the Department of Justice. It introduces a blueprint for addressing children's mental health needs in the United States. Available at www.surgeon-general.gov/topics/cmh/childreport.htm#pan2.

8. United States Department of Health and Human Services. Substance Abuse and Mental Health Services Administration (SAMHSA)

SAMSHSA's National Mental Health Information Center is a one-stop national clearinghouse for free information about mental health, including publications, references, and referrals to local and national resources and organizations.

See Goldstrom, Ingrid, Fan Jaiquan, Marilyn Henderson, Alisa Male, and Ronald W. Manderscheid. "The Availability of Mental Health Services to Young People in Juvenile Justice Facilities, in *Mental Health, United States, 2000*. Manderscheid, Ronald W. and Marilyn J. Henderson, eds. U.S. Department of

Health and Human Services: Substance Abuse and Mental
Health Services Administration. Available at http://mentalhealth.
samhsa.gov/publications/allpubs/SMA01-3537/chapter18.asp.

"In addition to its nationwide surveys of mental health
organizations and the people they serve, the National Reporting
Program of the Center for Mental Health Services (CMHS) continues to fill the gaps in information about the availability of
mental health services outside of the traditional mental health
sector. The survey discussed in this chapter builds upon earlier
successful inventories of mental health services availability in
State prisons (Goldstrom, Rudolph, & Manderscheid, 1992) and
in local jails (Goldstrom, Henderson, Male, & Manderscheid,
1998) and represents another step toward the completion of the
picture of the "de facto mental health system."

9. "Medicaid: Principles for Treatment of Children and Youth with
Emotional and Substance Use Disorders." National Association
of Children's Behavioral Health and National Association of
Psychiatric Health Systems Accountability for Children's
Mental Health. March 2006. Available at www.naphs.org/
WhatsNew/documents/PrinciplesforTreatmentFinal.pdf.

"Because each child is unique and because individual needs
change and evolve over time, children and youth with behavioral
disorders must have access to a comprehensive array of behavioral
health services including twenty-four-hour care and treatment
and non-twenty-four-hour care and treatment." The report goes
on to recommend Medicaid Action steps to Congress.

10. Cohen, Mark A. "The Monetary Value of Saving a High Risk
Youth." *The Journal of Qualitative Criminology* 14 (1):5–33.

11. Huston, A. C., et al., *Big World, Small Screen: The Role of Television
in American Society*. Lincoln, NE: University of Nebraska Press, 1992.

12. Provenzo, Eugene. *Video Kids: Making Sense of Nintendo*.
Cambridge, MA: Harvard University Press, 1991.